MW01156974

AMERICAN POPULATION
BEFORE THE
FEDERAL CENSUS OF 1790

PREPARED UNDER THE AUSPICES OF THE
COLUMBIA UNIVERSITY COUNCIL FOR RESEARCH
IN THE SOCIAL SCIENCES

AMERICAN POPULATION BEFORE THE FEDERAL CENSUS OF 1790

BY

EVARTS B. GREENE

DE WITT CLINTON PROFESSOR
OF AMERICAN HISTORY
COLUMBIA UNIVERSITY

AND

VIRGINIA D. HARRINGTON

PREFACE

For the student of American population before the first Federal Census was taken in 1790, there have hitherto been two compilations of major importance. The first was made by the late Franklin B. Dexter in his "Estimates of Population in the American Colonies," contributed to the American Antiquarian Society in 1887 and published in its *Proceedings, New Series* V, 22-50 (Worcester, 1889). This essay was subsequently included in a privately printed volume entitled *A Selection from the Miscellaneous Historical Papers of Fifty Years* (New Haven, 1918). Dexter's study, which included a limited amount of critical discussion, was chiefly concerned with population before 1776 and does not deal with the political subdivisions of the colonies and states.

In 1909 the United States Bureau of the Census issued a compilation entitled *A Century of Population Growth*, edited by Mr. W. A. Rossiter, Chief Clerk of the Census. This contained a considerable amount of material on American population before 1790. Chapter I of this volume summarized the information available for the area included in the first Federal Census, introducing some data not included in Dexter's essay, notably certain estimates of urban population. Under the head of "General Tables" are included (Tables 76-103 inclusive) official enumerations for seven of the original thirteen states: New Hampshire, Massachusetts, Rhode Island, Connecticut, New York, New Jersey, and Maryland. In these tables population is grouped not only in local subdivisions but under certain other categories, including age, sex, race, and servile or free status.

These earlier compilations of Dexter and Rossiter have proved their usefulness to scholars and have been frequently cited, but much additional material has since been made available for particular colonies and states. The plan of the present work is to assemble in a single volume: (1) the data contained in the earlier compilations; (2) the new material now scattered through a large number of publications, official and unofficial; (3) some additional data

drawn from such manuscript collections as those of the Public
Record Office in London, the Library of Congress, and the New
York Public Library. Enumerations are limited to population
within the territorial limits of the United States in 1790 when the
first Federal Census was taken. For purposes of comparison, some
figures have been reproduced from that census.

Though some explanatory matter will be found in the footnotes,
no systematic interpretation of the material has been attempted;
for the present it has seemed best simply to provide the student
with data from which he may draw his own inferences. This statement applies, for instance, to the enumeration of taxable persons,
of males liable to military service, or of the number of houses, without adding estimates, more or less conjectural, of total population
as calculated from the numbers in these special categories.

The statistics here presented obviously vary considerably in
value, ranging from mere estimates of more or less informed contemporaries to the official enumerations of governments. Estimates
must, of course, always be used with caution, and even official
enumerations varied considerably in the accuracy with which they
were taken. It will be seen that data drawn from different sources
as to the growth of population in any particular period do not
always harmonize with each other. Though some material of
questionable value has thus been included, a considerable number
of contemporary estimates have been omitted as more likely to
confuse than to enlighten the reader. Estimates by secondary
authorities have not generally been reproduced, except when they
appeared to be based on sources not readily available, or in a few
special cases like that of Bancroft, whose figures have been frequently used by later writers. Finally, to assist the student in
appraising the value of the material here included, there is for
each item a specific indication of the source from which it has been
taken.

The statistical matter is prefaced by a bibliography in the usual
form; but in order to keep the size of the volume within moderate
limits, the detailed citations have been given in the most abbre-
viated form possible, especially in the case of those authorities
which are most frequently cited. A key to these abbreviations is
provided with the bibliography.

Though pains have been taken to verify statistics and citations, some errors have doubtless escaped notice. Corrections are accordingly invited, with a view to a revised edition if the demand is sufficient to justify it. The present compilation is mainly the work of my research assistant, Miss Virginia D. Harrington. Acknowledgments are also due to others who have been helpful at various stages of the undertaking: to Mrs. Bernice L. Becknell for assistance in the preliminary stages of the work; to Dr. Louise Kennedy for expert editorial service in preparing the manuscript for the press and in checking statistical data; and to Dr. Stella Sutherland, who has permitted the use of material gathered for her study of American population in the Revolutionary era. Finally it should be said that this research has been aided by grants from the Columbia University Council on Research in the Social Sciences, and its publication in this form has been made possible by the liberal coöperation of the Columbia University Press.

EVARTS B. GREENE

COLUMBIA UNIVERSITY
May, 1932

CONTENTS

BIBLIOGRAPHY

MANUSCRIPT MATERIAL

British Museum
Additional MS. 12413. Edward Long, History of Jamaica: III.
Additional MS. 30372.
British Public Record Office
Colonial Office Papers (CO5): 358, 368, 371, 372, 375, 376, 378, 379, 388, 393, 394, 578, 582, 583, 762, 855, 864, 865, 868, 872, 880, 888, 1285.
Historical Society of Pennsylvania Transcripts
Plantations General: Vols. E, R, and S.
Proprieties: Vols. C, Q, R, S, and V.
Journal of the Board of Trade: Vol. X.
Library of Congress Transcripts
Colonial Office Papers (CO5): 9, 67, 216, 1099, 1309, 1310, 1312, 1313, 1314, 1316, 1317, 1319, 1320, 1322, 1325, 1326, 1327, 1328, 1330, 1332.
Egerton MS. 2395.
Kings MS. 205.
Archives Nationales, Colonies: A8, C13, G1: 464.
Force Transcripts
Maryland Records, Miscellaneous, 1755-75.
New Hampshire, Miscellaneous, 1752-64.
New York Public Library
Chalmers MSS.

PRINTED MATERIAL

Adams, John. Works of John Adams, Second President of the U. S. (ed. C. F. Adams). 10 vols. Boston, 1850-56.
Albach, James R. Annals of the West. Pittsburgh, 1857.
American Antiquarian Society Transactions and Collections (Archaeologia Americana). 12 vols. Worcester, 1820-1911.
American Antiquarian Society Proceedings. 6 vols. Worcester, 1849-.
American Historical Association Reports. 59 vols. Washington, 1889-.
Anderson, Adam. Historical and Chronological Deduction of the Origin of Commerce from the Earliest Accounts. Dublin, 1790.
Anderson, James S. M. History of the Church of England in the Colonies. 3 vols. London, 1856.

Andrews, Charles McLean. Guide to the Manuscript Materials for American History to 1783 in the Public Record Office of Great Britain. 2 vols. Washington, 1912-14.

Anon. History of North America. London, 1776.

—— The North American and West Indian Gazetteer. London, 1776.

—— State of British and French Colonies of North America. London, 1755.

Arnold, Samuel Greene. History of the State of Rhode Island and Providence Plantations. 2 vols. New York, 1859-60.

Ashe, Samuel A'Court. History of North Carolina. 2 vols. Greensboro, N. C., 1908-25.

Atwater, Edward E. History of the Colony of New Haven and Its Absorption into Connecticut. Meriden, Conn., 1902.

Bancroft, George. History of the Formation of the Constitution of the United States. 2 vols. New York, 1882.

—— History of the United States of America. 6 vols. New York, 1887.

Barry, John Stetson. History of Massachusetts. 3 vols. Boston, 1855-57.

Bartlett, John R. Census of the Inhabitants of the Colony of Rhode Island and Providence Plantations for 1774. Providence, 1858.

Baylies, Francis. Historical Memoir of the Colony of New Plymouth, 1608-1692. 2 vols. Boston, 1866.

Belknap, Jeremy. American Biography. 2 vols. Boston, 1794-98.

—— History of New Hampshire (ed. John Farmer). Dover, N. H., 1862.

Benton, Josiah Henry. Early Census-Making in Massachusetts. Boston, 1905.

Berkeley, Sir William. A Discourse and View of Virginia. London, 1663. (Facsimile: Norwalk, Conn., 1914.)

Beverly, Robert. History and Present State of Virginia. London, 1705.

Boggess, Arthur C. The Settlement of Illinois, 1778-1830. Chicago, 1908.

Bolton, Robert. History of the County of Westchester. 2 vols. New York, 1848.

Boston, Record Commissioners of. Reports. 39 vols. Boston, 1881-1909. [Cited as Boston Records.]

Bourne, Edward E. History of Wells and Kennebunk from Earliest Settlement to 1820. Portland, 1875.

Brissot de Warville, J. P. New Travels in the United States of America. London, 1792.

Brodhead, J. R. History of the State of New York. 2 vols. New York. Vol. I, rev. ed., 1874 [1st ed., 1853]; Vol. II, 1871.

Brookhaven. Records of the Town of Brookhaven, Suffolk Co., N. Y. Patchogue, 1880.

Brown, Alexander. First Republic in America. Boston and New York, 1898.

—— Genesis of the United States. Boston and New York, 2 vols. 1890.

Brumbaugh, Gaius Marcus. Maryland Records, Colonial, Revolutionary, County and Church, from Original Sources. Vol. I-. Baltimore, 1915-.

Burke, Edmund. An Account of the European Settlements in America. 2 vols. London, 1777.

Burnaby, Andrew. Travels through the Middle Settlements of North America in the Years 1759-1760. London, 1798.

Byrd, William. History of the Dividing Line between Virginia and North Carolina. 2 vols. Richmond, 1866.

Carroll, Bartholomew Rivers. Historical Collections of South Carolina. 2 vols. New York, 1836.

Chalmers, George. History of the Revolt of the American Colonies. 2 vols. Boston, 1845.

—— Political Annals of the Present United Colonies, 1607-1763. Two books (Book II in N. Y. Hist. Soc. Colls., I, 1-176). London, 1780; New York, 1868.

Chase, G. W. Abstract of the Census of Massachusetts, 1860. Boston, 1863.

Chastellux, Marquis de. Voyage . . . dans l'Amérique Septentrionale. 2 vols. Paris, 1788.

Chickering, Jesse. Statistical View of the Population of Massachusetts, 1765-1840. Boston, 1846.

Clark, Samuel A. History of St. John's Church, Elizabeth Town, New Jersey. Philadelphia and New York, 1857.

Clinton, George. Public Papers (ed. Hugh Hastings). 10 vols. New York and Albany, 1899-1914.

Coffin, Joshua. Sketch of the History of Newbury, Newburyport and West Newbury. Boston, 1845.

Connecticut Colonial Records, 1636-1776 (ed. J. J. Hoadley and others). 15 vols. Hartford, 1850-90.

Connecticut Historical Society Collections. 23 vols. Hartford, 1860-1930.

Controversy between New York and New Hampshire respecting the Territory Now the State of Vermont: Letters and Documents. 1749-69.

Cothren, William. History of Ancient Woodbury, Connecticut. Waterbury, Conn., 1854.

Dalcho, Frederick. Historical Account of the Protestant Episcopal Church in South Carolina. Charleston, 1820.

Dally, Joseph P. Woodbridge and Vicinity. New Brunswick, N. J., 1873.

Dankers, Jaspar, and Peter Sluyter. Journal of a Voyage to New York and a Tour in several of the American Colonies in 1679-1680 (trans. from Dutch by Henry C. Murphy). Brooklyn, 1867.

De Bow, J. D. B. Industrial Resources, etc., of the Southern and Western States. 3 vols. New Orleans, 1852-53.

xiv   BIBLIOGRAPHY

De Brahm, John Gevar William. History of the Province of Georgia. Wormsloe, 1849.

Dedham Town Records (ed. D. G. Hill). 5 vols. Dedham, 1886-99.

De Witt, Francis. Abstract of the Census of the Commonwealth of Massachusetts. Boston, 1857.

Diffenderffer, Frank R. German Immigration into Pennsylvania through the Port of Philadelphia. Lancaster, Pa., 1900.

Dinwiddie, Robert. Official Records (in Va. Hist. Soc. Colls., III and IV). 2 vols. Richmond, 1883-84.

Dix, Morgan. History of the Parish of Trinity Church in the City of New York. 4 vols. New York, 1898-1906.

Douglass, William. A Summary, Historical and Political, of the British Settlements in North America. 2 vols. London, 1755.

Drake, Samuel A. History of Middlesex County, Massachusetts. 2 vols. Boston, 1880.

Dunlap, William. History of the New Netherlands, Province of New York, and State of New York, to the Adoption of the Federal Constitution. 2 vols. New York, 1839-40.

Durfee, Job. Discourse Delivered before the Rhode Island Historical Society. Providence, 1847.

Dutchess County, New York. Book of the Supervisors. 2 vols. Poughkeepsie, 1909.

Elliot, Jonathan. Debates in the Several State Conventions on the Adoption of the Federal Constitution. 4 vols. Washington, 1836.

Ellis, Charles M. History of Roxburytown. Boston, 1847.

Essex County, Massachusetts, History of (ed. Henry M. D. Wheatland). Boston, 1878.

Essex Institute Historical Collections. Salem, 1859-.

Farmer, John. Historical Memoir of Billerica, Massachusetts. Amherst, N. H., 1816.

Farrand, Max (ed.). Records of the Federal Convention of 1787. 3 vols. New Haven, 1911.

Felt, Joseph B. Statistics of Population in Massachusetts (in American Statistical Association Collections, I, 121-216). Boston, 1897.

Field, Edward. Tax Lists of the Town of Providence, 1686, 1689. Providence, 1895.

Filson Club. Publications. 35 vols. Louisville, Ky., 1884-.

Foote, Rev. William Henry. Sketches of Virginia. 2 vols. Philadelphia, 1850-55.

Force, Peter. Tracts and Other Papers. 4 vols. Washington, 1836-46.

Franklin, Benjamin. Works (ed. Sparks). 10 vols. Boston, 1836-40.

——— Writings (ed. Smyth). 10 vols. New York, 1905-7.

Fuller, Thomas. History of the Worthies of England (ed. P. A. Nuttall). 3 vols. London, 1840.

BIBLIOGRAPHY   xv

Furman, Gabriel. Antiquities of Long Island. New York, 1875.
Georgia Colonial Records (ed. A. D. Candler and others). 25 vols. Atlanta, 1904-15.
Georgia Historical Society Collections. 9 vols. Savannah, 1840-1916.
Georgia Revolutionary Records (ed. A. D. Candler). 3 vols. Atlanta, 1908.
Gilman, Arthur (ed.). The Cambridge of 1776. Cambridge, 1876.
Gowans, William. Bibliotheca Americana. New York, 1845-69.
Great Britain. Acts of the Privy Council, Colonial Series. 6 vols. London, 1908-12.
—— Royal Commission on Historical Manuscripts: Reports on Collection of MSS. of Private Families, Corporations and Institutions. 76 vols. London, 1871-.
—— Journal of the Commissioners for Trade and Plantations, April 1704-December 1749. 8 vols. London, 1920-31.
—— Calendar of State Papers, Colonial Series (ed. W. N. Sainsbury and others). Vol. I-. London, 1860-.
Griffith, Thomas W. Annals of Baltimore. Baltimore, 1829.
Hall, Edwin. Ancient Historical Records of Norwalk, Conn. Norwalk, 1847.
Halsey, Francis W. Tour of Four Great Rivers, the Hudson, Mohawk, Susquehanna, and Delaware, in 1769. New York, 1906.
Hawkins, Ernest. Historical Notices of the Missions of the Church of England in the North American Colonies. London, 1845.
Hawks, Francis L. History of North Carolina. 2 vols. Fayetteville, N. C. 1857-58.
Hazard, Ebenezer. Historical Collections. 2 vols. Philadelphia, 1792-94.
Hazard, Samuel. Register of Pennsylvania. 16 vols. Philadelphia, 1828-36.
Hildreth, Samuel Prescott. Pioneer History. Cincinnati and New York, 1848.
Hilliard d'Auberteuil, M. R. Essais historiques et politiques sur les Anglo-Américains. Brussels, 1782.
Hills, George Morgan. History of the Church in Burlington, New Jersey. Trenton, 1885.
Holmes, Abiel. Annals of America, 1492-1826 (2d ed.). 2 vols. Cambridge, 1829.
Hotten, John Camden. Original Lists of Persons of Quality, 1600-1700. London, 1874.
Hough, F. B. Census of the State of New York for 1855. Albany, 1857.
Howell, George Rogers. Early History of Southampton, L. I., New York. Albany, 1887.
Humphrey, George P. American Colonial Tracts. 2 vols. Rochester, 1897-98.

Humphreys, David. An Historical Account of the Incorporated Society for the Propagation of the Gospel. London, 1730.

Hutchinson, Thomas. History of the Colony [and Province] of Massachusetts Bay. 3 vols. London, 1765, 1768, 1828.

Illinois State Historical Library. Illinois Historical Collections. 21 vols. Springfield, Ill., 1903-.

Imlay, Gilbert. Topographical Description of the Western Territory of North America. London, 1797.

Indiana Historical Society. Publications. Indianapolis, 1897-1931.

Indiana Magazine of History. 14 vols. Bloomington, Ind., 1917-30.

Izard, Ralph. Account of a Journey to Niagara, Montreal, and Quebec in 1765. New York, 1846.

Jay, John. Correspondence and Public Papers (ed. H. P. Johnston). 4 vols. New York, 1890-93.

Jefferson, Thomas. Writings (ed. P. L. Ford). 10 vols. New York, 1892-99.

Johnson, Amandus. Swedish Settlements on the Delaware, Their History and Relation to the Indians, Dutch, and English, 1638-1664. 2 vols. New York, 1911.

Johnson, Edward. Wonder-Working Providence (ed. W. F. Poole). Andover, 1867.

Johnston, George. History of Cecil County, Maryland. Elkton, Md., 1881.

Jones, Charles C., Jr. History of Georgia. 2 vols. Boston, 1883.

Judd, C. Parkman. Historical Address (in Memorial of the Reunion of the Natives of Westhampton, Mass., pp. 10-31). Waltham, Mass., 1866.

Judd, Sylvester. History of Hadley. Northampton, Mass., 1863.

Kalm, Peter. Travels into North America (trans. J. R. Foster). 3 vols. Warrington, 1770-71; 2 vols. London, 1771.

Kidder, F., and A. A. Gould. History of New Ipswich from Its First Grant in 1736 to the Present Time. Boston, 1852.

Lancaster County Historical Society. Historical Papers and Addresses. 34 vols. Lancaster, Pa., 1897-.

Laurens, Henry. Correspondence (from Materials for History, 1st Series, ed. Frank Moore). New York, 1861.

Lee, F. D., and J. L. Agnew. Historical Records of the City of Savannah. Savannah, 1869.

Letters of Brunswick and Hessian Officers during the American Revolution (ed. W. L. Stone). Albany, 1891.

Luquer, Rev. Lea. Centennial Address Delivered in St. Matthew's Church, Bedford, N. Y. New York, 1876.

McCrady, Edward. South Carolina under the Proprietary Government, 1670-1719. New York, 1897.

———— South Carolina under the Royal Government, 1719-1776. New York, 1901.

MacDonald, James M. Two Centuries in the History of the Presbyterian Church, Jamaica, L. I. New York, 1862.

McSherry, James. History of Maryland. Baltimore, 1849.

Magazine of American History. 30 vols. New York, 1877-93.

Maine, Documentary History of (Maine Historical Society Collections, 2d Series). 24 vols. Portland, 1869-1916.

Maine Historical Society. Collections. Portland, 1831-.

Mandrillon, Joseph. Le Spectateur américain. Amsterdam and Brussels, 1785.

Martin, François-Xavier. History of North Carolina. 2 vols. New Orleans, 1829.

Maryland Archives (ed. by William Hand Brown and others). 46 vols. Baltimore, 1883-1929.

Maryland Historical Magazine (Maryland Historical Society). Baltimore, 1906-.

Massachusetts Colonial Society. Publications and Transactions. Boston, 1895-.

Massachusetts Historical Society. Collections. 77 vols. Boston, 1792-.

Massachusetts Historical Society. Proceedings. Boston, 1791-.

Massachusetts Provincial Congress. Journals. Boston, 1838.

Mather, Cotton. Magnalia Christi Americana, or the Ecclesiastical History of New England. London, 1702.

Mead, Daniel M. History of the Town of Greenwich, Fairfield Co., Connecticut. New York, 1857.

Mease, James. Picture of Philadelphia. Philadelphia, 1811.

Michigan Pioneer Collections. 39 vols. Lansing, 1877-1915.

Mills, Robert. Statistics of South Carolina. Charleston, 1826.

Mississippi Provincial Archives, 1763-1766. 2 vols. Nashville, 1911, and Jackson, 1927.

Mittelberger, Gottlieb. Journey to Pennsylvania in the Year 1750 and Return to Germany in the Year 1754 (trans. C. T. Eben). Philadelphia, 1898.

Monette, John W. History of the Discovery and Settlement of the Valley of the Mississippi. 2 vols. New York, 1848.

Morris, Lewis. Papers (New Jersey Historical Collections, IV). New York, 1852.

Morse, Jedidiah. American Geography. Boston, 1792.

Morton, Oren T. History of Rockbridge County, Virginia. Staunton, Va., 1920.

Munsell, Joel. Annals of Albany. 10 vols. Albany, 1850-59.

New England Historical and Genealogical Register (ed. Wm. Cogswell and others). Boston, 1847-.

New Hampshire Historical Society. Collections. Concord and elsewhere. 1824-.

New Hampshire Provincial Papers (ed. N. Bouton and others). 33 vols. Concord and elsewhere. 1867-1915.

New Haven Records (ed. C. J. Hoadley). 2 vols. Hartford, 1857-58.

New Jersey Archives (ed. W. A. Whitehead and others). Documents Relating to the Colonial History of New Jersey. 33 vols. (1st Series), 5 vols. (2d Series). Newark, 1880-.

New Jersey (Dept. of State). Compendium of Censuses, 1726-1905. Trenton, 1906.

New Jersey Historical Society Proceedings. 46 vols. Newark, 1847-.

New York, Documentary History (ed. E. B. O'Callaghan). 4 vols. Albany, 1849-51.

New York, Documents Relative to the Colonial History of (ed. E. B. O'Callaghan and B. Fernow). 15 vols. Albany, 1856-87.

New York Calendar of Historical Manuscripts Relating to the War of the Revolution in the Office of the Secretary of State. 2 vols. Albany, 1868.

New York City. Minutes of the Common Council, 1675-1776. 8 vols. New York, 1905.

New York Directory for 1786, Prefaced by a General Description by Noah Webster (ed. David Franks). New York, 1905.

New York Historical Society Collections. New York, 1868-.

New York Holland Society Year Book. New York, 1886.

New York State Ecclesiastical Records (ed. Hugh Hastings). 7 vols. Albany, 1901-16.

New York State Library. Bulletin (University of the State of New York). Nos. 1-78. Albany, 1898-1927.

North Carolina Colonial Records (ed. W. L. Saunders). 10 vols. (Vols. XI-XXVI, State Records). Raleigh, 1886-90.

North Carolina Historical and Genealogical Register (ed. J. R. B. Hathaway). 3 vols. Wenton, 1900-1903.

North Carolina State Records (ed. W. W. Clark). 26 vols. Winston, 1895-; Goldsboro, 1905-.

North Carolina University Publications. James Sprunt Historical Monographs and Publications. 17 vols. Chapel Hill, N. C., 1900-1922.

O'Callaghan, E. B. History of New Netherland. 2 vols. New York, 1846-48.

Ogilby, John. America. London, 1671.

Oldmixon, J. British Empire in America. 2 vols. London, 1708.

Onderdonk, Henry. Antiquities of the Parish Church, Jamaica (Including Newtown and Flushing). Jamaica, N. Y., 1880.

Orcutt, Rev. Samuel. History of Torrington, Connecticut. Albany, 1878.

Oyster Bay Town Records (ed. John Cox, Jr.). 2 vols. New York, 1916-24.

Paige, Lucius R. History of Cambridge, Massachusetts, 1630-1877. Boston, 1877.

Palfrey, J. G. History of New England. 5 vols. (Vol. V by F. W. Palfrey.) Boston, 1890-97.

Palmer, Peter S. History of Lake Champlain. Albany, 1866.

Parker, Cortlandt. Historical Address (in Bicentennial Celebration of the Board of American Proprietors of East New Jersey). Newark, 1885.

Pennsylvania, Votes and Proceedings of the House of Representatives of the Province of. 6 vols. Philadelphia, 1752-76.

Pennsylvania Archives (ed. Samuel Hazard and others). 100 vols. Philadelphia and Harrisburg, 1852-1914.

Pennsylvania Colonial Records (ed. Samuel Hazard and others). 16 vols. Philadelphia and Harrisburg, 1851-53.

Pennsylvania German Society Proceedings and Addresses. Lancaster, Pa., 1891-.

Pennsylvania Historical Society Memoirs. Philadelphia, 1826-95.

Pennsylvania Magazine of History and Biography (Penna. Hist. Soc.). Philadelphia, 1877-.

Perry, William Stevens (ed.). Historical Collections Relating to the American Colonial Church. 5 vols. Hartford, 1870-78.

Peyton, J. Lewis. History of Augusta County, Virginia. Staunton, 1882.

Pitkin, Timothy. A Statistical View of the Commerce of the United States of America. New York, 1817.

Pitman, Philip. Present State of the European Settlements on the Mississippi (ed. F. H. Hodder). [London, 1770.] Cleveland, 1906.

Plymouth Colony Records (ed. N. B. Shurtleff). 12 vols. Boston, 1859-61.

Plymouth Town Records. 2 vols. Plymouth, 1889-92.

Pownall, Thomas. Three Memorials Most Humbly Addressed to the Sovereigns of Europe, Great Britain, and North America. London, 1784.

Prince Society Publications. 36 vols. Boston, 1865-1920.

Proud, Robert. History of Pennsylvania. 2 vols. Philadelphia, 1797-98.

Providence Early Records. 20 vols. Providence, 1892-1909.

Purchas, Samuel. Purchas his Pilgrimes. 4 vols. London, 1625.

Ranck, George W. History of Lexington, Kentucky. Cincinnati, 1872.

Rhode Island Colonial Records (ed. J. R. Bartlett). 10 vols. Providence, 1856-65.

Rhode Island Historical Society Collections. Providence, 1827-.

Roberts, Ellis H. New York. 2 vols. Boston and New York, 1896.

Robin, Abbé. New Travels through North America, 1781. Philadelphia, 1783.

Rockey, J. L. (ed.). History of New Haven County, Connecticut. 2 vols. New York, 1892.

Scharf, J. Thomas. History of Delaware, 1609-1888. 2 vols. Philadelphia, 1888.

—— History of Maryland. 3 vols. Baltimore, 1879.

Schenk, Mrs. Elizabeth H. History of Fairfield, Fairfield County, Conn. 2 vols. New York, 1889-1905.

Schoolcraft, Henry Rowe. History, Condition and Prospects, of Indian Tribes of the United States. Philadelphia, 1860.

Schoonmaker, Marius. History of Kingston, New York. New York, 1888.

Sewall, Samuel. History of Woburn, Middlesex County, Mass. Boston, 1868.

Shattuck, Lemuel. Report of the Committee of the City Council, 1845. Boston, 1846.

Shirley, William. Correspondence (ed. C. H. Lincoln). 2 vols. New York, 1912.

Slaughter, Rev. Philip. History of St. George's Parish in the County of Spotsylvania (ed. R. A. Brock). Richmond, 1890.

Smith, Captain John. The Tours, Travels, Adventures and Observations of. 2 vols. Richmond, 1819.

—— Works, 1608-1631 (ed. Edward Arber). Birmingham, 1884.

Smith, William. History of New York. Albany, 1814.

Smyth, J. F. D. Tour in the United States. 2 vols. London, 1784.

Southampton Town Records. 4 vols. Sag Harbor, N. Y., 1874-93.

South Carolina Historical and Genealogical Magazine (South Carolina Historical Society). Charleston, 1900-.

South Carolina Historical Society Collections. 5 vols. Charleston, 1857-97.

Spotswood, Alexander. Official Letters (from Va. Hist. Soc. Colls., I and II). 2 vols. Richmond, 1882-85.

Stevens, William Bacon. History of Georgia. 2 vols. New York, 1847, and Philadelphia, 1859.

Stiles, Ezra. Discourse on the Christian Union. Brookfield, 1799.

—— Itineraries and Correspondence. New Haven, 1916.

Stiles, Rev. Henry R. History and Genealogy of Ancient Windsor, Conn. 2 vols. Hartford, 1891-92.

Stone, E. M. History of Beverly. Boston, 1843.

Stone, W. L. (ed.) see Letters of Brunswick and Hessian Officers.

Sullivan, James. History of the District of Maine. Boston, 1795.

Temple, J. H. History of the Town of Whately, Massachusetts. Boston, 1872.

Thomas, Gabriel. Historical and Geographical Account of the Province and County of Pennsylvania, and of West New Jersey in America. London, 1698.

Thwaites, Reuben G. Early Western Travels. 32 vols. Cleveland, 1904-1907.

Tisbury Town Records (ed. S. W. Swift and J. W. Cleveland). Boston, 1903.

Trumbull, Benjamin. Complete History of Connecticut, 1630-1764. 2 vols. New Haven, 1818.

Trumbull, J. Hammond, ed. Memorial History of Hartford County, Conn., 1633-1884. 2 vols. Boston, 1886.

Tucker, George. History of the United States. 4 vols. Philadelphia, 1856-57.

U.S. Bureau of the Census. Heads of Families at the First Census of 1790. 12 vols. Washington, 1907-8.

Updike, Wilkins. History of the Episcopal Church in Narragansett, R. I. 3 vols. New York, 1847; Boston, 1907.

Vass, Rev. L. C. History of the Presbyterian Church in New Bern, N. C. Richmond, 1886.

Vermont Historical Society Proceedings. 19 vols. Montpelier and Burlington, 1861-1931.

Vinton, Rev. Francis. Orations on the Annals of Rhode Island and Providence Plantations (Addresses and Orations, Vol. VII, No. 8). New York, 1864.

Virginia. Journals of the House of Burgesses (ed. by R. McIlwaine). 13 vols. Richmond, 1913-15.

—— Statutes at Large from 1619 (ed. William Waller Hening). 13 vols. Richmond, 1819-23.

Virginia Calendar of State Papers (ed. W. P. Palmer and others). 11 vols. Richmond, 1875-93.

Virginia Colonial Records (Senate Document). Richmond, 1874.

Virginia Historical Register and Literary Advertiser (ed. William Maxwell). 6 vols. Richmond, 1848-53.

Virginia Historical Society Collections, New Series (ed. R. A. Brock). 11 vols. Richmond, 1882-92.

Virginia Magazine of History and Biography (Virginia Historical Society). Richmond, 1893-.

Walker, George Leon. History of the First Church in Hartford, 1633-1883. Hartford, 1884.

Warden, D. B. Statistical, Political, and Historical Account of the United States. 3 vols. Edinburgh, 1819.

Waters, Thomas Franklin. Ipswich in the Massachusetts Bay Colony. Ipswich, Mass., 1905.

Watson, Elkanah. Memoirs, 1777-1842 (ed. W. C. Watson). New York, 1857.

Watson, John F. Annals and Occurrences of New York City and State in the Olden Times. Philadelphia, 1846.

—— Annals of Philadelphia and Pennsylvania. Rev. and enlarged ed., 3 vols. [Vol. III added by W. P. Hazard]. Philadelphia, 1898. [1st ed., 2 vols., 1857].

Webster, Noah. N. Y. Directory for 1786, see New York Directory for 1786.

Weston, P. C. J. (ed.). Documents Connected with the History of South Carolina. London, 1856.

Weston Tax Lists, 1757-1827 (ed. Mary F. Peirce). Boston, 1897.

Wheeler, George Augustus, and Henry Warren Wheeler. History of Brunswick, Topsham, and Harpswell, Maine. Boston, 1878.

White, George. Historical Collections of Georgia. New York, 1855.

Whitehead, William A. East Jersey under the Proprietary Governments. 2d ed., Newark, 1875.

Williamson, William D. History of the State of Maine. 2 vols. Hallowell, 1832.

Willis, William. History of Portland, from 1632-1864. Portland, 1865.

—— Journals of the Rev. Thomas Smith and the Rev. Samuel Deane, Pastors of the First Church in Portland. Portland, 1849.

Winsor, Justin. Memorial History of Boston. 4 vols. Boston, 1880-81.

—— The Mississippi Basin, 1697-1763. Boston and New York, 1895.

—— Narrative and Critical History of America. 8 vols. Boston and New York, 1884-89.

Winthrop, John. History of New England (ed. James Savage). 2 vols. Boston, 1853.

Wisconsin State Historical Society. Collections. Madison, 1855-.

Wisconsin Historical Society. Proceedings. Madison, 1874-.

Wood, William. New England's Prospect. London, 1634.

Worthington, Erastus. History of Dedham. Boston, 1827.

Wynne, J. H. General History of the British Empire in America. 2 vols. London, 1770.

Yorge, Samuel H. The Site of Old "James Towne," 1607-1698. Richmond, 1904.

NOTE ON METHODS OF CALCULATION

Most of the estimates of population during the colonial period were computed on the basis of the number of militia, polls, taxables and tax lists, and families and houses, from which by multiplying by the ratio each group held to the whole population, the total number of inhabitants was estimated.

Militia: generally estimated at 5 to 1. — Gov. Dudley of Massachusetts in 1709 estimated the militia at 5 to 1, although in 1720 the Lords of Trade put it at 6 to 1, and in 1763 Gov. Bernard set it at 4 to 1. Felt, in *Statistics of Population in Mass.*, thought the ratio should be 5⅓ to 1, and Dexter thought it to be between 4½ and 5½ to 1. The modern statisticians hold that the ratio of men of military age to the whole population is 5 to 1, and in a country where recent immigrants made up so large a proportion of the inhabitants, it would not be any smaller and possibly would be larger, since there would be a tendency for the population to be concentrated between the ages of 16 and 60.

Polls, taxables, and *tax lists*: estimated at 4 to 1. — Polls were usually all men above 21, residents; sometimes, all above 16. Taxables might sometimes include nonresidents. There is general agreement among contemporaries such as Gov. Bernard (Ans. Quer., 1763), and modern students such as Felt, that they represented about one-fourth of the population. The taxables in the South were all white males above 16 and all negro males and females above 16. They were about one-third of the total population. *See* Virginia, p. 000.

Families: average size, 5.7 to 6. — The average size of the family by the census of 1790 was 5.7. It would hardly have been any smaller in the colonial period, and might have been somewhat larger, but certainly no more than 6 persons to a family. Brissot de Warville, *New Travels*, 362 ff., says that by the "general convention" of 1787 the family was estimated at 6 persons. Felt used 5½.

Houses: at least 7 to 1. — Gov. Bernard in 1763 estimated 5 or 6 persons to each house, but from the census of 1763-65 in Massachusetts it is apparent that more than one family frequently lived in one house. Felt multiplied the number of houses by 7.15.

AMERICAN POPULATION
BEFORE THE
FEDERAL CENSUS OF 1790

ABBREVIATIONS

Ans. Quer.	ANSWERS TO QUERIES
BT	BOARD OF TRADE
CO	COLONIAL OFFICE PAPERS
Conn. CR	CONNECTICUT COLONIAL RECORDS
Conn. HSC	CONNECTICUT HISTORICAL SOCIETY COLLECTIONS
CSPC	CALENDAR OF STATE PAPERS, COLONIAL SERIES: AMERICA AND WEST INDIES
CVSP	CALENDAR OF VIRGINIA STATE PAPERS
Ga. CR	GEORGIA COLONIAL RECORDS
Ga. HSC	GEORGIA HISTORICAL SOCIETY COLLECTIONS
HSPT	HISTORICAL SOCIETY OF PENNSYLVANIA TRANSCRIPTS
Humphreys, S. P. G.	HISTORICAL ACCOUNT OF THE SOCIETY FOR THE PROPAGATION OF THE GOSPEL
LC MS.	LIBRARY OF CONGRESS MANUSCRIPTS
LCT	LIBRARY OF CONGRESS TRANSCRIPTS
MHSC	MASSACHUSETTS HISTORICAL SOCIETY COLLECTIONS
MHSP	MASSACHUSETTS HISTORICAL SOCIETY PROCEEDINGS
N.C. CR	NORTH CAROLINA COLONIAL RECORDS
N.H. HSC	NEW HAMPSHIRE HISTORICAL SOCIETY COLLECTIONS
N.J. HSP	NEW JERSEY HISTORICAL SOCIETY PROCEEDINGS
NYCD	DOCUMENTS RELATING TO THE COLONIAL HISTORY OF NEW YORK
NYDH	DOCUMENTARY HISTORY OF NEW YORK
NYHSC	NEW YORK HISTORICAL SOCIETY COLLECTIONS
NYPL	NEW YORK PUBLIC LIBRARY
Pa. CR	PENNSYLVANIA COLONIAL RECORDS
Plymouth CR	PLYMOUTH COLONY RECORDS
Repr.	REPRESENTATION
Rept.	REPORT
R.I. CR	RHODE ISLAND COLONIAL RECORDS
R.I. HSC	RHODE ISLAND HISTORICAL SOCIETY COLLECTIONS
S.C. HSC	SOUTH CAROLINA HISTORICAL SOCIETY COLLECTIONS
S.P.G.	SOCIETY FOR THE PROPAGATION OF THE GOSPEL
Va. CR	VIRGINIA COLONIAL RECORDS
Va. HSC	VIRGINIA HISTORICAL SOCIETY COLLECTIONS
Vt. HSP	VERMONT HISTORICAL SOCIETY PROCEEDINGS

GENERAL ESTIMATES
OF THE
THIRTEEN COLONIES AS A WHOLE [1]

1625   1,980 colonists in America, including 180 in Plymouth and 1,800 in Va. Chalmers, *Revolt*, I, 29.

1641   50,000 English inhabitants ("mannen"). Peters to W. Ind. Co., in NYCD, I, 567.

1663   200,000 English in Am. Berkeley, *Discourse and View of Va.*, 10.

1665 [2]   80,000 population in Va. in 1659; 27,000 fighting men in Long Island and New Eng.; 2,500 fighting men in Plymouth; 4,300 fighting men in Conn.; 5,400 in New Haven and Providence Plantations. "General Desc. of Am.." in CSPC, 1661-68, 350, No. 1110.

1671   50,400 men, total forces by land: 1,500 in N.Y., Long Island, and N.J.; 14,000 in Conn.; 1,000 in Providence; 1,000 in Plymouth; 30,000 in Mass.; 1,800 in N.H.; 1,000 in Me., and 100 in Kennebec. Col. Cartwright to Council for Foreign Plantations, June 21, 1671, in CSPC, 1669-74, 232, No. 566. [Southern colonies not included.]

1688   200,000 inhabitants: Mass. with Plymouth and Me. 44,000; N.H. 6,000; R.I. with Providence 6,000; Conn. 17,000 to 20,000; New Eng. total 75,000; N.Y. 20,000; N.J. 10,000; Pa. and Del. 12,000; Md. 25,000; Va. 50,000; the two Carolinas and Ga. 8,000. Bancroft, I, 602, or II, 175 in 1879 ed.

        250,000 inhabitants. Chalmers, *Revolt*, I, 217.

1693   28,700 men able to bear arms: Va. 6,000 men; Md. 4,000; Pa. 2,000; Conn. 3,000; New Eng. 9,500; R.I. 1,200; N.Y. 3,000. "Estimate of the annual charge for the defence of Albany and of quotas to be furnished by the Various Colonies," in CSPC, 1693-96, 173, No. 611, iii.

1699   32,000 freemen estimated to be in the colonies: New Eng., Conn., and R.I. 16,000; N.Y. 4,000; the Jerseys 2,000; Pa. 2,000; Md. 3,000; Va. 5,000. "Col. Hamilton's Plan," in NYCD, IV, 680.

---

[1] No secondary estimates are included in this section except those of Chalmers, because he used the British State Papers extensively but frequently gave no citation; Bancroft, because of the frequency with which his figures have been quoted; and Tucker, because he arrived at his results by a method of estimation different from that used by other writers.

[2] The date is uncertain, but the editor places it at 1665.

1700   250,000 total population:[3] New Eng. 90,000; N.Y., the Jerseys, Pa.,
       Del., and Md. 80,000; Va. and Carolinas 80,000. Tucker, U.S., I,
       54.

1701   60,000 families. Memorandum from M. d'Iberville, "Archs. de la
       Marine," in *Rept. on Canadian Archs.*, *1905*, I, 523.
       262,000 total population: Conn. 30,000; Md. 25,000; Mass. 70,000;
       N.H. 10,000; N.J. 15,000; N.Y. 30,000; N.C. 5,000; Pa. 20,000;
       R.I. 10,000; S.C. 7,000; Va. 40,000. Memorials of Gov. Dudley,
       Col. Morris, and Col. Heathcote, in Humphreys, S.P.G., 41-42.
       238,000 souls: S.C. 7,000; N.C. 5,000; Va. 40,000; Md. 25,000; Pa.
       15,000; W.N.J. 2,000; E.N.J. 6,000; N.Y. 25,000; Conn. 30,000;
       Mass. 70,000; N.H. 3,000; R.I. (incl. Providence) 5,000; Narra-
       gansett or King's Province 3,000; Me. 2,000. "Acct. of the State
       of Religion in the Eng. Plantations in North Am.," by Col. Dud-
       ley, in Hawkins, *Hist. Notices*, 23-25.

1702   270,000 white inhabitants. Bancroft, II, 78.

1708   80,000 men in the several provinces. Col. Quary to BT, Jan. 10,
       1708, in CSPC, 1706-8, 638, No. 1273.

1709   150,000 souls from Pemaquid to Delaware River. Gov. Dudley, Ans.
       Quer., Mar. 1, 1709, in CSPC, 1708-9, 237, No. 391.

1715   434,600 total population: 375,750 whites; 58,850 Negroes.

Colony	White	Negro	Whole
N. H.	9,500	150	9,650
Mass.	94,000	2,000	96,000
R. I.	8,500	500	9,000
Conn.	46,000	1,500	47,500
N. Y.	27,000	4,000	31,000
N. J.	21,000	1,500	22,500
Pa.	43,300	2,500	45,800
Md.	40,700	9,500	50,200
Va.	72,000	23,000	95,000
N. C.	7,500	3,700	11,200
S. C.	6,250	10,500	16,750
Total	375,750	58,850	434,600

       Chalmers, *Revolt*, II, 7. Cf. Bancroft, II, 238.

1726   178,000 inhabitants: Me. 4,000; N.H. 7,000; Mass. 35,000; R.I.
       10,000; Conn. 20,000; N.Y. 20,000; Jersey 10,000; Pa. 15,000;
       Md. 6,000; Va. 30,000; N.C. 5,000; S.C. 16,000. Wendell Papers,
       in *N. E. Hist. Gen. Reg.*, XX, 7-9.

1727   502,000 white inhabitants. Chalmers, *Revolt*, II, 116.

[3] Tucker bases this estimate on the census of 1790, assuming an average duplication
of the entire population every 22¼ years.

1740 135,000 militia: New Eng. and Nova Scotia 38,000; Conn. and R.I. 8,000; N.Y. and the Jerseys 10,000; Pa. and the lower counties 50,000; Md. 10,000; Va. 12,000; N.C. 2,000; S.C. 4,000; Ga. 1,000. Rept. of Robt. Dinwiddie to BT, in *N.J. Archs.*, VI, 89, citing *Pls. Genl.*, X, N: 45.

1749 1,046,000 inhabitants: N.H. 30,000; Mass. 220,000; R.I. 35,000; Conn. 100,000; N.Y. 100,000; N.J. 60,000; Pa. and Del. 250,000; Md. 85,000; Va. 85,000; N.C. 45,000; S.C. 30,000; Ga. 6,000. Pitkin, *Statistical View*, 12.

1750 1,260,000 total inhabitants: 1,040,000 whites; 220,000 blacks. Bancroft, II, 390n.

1754 1,485,634 total souls: 1,192,896 whites; 292,738 blacks. Estimate of BT to the King, in Chalmers, *Revolt*, II, 273.[4] 1,428,000 total inhabitants: 1,165,000 whites; 263,000 blacks. Bancroft, II, 389-91.

1755 1,058,000 total white inhabitants according to reports to BT, as follows:

Colony	Date of Return	Whites	Militia	Men Capable of Bearing Arms
Ga.	1752	3,000	5,000	
S. C.	1755	25,000	.....	13,000
N. C.	1755	50,000	28,000	
Va.	1755	125,000	12,500	
Md.	1749	100,000		
Pa.	Estimated a	220,000 b	.....	25,000
Conn.	Do.	100,000		
R. I.	Do.	30,000		
N. J.	1755	75,000	10,000	
N. Y.	Estimated a	55,000	.....	12,000
Mass. Bay	Do.	200,000	.....	40,000
N. H.	1755	75,000	6,000	
		1,058,000		
Nova Scotia	1754	4,000	1,200	
		1,062,000		

NYCD, VI, 993; also in Anon., *State of British and French Colonies in North Am., 1755*, 139.

a No returns from Pa., Conn., and R.I. since 1730, nor from N.Y. and Mass. Bay since 1738, but estimates are taken from the "best accounts."
b Of these 100,000 are Germans and other foreign Protestants.
4 Bancroft says these figures included Nova Scotia. See Bancroft, II, 390.

1,471,000 total inhabitants: 1,318,000 whites; 153,000 blacks, as follows: N.H. 30,000; Mass. (incl. Me.) 220,000; R.I. (incl. Providence) 35,000; Conn. 100,000; N.Y. 100,000; N.J. 60,000; Pa. (incl. Del.) 360,000 (100,000 fighting men); Md. 140,000 (40,000 Negroes); Va. 230,000; N.C. 80,000; S.C. 110,000 (50,000 Negroes); Ga. 6,000. Gov. Dobbs to BT, in N.C. CR, V, 471-73.[5]

1757   1,000,000 English upwards, of which 80,000 were immigrants. Franklin, Works (Sparks), II, 319.

1760   1,695,000 inhabitants: 1,385,000 whites; 310,000 blacks. Bancroft, II, 390n.

1765   2,240,000 inhabitants, and 560,000 men, white and black, able to bear arms, as follows:

Colony	Men	Inhabitants
Mass.	70,000	280,000
N. H.	20,000	80,000
Conn.	45,000	180,000
R. I.	15,000	60,000
N. Y.	25,000	100,000
E. and W. N. J.	20,000	80,000
Pa. and Del.	100,000	400,000
Va. and Md.	180,000	720,000
N. C.	30,000	120,000
S. C.	45,000	180,000
Ga. and E. and W. Fla.	10,000	40,000

On map labeled "Distance in Am. in Eng. Miles, Done by Hugh Finlay, Esq., One of the Post-Masters General of Am.," in LC MS., Am. B-1765; also in The North Am. and W. Ind. Gazetteer, xxiv.[6] The list of men able to bear arms is also in N.Y. Gazette or Weekly Post Boy, Dec. 19, 1765.

1766   250,000 fighting men, at least. Franklin, "Letters concerning the Stamp Act," Writings (Smyth), IV, 394.

300,000 males, 16 to 60 years of age. Franklin, "Examination before the House of Commons," ibid., IV, 416.

1770   2,312,000 total population: 1,850,000 whites; 462,000 blacks. Bancroft, II, 390.

1774   2,141,307 population, although Congress Estimate is 3,026,678. Pownall, Memorial, 62-63.

3,016,678 total population according to informal estimate of mem-

---

[5] Gov. Dobbs criticizes estimates of the author of the British and French Colonies in Am. (see above) and recomputes the population of the southern colonies, basing his estimates on available returns of taxables, militia, etc. He is suggesting a revision of taxes, with a poll tax for each colony.

[6] The Gazetteer says this list was published in N.J. in 1765.

bers of Congress, as follows: N.H. 150,000; Mass. 400,000; R.I. 59,678; Conn. 192,000; N.Y. 250,000; N.J. 130,000; Pa. and Del. 350,000; Md. 320,000; Va. 640,000; N.C. 300,000; S.C. 225,000. Adams, *Works*, VII, 302-4.[7] Cf. d'Auberteuil, *Essais historiques et politiques*, 112; "Junius" in *N.H. Gazette*, Jan. 9, 1776, in *N.H. Prov. Papers*, VIII, 26; *Chalmers Coll.*, Md., I, NYPL; Gov. Trumbull to Baron J. D. Vander Capellan, Aug. 3, 1779, in MHSC, 1st Ser., VI, 179; "The Crisis Extraordinary," by Commonsense, in *N.J. Archs.*, 2d Ser. V, 57; Bancroft, II, 390; Jay to Florida Blanca, Apr. 25, 1780, in *Corr. of John Jay*, I, 283; and Long MSS., "History of Jamaica," III, 34, in *Brit. Mus. Add. MSS.*, 12413.

2,590,000 total population Aug. 1, 1774: Mass. 360,000; N.H. 80,000; Conn. 200,000; R.I. 50,000; N.Y. 180,000; N.J. 130,000; Pa. 300,000; Del. 40,000; Md. 220,000; Va. 560,000; N.C. 260,000; S.C. 180,000; Ga. 30,000. Tucker, *U.S.*, I, 96.[8]

2,600,000 total population: 2,100,000 whites; 500,000 blacks. Bancroft, IV, 62.[9]

1,911,000 European inhabitants in North Am. (including 17,000 in Nova Scotia): Nova Scotia 17,000; Conn. 191,392; Mass. 400,000; R.I. 35,939; N.Y. 148,000; N.H. 100,000; Va. 300,000; Pa. 300,000; Md. (1762) 114,332; Ga. 18,000; N.J. 77,000; S.C. 60,000. Knox MSS., Miscellaneous Papers,[10] in *Hist. MSS. Comm. Rept. 1909, Various Colls.*, V-VI, 288-89.

1775   2,418,000 total population: N.H. 100,000; Mass. 350,000; R.I. 58,000; Conn. 200,000; N.Y. 200,000; N.J. 130,000; Pa. 300,000; Del. 30,000; Md. 250,000; Va. 400,000; N.C. 200,000; S.C. 200,000. Clinton, *Public Papers*, I, 210 (69).[11]

2,803,000 inhabitants. De Bow, *Statistical View of U.S.*, 37n.

1783   2,389,300 population, according to Congressional computation: N.H. 82,200; Mass. 350,000; R.I. 50,400; Conn. 206,000; N.Y. 200,000; N.J. 130,000; Pa. 320,000; Del. 35,000; Md. 220,700;

[7] Adams explains that Ga. was not included as she was not represented in the first Congress. He then quotes Pownall's figures, but thinks these more nearly correct. These estimates were given in informal conversation, and are not in the Journals of Congress.

[8] Tucker bases his estimate on the census of 1790, q.v., supposing that the increase of the preceding ten years was 33⅓ per cent. Hence the population in 1780 would total 2,947,371. Then supposing the increase of the preceding six years had been 30 per cent, the natural increase being diminished and no gain allowed from immigration, the population for Aug. 1, 1774, would be 2,590,000.

[9] Bancroft bases this upon returns which he says were "but in part accessible to the Congress."

[10] The editor notes "A rough calculation on the MS. brings the total to 1,911,000, but the items do not exactly tally with those above. Md. is omitted and Conn. is given twice. Pa. is put at 300,000." The total of the figures given is 1,744,663, omitting Nova Scotia.

[11] No statement is made as to the source of these figures.

Va. 400,000; N.C. 200,000; S.C. 170,000; Ga. 25,000. Smyth, *Tour in the U.S.*, 413-14.[12]

1786   3,102,670 total inhabitants: N.H. 150,000; Mass. 400,000; R.I. 59,670; Conn. 192,000; N.Y. 250,000; N.J. 150,000; Pa. 300,000; Del. 50,000; Md. 320,000; Va. 650,000; N.C. 300,000; S.C. 225,000; Ga. 56,000. *Pa. Packet*, Dec. 11, 1786.

1787   2,776,000 total population: 2,568,000 population on which representation in Congress was based, i.e., taking only three-fifths of the Negro slaves in the southern states, as follows:[13]

N. H.	102,000	Md.	218,000	incl.	3/5	of	80,000	Negroes
Mass.	360,000	Va.	420,000	Do.			280,000	Do.
R. I.	58,000	N. C.	200,000	Do.			60,000	Do.
Conn.	202,000	S. C.	150,000	Do.			80,000	Do.
N. Y.	233,000	Ga.	90,000	Do.			20,000	Do.
N. J.	138,000		———				———	
Pa.	360,000		1,078,000	Do.			520,000	Do.
Del.	37,000							

1,490,000

C. C. Pinckney in S.C. House of Reps., Jan., 1788, in Elliott, *Debates*, IV, 277-86; and Farrand, *Recds.*, III, 253.

2,223,000 white inhabitants [14]: N.H. 82,000 to 102,000; Mass. 352,000; R.I. 58,000; Conn. 202,000; N.Y. 238,000; N.J. 138,000 to 145,000; Pa. 341,000; Del. 37,000; Md. 174,000, and 80,000 blacks; Va. 300,000, and 300,000 blacks; N.C. 181,000; S.C. 93,000; Ga. 27,000. "Returns of Numbers in Several States," Brearly Papers, in Farrand, *Recds.*, I, 573.

NEW ENGLAND

GENERAL

1632   2,000 English. Capt. Thos. Wiggin to Secy. Coke, in CSPC, VI, 156, No. 8.

1634   30,000 persons in the plantations beginning at New Plymouth and ending at Penobscott, whereof "New Plimouth may containe well nere 1,800, the Massachusetts more than 20,000, the rest of the Patents beinge planted with the residue." "Relation Concerning the Estate of New Eng.," in *N.E. Hist. Gen. Reg.*, XL, 72.

[12] The same figures are given for 1785 by Mandrillon, *Le Spectateur américain*, 332, except that Md. is put at 220,000, and Conn. at 206,900, which makes the total 2,389,500.

[13] Counting all Negroes, the total population of the southern states is 1,286,000 (Va. 532,000; N.C. 224,000; S.C. 182,000; Ga. 98,000) and of U.S. 2,776,000.

[14] If larger alternatives are used, 2,250,000.

1637 21,200 men, women, and children. Josselyn, "New Eng. Rarities," in *Am. Antiq. Soc. Colls.*, IV, 236.

1641 40,000 inhabitants. "Proposals of Mr. Peters to the Amsterdam W. Ind. Co.," in NYCD, I, 568.

1648 50-60,000 souls. "Mandamus in Appeal of Messrs. Cuyter and Melyn," in NYCD, I, 251.

1665 12,000 men may be mustered in New Eng., whereof two-thirds esteemed Masters and one-third servants; Mass. about 7,000, and the other four colonies about 5,000 more. Notes on New Eng. evidently submitted by the Commission of 1665.[1] Egerton MS., 2395, fol. 415, in LCT.

27,000 fighting men in Long Island and New Eng. *See* Thirteen Colonies: General, 1665.

1675 120,000 souls; 13,000 families; 16,000 that can bear arms.[2] Observations made by the Curious on New Eng. about 1673, in Chalmers, *Annals*, I, 434-35; also in *N.E. Hist. Gen. Reg.*, XXXVIII, 379.

7,000 or 8,000 foot and 8 or 10 troops of horse, each troop consisting of between 60 and 80 horse, in the militia. "An Acct. taken from Mr. Harris of New Eng.," in CSPC, 1675-76, 220, No. 543.

1676 150,000 inhabitants, including Hampshire and Me.; 30-40,000 able to bear arms. Edward Randolph's Rept.,[3] in CSPC, 1675-76, 464-65, No. 1067.

80,000 inhabitants in New Plymouth and Conn., and about 20,000 men able to bear arms. *Ibid.*, 1675-76, 468, No. 1067.

1686 22,000 men on the muster-rolls of the territory between Pemaquid and Delaware.[4] Letter from New. Eng., Boston, Nov. 1, 1694, in CSPC, 1693-96, No. 1467.

1688 75,000 inhabitants. *See* Thirteen Colonies: General, 1688.

1689 200,000 souls. "A Brief Relation of the State of New Eng.," Force, *Tracts*, IV, Tract XI, 5.

100,000 souls, and perhaps many more. Mather, "Vindication of New Eng.," in *Andros Tracts*, II: *Prince Soc. Pub.*, VI, 23.

1690 13,279 militia, as follows: Mass. 9,282; Conn. 3,061; R.I. 792;

[1] A further statement is made: "The size of the family is ordinarily 7, 8, or 9 persons," *Ibid.*, fol. 423.

[2] Felt comments: "The first item exceeds all reasonable bounds. Results from a calculation based on the last two items make the first much less. The families, multiplied by 5½ persons each, would afford the product of 71,500. The military, multiplied by 5⅓ would give 85,333 as the inhabitants of New Eng. The mean proportion of these two sums is 78,416 within a fraction." "Statistics of Population in Mass.," in *Amer. Statist. Assoc. Colls.*, I, 140-41.

[3] Felt, 141, considers this report highly extravagant.

[4] This territory would include N.Y. and N.J. as well as New Eng.

Me. 144; N.H. ——. Gov. Andros, May 13, 1690, in CO 5: 855, Bb, P: 23, pp. 202-5. Cf. CSPC, 1689-92, 261, No. 879.[5]

1693   9,500 men able to bear arms in New Eng. *See* Thirteen Colonies: General, 1693.

1697   10,000 or 15,000 families in New Eng. The Agents for N.Y. to BT, in CSPC, 1696-97, 353, No. 691.

1699   16,000 freemen in New Eng., Conn., and R.I. *See* Thirteen Colonies: General, 1699.

1700   90,000 total population in New Eng. *See* Thirteen Colonies: General, 1700.

1708   160,000 souls and 50,000 fighting men. Oldmixon, *British Empire*, I, 106.

       100,000 to 120,000 souls. Stiles, *Christian Union*, 141, quoting Thomas Brattle.

1740   38,000 militia in New Eng. and Nova Scotia. *See* Thirteen Colonies: General, 1740.

1743   200,000 souls, or a little less, two-thirds at least in number of all British subjects on the continent of North America. P. Bearcroft to M. J. Meadows, in Perry, *Hist. Colls. Re. Am. Col. Church*, III, 376.

1746   75,000 fighting men. Chalmers, *Revolt*, II, 243.

1755   436,936 inhabitants.[6] Holmes, *Annals*, II, 68, citing *Pemberton MS. Chron.*

1760   501,909 souls. Stiles, *Christian Union*, 142.[7]

1774   746,000 people, according to estimate lately taken by an order "from home": R.I. 60,000; N.H. 70,000; Conn. 196,000; Mass. 420,000. Charles Lee to Sir Charles Dovers, Lee Papers, in NYHSC, IV, 136.

PLYMOUTH

GENERAL

1620   102 souls landed from the *Mayflower*. Bradford, "Hist. of Plymouth Plantation," in MHSC, 4th Series, III, 447-55.

1621   50 persons remained. *Ibid.*, 91.

1624   180 persons. Smith, "Advertisements for the Unexperienced Planters of New Eng.," in MHSC, 3d Series, III, 27.

---

[5] Chalmers, *Annals*, II, 87-88, gives the same figures plus 250 for N.H.

[6] Governor Shirley of Mass., *Correspondence*, II, 240, estimated 1,200,000 people in the northern colonies for this year, which, even were he including New York and New Jersey in this district, is evidently a gross exaggeration.

[7] Stiles bases his estimate on censuses, polls, etc., of the colonies for preceding years.

1627 33 families and 22 unattached men. List for Division of Cattle, in
Baylies, *New Plymouth*, I, Pt. I, 261-64.
1629-1630 300 people. Patent to Bradford, in Hazard, *Hist. Colls.*, I,
300.
1630 400 or 500 people. Smith, "Advertisements," in MHSC, 3d Series,
III, 40.
1633 89 polls. Shurtleff, "Plymouth Col. Rates," in *N.E. Hist. Gen. Reg.*,
IV, 252-53.
81 persons were taxed for estates. List in Hazard, *Hist. Colls.*, I,
326-27.
1634 81 polls. Shurtleff, "Plymouth Col. Rates," in *N.E. Hist. Gen. Reg.*,
IV, 253-54.
1637 122 freemen, or "allowing a proportion of 4½ to 1, 549 persons."
Felt, 143.[1]
1643 219 freemen, and 621 men, 16-60, able to bear arms.

	Freemen	Able to Bear Arms
Plymouth	64	148
Duxbury	34	81
Scituate	31	105
Sandwich	12	69
Cohannet	15	
Yarmouth	16	52
Barnstable	22	61
Marshfield	11	51
Rehoboth	4	
Nawsett	10	
Taunton	..	55
	219	622

Plymouth CR, VIII, 174 ff.
1658[2] 303 freemen: Plymouth 62; Duxbury 39; Scituate 46; Sandwich 8;
Taunton 17; Yarmouth 14; Barnstable 42; Marshfield 28; Rehoboth 16; Eastham 21; Bridgewater 10. Plymouth CR, VIII,
197-202.
1665 2,500 fighting men. *See* Thirteen Colonies: General, 1665.
1671 1,000 total forces by land. *See* Thirteen Colonies: General, 1671.
1675 407 freemen: Yarmouth 19; Barnstable 44; Marshfield 32; Rehoboth 40; Eastham 34; Bridgewater 16; Dartmouth 6; Swanzey
12; Middleberry 8; Plymouth 54; Duxburrow 43; Scituate 50;

[1] Felt adds this note, *Ibid.*, 214, that the freemen should be multiplied by about 6
instead of 4½, giving a total of 732.
[2] The editor finds nothing in the records to indicate the year of this list, but thinks,
because of "internal evidence," not cited, that it is 1658.

Sandwich 11; Taunton 31; Others 7. *Publ. Col. Soc. Mass.,* XXIV, 149-55, citing LC MS.

7,000 inhabitants. Bancroft, I, 383.

1,300 houses in trading towns and ports. "An Acct. of New Eng.," in *N.E. Hist. Gen. Reg.*, XXXVIII, 380-81. See below.

1678   1,000 or 1,500 men able to bear arms. Gov. Andros, Ans. Quer., in NYCD, III, 262.

1680   1,200 listed men from 16 to 60. Gov. Winslow, Ans. Quer., May 1, 1680, in CSPC, 1677-80, 522, No. 1349.

1683-1684   441 freemen: Plymouth 55; Duxbury 40; Scituate 62; Sandwich 15; Taunton 44; Yarmouth 22; Barnstable 53; Marshfield 63; Eastham 35; Rehoboth 52. Plymouth CR, VIII, 202-10.

1685   1,439 Indians, "besides boys and girls under 12 years old, which are supposed to be more than three times so many." Census by Gov. Hinckley, Hinckley Papers, in MHSC, 4th Series, V, 133.

1690   1,392 militia men. Sir. Ed. Andros to BT, in Palfrey, IV, 136n.

Local

I. Account of Trading Towns and Ports, 1675 [a]

Place		Number of Houses
Secunk		100
Swansye		50
Taunton		150
Dartmouth	(Burnt)	
Sandwich		100
Yarmouth		150
Nawsett		100
Barnstable		100
Plymouth		105
Duxberry		100
Scituate		300
Green Harbor		100
		1,300 [1,355]

MASSACHUSETTS

General

1630   1,000 persons, about. Petition in behalf of the Gov. and Mass. Bay Co. to the Privy Council, in CSPC, V, 120, No. 106.

1,600 English. Smith, "Advertisements," in MHSC, 3d Series, III, 41.

a "An Acct of New Eng.," in *N.E. Hist. Gen. Reg.*, XXXVIII, 380-81.

300 planters. Higginson, "New England's Plantation," in Force, *Tracts*, I, Tract XII, 13.

506 people in whole colony; more than 80 of this number were cut off the next winter by disease. Felt, 138-39.

1632 2,000 people. Wiggin, Letter to Sir John Cooke, Nov., 1632, in MHSC, 3d Series, VIII, 322. Cf. Sir Joseph Williamson, "Original Notes Relative to New Eng.," Col. Papers, No. 45, in MHSP, X, 380; also in CSPC, 1661-68, 179, No. 625.

1633 4,000 souls. Wood, *New England's Prospect*, 52.

1634 4,000 people. John Winthrop to Sir Nathaniel Riche, May 22, 1634, in Kimbolton Papers, No. 421, in MHSP, XX, 43.

1637 7,912 inhabitants. Estimate arrived at as follows: In 1637 the General Court ordered 211 men proportionately from each town in Mass. Salem was assessed 24 of them, and had 900 inhabitants. Thus in proportion of 24 to 900, 211 men argue 7,912. Felt, 139. Cf. Hutchinson, *Mass. Bay*, I, 76n.

1639 8,592 inhabitants, reckoning the militia at 1,611 men, and the whole population at 5⅓ times that. Militia computed at 1,000 for the Boston district (Winthrop's *Journal*), and 611 for outlying towns. Felt, 139.[1]

1643 15,000 population. Estimated on military levy of New Eng. Confed., in which the quota of Mass. was five times that of Plymouth, which had 627 militia. Palfrey, II, 5.[2]

1654 16,026 population. Estimated as follows: In 1654 Conn. had 3,186 inhabitants (q.v.), and was assessed 33 men by Commissioners of the United Colonies, while Mass. was assessed 166. Therefore, proportionately Mass. had 16,026 inhabitants. Felt, I, 140.

1661 80,000 persons. Address from Mass. to Charles II, in Johnson, *Wonder-Working Providence*, CXXIV-CXXVIn. (Poole ed.)

1665 23,467 inhabitants, on basis of militia of 4,000 foot and 400 horse, multiplied by 5⅓. Probably included the few towns of N.H. and Me. Felt, I, 140.

25,000 inhabitants in Mass. Palfrey, II, 35.[3]

1667 30,000 fighting men. Notes Relative to Am., in CSPC, 1661-68, 532, No. 1660.[4]

1670 1,000 to 1,200 freemen, counting 1 freeman for every 4-5 adult males. (Based on lists of freemen.) Palfrey, III, 41n.

[1] Felt, *Ibid.*, 140, thinks estimate of *Universal Hist.*, XXIX, 288, for 1642 of 7-8,000 militia for New Eng., which would give Mass. a population of 20,000, too high.

[2] Rossiter, *Cent. Pop. Growth*, uses figure 16-17,000, also given by Palfrey, but F. B. Dexter thinks 15,000 safer.

[3] Dexter and Rossiter also give 30,000 for this year.

[4] Rossiter gives 30,000 as entire population for 1665. Dexter also adopts 30,000 from Palfrey.

1671 30,000 total forces by land. *See* Thirteen Colonies: General, 1671.

1675 5,680 houses: Hull 80; Hingham 250; Waymouth 250; Brantree
      250; Dorchester 350; Boston 2,500; Charlestowne 500; Salem
      500; Marblehead 50; Cape Ann 50; Ipswich 400; Newberry
      300; Salisbury 200. "An Acct. of New Eng.," in *N.E. Hist. Gen.
      Reg.*, XXXVIII, 381.

1678 8-10,000 militia. Gov. Andros, Ans. Quer., in NYCD, III, 262.[5]

1688 44,000 with Plymouth and Me. *See* Thirteen Colonies: General,
      1688.

1690 100,000 people, increase in 50 years from 4,000 first planters
      arriving before 1640. Mather, *Magnalia*, Book I, 23.
      9,282 militia. See p. 19. Gov. Andros to BT, May 13, 1690, in
      CO 5: 855, Bb, P:23, pp. 202-5.

1695 2,605 adult Indians. Mather, *Magnalia*, Book VI, 54, 56, 60.

1696 10,000 men fit to bear arms. Proc. of BT, in NYCD, IV, 185,
      citing BT, *Journal*, IX, 100.
      62,724 people. Estimated as follows: Stiles' estimate of New Eng.
      in 1696 was 100,000. Mass. quota against the French was 350
      out of a total of 558 for New Eng. Thus her proportion of
      100,000 is 62,724. Felt, 141-42. Cf. estimates in Barry, *Hist. of
      Mass.*, II, 49n;[6] Winsor, *Narr. Crit. Hist.*, V, 92; Palfrey, IV,
      135.

1700 9,304 militia men. Lord Bellomont to BT, in Palfrey, IV, 36n.

1701 80,000 souls, including Me. Humphreys, S. P. G., 42.
      70,000 population. *See* Thirteen Colonies: General, 1701.

1702 10,000 militia in 1702, and 50,000 souls. Gov. Dudley, Ans. Quer.,
      Mar. 1, 1709, in CSPC, 1708-9, 235, No. 391.

1704 7,750 men only. Rept. of Commissioners to Gov. Dudley, Dec. 28,
      1704, in CSPC, 1704-5, 668, No. 1424.

1707 10,000 freeholders. Gov. Dudley to the Queen, Nov. 10, 1707, in
      CSPC, 1706-8, 593, No. 1186. ii, citing CO 5: 864, No. 231.

1709 56,000 souls besides the blacks. Gov. Dudley, Ans. Quer., Mar. 1,
      1709, in CSPC, 1708-9, 235, No. 391, citing CO 5: 865, No. 22.

1710 10,917 militia, besides 500 in service. Repr. BT, in NYCD, V, 597;
      also in *BT Pls. Genl.*, E38; and *Kings MS.*, 205, p.l., in LCT.

1712 75,102 population. Estimate of Gov. Dudley, in Felt, 584.

1715 96,000 inhabitants: 94,000 whites, 2,000 Negroes. *See* Thirteen Col-
      onies: General, 1715.

[5] Felt, 584, compromises on 9,000 militia, and estimates 48,000 inhabitants, which he
considers too large if Andros meant only the territory then in the Commonwealth.
[6] Bases estimate on report to BT. in 1715 of 94,000 population. As population doubled
once in 25 or 30 years, the estimate for 1692 could not have exceeded 40,000 or 50,000.
Dexter and Rossiter use 60,000.

1718 94,000 souls: 15,611 militia; 1,200 Indians; 2,000 slaves mostly
Negroes. Gov. Shute, Ans. Quer., Feb. 17, 1719, from Baxter
MSS. in Me. *Doc. Hist.*, X, 106-7.

14,925 militia besides 300 officers, 500 in service, and 800 exempt;
1,200 Indians. *Kings MS.*, 205, fol. 9, p. 14, in LCT; also NYCD,
V, 597.

1721 94,000 souls.[7] Repr. BT to King, *Kings MS.*, 205, fol. 9, p. 14, in
LCT.

1726 22,000 ratable male polls. Gov. Belcher, Ans. Quer., Mar. 1736-37,
in CO 5: 879, Cc 38.

35,000 inhabitants. *See* Thirteen Colonies: General, 1726.

1728 20,000 militia. Gov. Belcher, Ans. Quer., Apr. 5, 1751, in Benton.
Early Census Making in Mass., 22.

1731 120,000 white inhabitants. Anderson, *Origin of Commerce*, III, 426.

1733 120,000 souls are not to be exceeded in Mass. Province, nor 25,000
fit to bear arms. Gov. Belcher to Chandos, 1733, from Belcher
Papers, I, in MHSC, 6th Series, VI, 383.

1735 35,427 white males from 16 and upwards; 2,600 Negroes.[8] Anon.,
State of British and French Colonies in North Am., 1755, 132-33.

144,308 total inhabitants. Estimated on basis of above by multiplying white males by 4 for total whites. Felt, 142.

1736 30,000 ratable male polls; females and those under 16, not ratable,
reckoned at 4 to 1; 2,000 Negroes, and 1,000 Indians. Gov. Belcher, Ans. Quer., Mar. 1736-37, in CO 5: 879, Cc 38.

1737 25,931 militia by exact count. Gov. Belcher to BT, Jan. 28, 1737-
38, in CO 5: 880, Cc 87.

1742 164,000 population. Pownall, *Memorial*, 58.

200,000 population on basis of 41,000 white polls. Douglass, *Summary*, I, 531, and II, 180.

1747 36,000 militia, or about 192,000 people. Cited from *Hist. of the
British Dominions*, in Felt, 142.

1749 220,000 people.[9] Holmes, *Annals*, II, 538.

220,000 inhabitants. *See* Thirteen Colonies: General, 1749.

1751 120,000 white inhabitants, and 2,000 Negroes. (On basis of militia
of 20,000 for 1728.) 3,000 "Praying Indians"; 300 fighting men
among other Indians of the province. Gov. Belcher, Ans. Quer.,
Apr. 5, 1751, in Benton, *Early Census Making in Mass.*, 22.

164,484 population. Pownall, *Memorial*, 58.

---

[7] The same figure, 94,000 souls, is given for 1722 by Felt, 142, and Douglass, *Summary*, I, 531, and Pownall, *Memorial*, 58.

[8] Felt, 142, says figure is based upon Provincial Acct. of polls.

[9] Dexter uses this figure from Pitkin, *Statistical View*, 12.

1754   200,000 population.[10] Gov. Shirley to Earl of Holderness, Jan. 7, 1754, in *Shirley Corr.*, II, 21.

1755   200,000 inhabitants; or 220,000 including Me. *See* Thirteen Colonies: General, 1755.

1758   45,764 men on the Alarm List of 32 regiments, of which 37,446 are by law obliged to train. Gov. Pownall to BT, Jan. 15, 1758, in CO 5: 888, Ii, p. 25.

1759   41,000 fencible men; but the train band list did not amount to more than 35,000. Gov. Bernard, Ans. Quer., Sept. 5, 1763, in *Kings MS.*, 205, fol. 203, pp. 412-13, in LCT.

1760   200,000 souls. Burnaby, *Travels*, 104.

1761   216,000 population. Pownall, *Memorial*, 58.

       152,000 total population, as follows: ratable polls, 57,000; add one-third for males under 16, and those unable to pay, equals 76,000; plus an equal number of females, equals 152,000.

       160,000 total population, on basis of number of houses: 32,000 houses multiplied by 5 equals 160,000.

       176,000 total population, if houses are multiplied by $5\frac{1}{2}$.

       192,000 total population, if houses are multiplied by 6.

       Various estimates by Gov. Bernard, Ans. Quer., Sept. 5, 1763, in *Kings MS.*, 205, fol. 201, p. 409; fol. 202, p. 410, in LCT; and in Benton, *Early Census Making in Mass.*, 54-55; also in CO 5: 891, Ll, pp. 67-68.

       53,940 ratable polls. 31,976 dwelling houses, according to valuation in 1761. Encl. in Gov. Hutchinson's letter to Earl of Dartmouth, Oct. 1, 1773, in CO 5: 762, p. 811.

       54,000 ratable polls, or 270,000 total population.[11] Gov. Hutchinson to Earl of Dartmouth, Oct. 1, 1773, in CO 5: 762, p. 787.

1763   200,000 souls; Negroes and mulattoes, 2,221; 370 families of Indians. "As all returns before mentioned were taken in order to make a rate of taxes . . . they are certainly short of the truth." Gov. Bernard, Ans. Quer., Sept. 5, 1763, in *Kings MS.*, 205, fol. 201, p. 409; 202, p. 410, in LCT.

1763-   241,024 total population: 235,810 whites; 5,214 blacks, according

[10] Gov. Shirley noted decrease in population of Mass. due to lack of immigration, loss of land to N.H. and R.I. in boundary disputes, and losses during wars. He probably does not overestimate the Mass. population, as he is protesting against what he considers an unfair military levy.

[11] Gov. Hutchinson continues: "These estimates are not to be depended upon, every town being desirous of keeping both Inhabitants and Estate as low as possible . . . but as this has always been the case a pretty good judgment may be made of the increase of the Province. . . . Both returns are supposed to be somewhat short of the full number, and it is thought by many not too large a computation when the number of males and females of all ages are made to be five times the number of polls in these estimates."

1765 to census. "Dr. Belknap's Ans. to Judge Tucker's Quer. Respecting Slavery, etc.," in MHSC, 1st Series, IV, 198.

241,813 total population according to Census of 1763-65. Felt, 157.

244,016 total population. Chase, *Abstract of Census of Mass., 1860*, 261.

238,226 total population.[12] Benton, *Early Census Making in Mass.*, 72-104. See page 21 below.

1765 250,000 souls; 5,500 blacks, and 1,500 Indians. Gov. Hutchinson's Ans. Quer., Oct. 1, 1773, in CO 5: 762, pp. 801-2.

255,000 population. Pownall, *Memorial*, 58.

280,000 inhabitants; 70,000 men able to bear arms. *See* Thirteen Colonies: General, 1765.

1770 266,565 inhabitants, reckoning an average rate of increase of 9.1811 per cent in five years over census figures of 1763-65. Chickering, *Statistical View*, 9.

1771 73,000 ratable polls or 365,000 inhabitants. Gov. Hutchinson to Earl of Dartmouth, Oct. 1, 1773, in CO 5: 762, p. 787.

292,000 population. Pownall, *Memorial*, 58.

1772 73,478 polls: ratable 71,779; non-ratable, 1,699.[13] Felt. 132, 157. See page 30.

1773 300,000 population, even allowing for emigration of many families to the frontier towns in N.Y. and N.H.; 6,000 blacks, and 1,500 Indians. Gov. Hutchinson, Ans. Quer., Oct. 1, 1773, in CO 5: 762, pp. 801-2. Cf. Pownall, *Memorial*, 58.

1774 400,000 total population; or 360,000. *See* Thirteen Colonies: General, 1774.

1775 291,039 inhabitants at rate of 9.1811 per cent increase in five years. Chickering, *Statistical View*, 9. See above, 1770.

352,000 inhabitants. De Witt, *Abstract of Census in Mass.*, 1855.

350,000 total population. *See* Thirteen Colonies: General, 1775.

1776 338,667 total population: 333,418 whites; 5,249 blacks,[14] according to census by counties and towns. See pages 30, 31. Felt, 165, 213.

290,000 total population for Mass., deducting the three Me. counties, York, Cumberland, Lincoln. Thus 47,279 whites from 333,418 equals 286,139, and 241 blacks from 5,249 equals 4,761.[15] Chickering, *Statistical View*, 9.

---

[12] Felt and Chase both draw their figures from the census as published in the *Columbian Centinel*, Aug. 17, 1822 — the Dana MS. Benton reprints the Crane MS., which was found about 1900. See note to table, page 000. Felt discovered errors in the added totals of his version, which when corrected made the total whites 242,780. There are also errors in the Crane MS. The correct total is 245,627.

[13] The author states the figures are drawn from a MS. of credible authority and also mentions another list giving a total of 71,728 polls.

[14] Author also (*Ibid.*, 158) mentions a document issued by the legislature in 1782 which states results of census as 338,627.

[15] According to Felt (q.v.) 241 represents returns for Negroes in York Co. only. The

349,094 total population including Me.: 343,845 whites and 5,249
blacks. See page 30. *Journals Prov. Cong. Mass.*, 755; also "Dr.
Belknap's Ans. to Judge Tucker's Quer. Respective Slavery,
etc.," in MHSC, 1st Series, IV, 198.[16]

1777 343,876 total white population including Me. counties. Morison,
Mass. Const. Conventions, in MHSP, L, 248. See page 30. (Abstract of Census in *Mass. Archs.*, 332:99.)

75,689 polls; 796 strangers; 1,099 Quakers; see page 31. Felt, 165.

1778 76,445 polls in valuation. Felt, 165. See page 31.

345,843 total white inhabitants, estimated on basis of 4½ times
76,854 polls. *Ibid.*, 132, quoting document issued by legislature,
1782.

1780 317,760 population on basis of an average rate of 9.1811 per cent
increase in five years. Chickering, *Statistical View*, 9.

1781 77,388 polls in valuation. Felt, 165. See page 31.

358,402 white inhabitants on basis of 4½ times 79,645 polls. *Ibid.*,
132, quoting document issued by legislature, 1782.

1783 350,000 population. *See* Thirteen Colonies: General, 1783.

1784 357,510 total inhabitants: 353,133 whites; 4,377 blacks, by census.
"Dr. Belknap's Ans. to Judge Tucker's Quer. Respecting Slavery,
etc.," in MHSC, 1st Series, IV, 198. Cf. Morse, *American Geography*, 172. See page 46.

90,757 polls; 789 maintained by the towns; total 91,546, multiplied
by 4 is 366,184 inhabitants. Felt, 170.[17] See page 40.

77,034 polls for Mass., deducting 13,723 for Me. counties.

346,653 inhabitants, multiplying polls by 4½. Chickering, *Statistical
View*, 10.

1785 346,934 inhabitants, at average rate of 9.1811 per cent increase in
five years. Chickering, *Statistical View*, 9.

330,836 whites; 4,188 blacks. Baxter MSS., from Sec'y's office, in
Me. Doc. Hist., XXI, 63. Cf. Webster, in *N.Y. Directory for
1786*, 21.

1786 352,171 whites; 4,371 blacks, by returns made into Sec'y's office of
number of inhabitants. Gov. Bowdoin's Message, from Baxter
MSS., in *Me. Doc. Hist.*, XXI, 153.

400,000 inhabitants. *See* Thirteen Colonies: General, 1786.

1787 360,000 total population, or 352,000 whites. *See* Thirteen Colonies:
General, 1787.

aggregate returns for the three Me. counties would be 619, which, deducted, would give
Mass. proper a total population of 290,769. Chickering cites these figures to show the
near agreement of the actual census with his own estimate for 1775.

[16] Cf. *The North Am. and W. Ind. Gazetteer*, under "Mass. Bay"; and Anon., *Hist.
of North Am.*, 78.

[17] The author also mentions (*ibid.*, 170) a MS. document in the Mass. Hist. Soc.
which gives the total figure at 357,511 but cites nothing more definite.

1790 378,787 total inhabitants by census, as follows:[18] number of families, 65,779; free white males over 16, 95,453; free white males under 16, 87,289; free white females, 190,582; other free persons, 5,463. U.S. Bureau of Census, *Heads of Families*, Mass., 9-10. See page 46.

LOCAL

I. MILITIA FOR 1690 [a]

Suffolk		Suffolk — Continued		Middlesex One-half	
Boston [b]	954	Medfield [f]	98	Watertown	151
Roxberry [c]	129	Hull [g]	53	Cambridge [h]	118
Dorchester [d]	149	Muddy River	51	Cambridge Vill.	77
Braintree	139	Wrentham	44	Charlestown [i]	98
Weymouth	116	Mendham	52	Charlestown	91
Hingham	119	Horse:		Redding	75
Dedham [e]	111	Weymouth	56	Oborne	142
Milton	78		1,195	Medfield	20
			[2,149]		

a CO5: 855, Bb, P: 23, pp. 202-5.

b Boston in *1664* had 14,300 souls: CSPC, 1661-1668, 532, No. 1660; in *1674*, 989 on tax lists containing 691 ratables and 298 non-ratables: Incomplete Lists, in *Boston Recds.*, I, 20-59; 1,330 polls in *1687*: Shattuck, *Rept. to City Council*, 1845, 5; 1,499 polls in *1688*: *Boston Recds.*, I, 134-45; 972 heads in *1691*: Tax List, in *ibid.*, I, 148-57.

c Roxbury had 70 ratable polls in *1639*: Ellis, *Hist. Roxbury Town*, 17-19; 80 families in *1657*: Hutchinson Papers in MHSC, 3d ser., I, 50.

d Dorchester had 120 families in *1657*: Hutchinson Papers in MHSC, 3d ser., I, 50; 200 or more houses in *1663*: Josselyn, "Voy. to New Eng.," in MHSC, 3d ser., III, 318.

e Dedham had 61 taxables in *1642*: Worthington, *Hist. Dedham*, 42. The rate lists show 91 taxables for *1648*; 92 for *1649*; 79 for *1651*; 71 for *1652*; 90 for *1653*; 87 for *1659*; 88 for *1660*; 93 for *1661*; 81 for *1662*; 97 for *1663*; 96 for *1664*; 91 for *1665*; 67 for *1666*; 94 for *1667*; 104 for *1668*; 80 for *1669*; 99 for *1670*; 98 for *1671*; 91 for *1672*; 104 for *1673*; 87 for *1674*; 94 for *1675*; 99 for *1676*; 95 for *1677*; 90 for *1678*; 103 for *1679*; 110 for *1680*; 108 for *1681*; 113 for *1682*; 114 for *1683*; 122 for *1684*; 114 for *1685*; 115 for *1686*; 117 for *1687*; 119 for *1689*; 129 for *1690*; 101 for *1692*; 124 for *1693*; 126 for *1694*; 127 for *1695*; 122 for *1696*; 131 for *1697*; 128 for *1698*; 134 for *1699*; 146 for *1700*; 125 for *1701*; 139 for *1702*; 127 for *1703*; 159 for *1704*; 162 for *1705*; 142 for *1706*. *Dedham Town Recds.*: Lists for *1648-53* in III, 152-53, 160-61, 183-84, 205, 213-14; for *1659-71* in IV, 6-7, 25-26, 37-38, 50, 68-69, 90-91, 104-5, 119-20, 138-39, 158-59, 176-77, 200-1, 207-8; for *1672-1706* in V, 2-3, 7-8, 19-20, 32-33, 41-42, 55-56, 70-71, 83-84, 99-100, 110-11, 130-31, 141-42, 153-55, 171-72, 187-88, 200-201, 204-5, 211-12, 214-17, 223-24, 227-28, 233, 240, 246-47, 254, 265-66, 275-76, 290-91, 299-300, 310-11, 325-26, 347-48, 359.

f Medfield had 40 families in *1657*: Hutchinson Papers, in MHSC, 3d Series, I, 50.

g Hull had 20 houses in *1644*: Winthrop, *Hist. New Eng.*, II, 214.

h Cambridge had 85 houses in *1635*: Gilman, *Cambridge of 1776*, 6; 135 on rate list in *1647*: Paige, *Hist. Cambridge*, 439; 169 taxables and 121 families in *1680*; 191 taxables in *1688*: Drake, *Hist. Middlesex Co.*, I, 326.

i Charlestown had 58 inhabitants in *1633*: Charlestown Recds., in *N.E. Hist. Gen. Reg.*, XX, 109; 200 families with 240 males in *1679*: Paige, "Middlesex Statistics" in *N.E. Hist. Gen. Reg.*, V, 171-74; 319 polls in *1688*: Jeffries Family Papers in *N.E. Hist. Gen. Reg.*, XXXIV, 269.

18 Rossiter gives 378,556 for Mass.; 96,643 for Me.; total 475,199. The 1790 census total is incorrect; see page 46.

I. MILITIA FOR 1690 — *Continued*

Middlesex One-half — *Continued*		*Essex One-half —* *Continued*		*Essex One-half —* *Continued*	
Malden	73	Ipswich o	129	Andover	106
Horse: [1]	80	Ipswich	175	Amesbury	96
[2]	60	Lynn	120	Bradford	48
	————	Marblehead	206	Boxford	33
	985	Beverly p	137	Horse:	
Middlesex One-half		Gloucester	77	Newbury and	
Groton j	58	Warham	70	Rowley	78
Malborough	68	Salem Village	82	Haverhill ⎫	
Chelmsford	98	Horse:		Salsbury ⎬	45
Dunstable	31	Salem	40	Amesbury ⎫	
Billerica k	105	Ipswich	71	Andover ⎪	
Lancaster	58	Lynn	57	Topsfield ⎬	51
Sherborne	63	Beverly	37	Bradford ⎭	
Sudbury	103		————		
Concord l	162		1,445		1,112
Stow m	29				[1,117]
Horse:		*Essex One-half*		*Cornwall*	
Sudbury	104	Newberry q	129	Newton and	
	————	Newberry	116	Sagadahoc	94
	879	Salsbury	112	New Dartmouth	47
Essex One-half		Rowley r	115	James Town and	
Salem n	129	Haverhill	113	New Harbor	60
Salem	115	Topsfield s	75		————
					201

j Groton had 4 or 5 families in *1661*; 60 families and 300-350 inhabitants in *1676*; 40 families in *1680*: Green, "Pop. of Groton," in MHSP, 2d Series, IV, 136-38.

k Billerica had 48 families and 47 houses in *1675*; 60 ratables in *1679*; 50 families able to pay taxes, 10 aged persons, poor, and widows in *1680*: Farmer, *Hist. Mem. Billerica*, 11; 103 polls, 12 impotent persons in *1688*: Jeffries Family Papers, in *N.E. Hist. Gen. Reg.*, XXXI, 303-7.

l Concord in *1679* had 120 ratable males: Paige, "Middlesex Statistics," in *N.E. Hist. Gen. Reg.*, V, 171-74.

m Stow in *1688* had 34 taxables: Jeffries Family Papers, in *N.E. Hist. Gen. Reg.*, XXXII, 81.

n Salem in *1632* had 40 families: Bentley, "Desc. of Salem," in MHSC, 1st ser., VI, 223; 226 families, 884 to 901 inhabitants, in *1637*: Orig. Recds. in *Essex Inst. Hist. Colls.*, XLII, 379; 85 houses and 300 polls in *1678*: Bentley, "Desc. of Salem," in MHSC, 1st Series, VI, 223.

o Ipswich had 127 freemen in *1673*: *Essex Inst. Hist. Colls.*, XLV, 355-56; 146 families in *1646*: Nason, "Hist. Ipswich," in *Hist. Essex Co.*, 203; 125 freemen in *1679*: Water, *Ipswich in Mass. Bay Colony*, 91-93.

p Beverly had 600 in population in *1668*: Stone, *Hist. Beverly*, 197.

q Newbury in *1691* had 250 ratable polls: Coffin, *Hist. Newbury, Newbury Port*, 156.

r Rowley in *1662* had 87 ratables: List, in *N.E. Hist. Gen. Reg.*, XV, 253-54.

s Topsfield had 46 on rate list in *1668*: List in *Essex Inst. Hist. Colls.*, XXXIII, 194-95; 91 taxables in *1687*; 98 taxables in *1688*: Jeffries Family Papers in *N.E. Hist. Gen. Reg.*, XXXV, 34-37; 100 polls in *1723-25*: List in *Essex Inst. Hist. Colls.*, XXXIII, 194-96.

I. MILITIA FOR 1690 — Continued

Plymouth		Bristol — Continued		Hampshire — Cont.	
Plymouth t	155	Swansey	101	Enfield	36
Bridgewater	88	Little Compton	82	Horse:	
Duxberry	82		—	Springfield	65
Middleborough	33		780		—
Scituate	173	Hampshire			654
Marshfield	80	Springfield	98	Barnstable	
	606	[611] Hadley u	62	Eastham	119
Bristol		Northampton	110	Yarmouth	118
Bristol	108	Hatfield v	82	Barnstable	134
Freetown	31	Deerfield	51	Sandwich	100
Dartmouth	96	Northfield	34		471
Rehoboth	166	Suffield	60	Total	9,282w
Taunton	196	Westfield	56		[9,292]

II. CENSUS OF 1765 a

A. COUNTY TOTALS ONLY

County	Dana MS.	Crane MS.
Suffolk	34,997	36,352
Essex	42,706	43,707
Middlesex	32,710	33,814
Hampshire	18,472	17,298
Worcester	31,239	30,464
Plymouth	20,733	22,350
Barnstable	11,691	12,471
Bristol	20,900	18,070
York	10,465	10,719
Duke's	2,180	2,739
Nantucket	2,820	3,526
Cumberland	7,366	7,474
Lincoln	2,623	3,624
Berkshire	2,911	3,019
	241,813	238,226 [245,627]

t Plymouth in 1689 had 75 freemen: "Notes on Plymouth," in MHSC 2d Series, III, 170.

u Hadley had 48 taxables in 1670; 50 families in 1675; 79 taxables in 1681; 57 taxables in 1682; 60 families in 1685; 82 taxables in 1686: Judd, Hist. of Hadley, 92, 152, 198, 211, 212.

v Hatfield had 60 freemen in 1678: List from County Recorder's Book, in N.E. Hist. Gen. Reg., IV, 25.

w In the original MSS., Boston is omitted from the total for Suffolk County, but not from the grand total. There are also errors in the figures for Essex and Plymouth Counties, possibly in making the copy for the Board of Trade.

a The Dana MS. was published in the Columbian Centinel, Aug. 17, 1822. As printed in Felt, Statistics of Pop. in Mass., it does not include colored persons, but only houses, families, and whites. The Crane MS. was discovered about 1900, and is published in Benton, Early Census Making in Mass. It included, as was required in the order for

B. Number of Houses, Families, and Inhabitants by County and Town[b]

County	Houses	Families	Total Inhabitants
1. *Suffolk*			
Boston [c]	1,676	2,069	15,520
Roxbury	212	212	1,493
Dorchester [d]	204	245	1,360
Milton	124	141	948
Braintree	327	357	2,445
Weymouth	203	248	1,258
Hingham	375	426	2,506

taking the census, not only these classifications, but also Indians, Negroes, mulattoes, and French Neutrals. On comparison, it appeared that the larger figures given in the Crane MS. were accounted for by the inclusion of these other groups. It was decided, therefore, to use the Crane MS. in giving the total population for the towns. It will be seen that in some cases the county totals given above are greater in the Dana than in the Crane MS. (i.e., Hampshire, Bristol, and Worcester) due to the fact that no returns are given in the latter for a few towns that are included in the former. In such cases the figures found in the Dana MS. are given in footnotes. The sum total of the Crane MS. would seem to be less than that of the Dana, but apparently errors have been made in addition. The correct figures are given in brackets at the right. If the omitted towns were included, the result would be even larger. Rossiter, *Cent. Pop. Growth*, gives 245,718 for Mass. and 23,993 for Me., a total of 269,711, from Chickering, *Statistical View*, 7.

b The Me. counties are Lincoln, York, and Cumberland (q.v.). Me. in *1630* had 84 families at Pemaquid, St. George's, and Sheepscot: Davis's account, in Sullivan, *Hist. Me.*, 167. In *1664* there were about 700 men in the militia: Palfrey, III, 39n., 40n. In *1673* there were 175 families, 20 at and near Sagadahock, 31 on the east side of Sagadahock to Merry Meeting, 6 from Cape Nawagen to Pemaquid, 15 in Pemaquid, 10 at New Harbour, 1 at St. George's, 1 on east side of Inisquamego, 12 between the Kennebec and Georges Rivers, 50 in Sheepscot town, 10 between Sheepscot and Damariscotta Rivers, 7 or 8 at Damariscotta, 12 at Misconcus, Pemaquid, and Round Pond: Sullivan, *Hist. Me.*, 391. In *1675* there were 700 militia, 180 men at Kittery, 80 at York, 80 at Wells and Cape Porpus, 100 at Saco and Winter Harbour, 100 at Blackpoint, 80 at Casco Bay, and 80 at Sagadahock: Chalmers, *Annals*, I, 507. Bancroft estimates 4,000 inhabitants for same year: Bancroft, I, 383. In *1704* there were 104 taxables: Baxter MSS., in *Me. Doc. Hist.*, IX, 174-77; 2,300 polls in *1743*: Felt, 146; 2,855 militia in *1744*: Douglass, *Summary*, I, 390.

c Boston had 6,700 inhabitants in *1700*: Shattuck, *Rept. to City Council*, 5; 3,000 men in *1701*: "Projects vs. New Eng.," in NYCD, IX, 726; 10,567 inhabitants according to census in *1722*; 13,000 inhabitants, of which 11,900 were whites and 1,100 Negroes, in *1730*; 3,637 polls or about 16,000 inhabitants in *1735*: Shattuck, *Rept. to City Council*, 3-5; 3,395 ratable polls in *1738*; 3,231 in *1739*; 3,043 in *1740*: Scudder, "Life in Boston in Prov. Period," in Winsor, *Mem. Hist. Boston*, II, 459; 17,000 inhabitants, of which 15,626 were white and 1,374 colored in *1740*: Shattuck, *Rept. to City Council*, 5; 2,972 ratable polls in *1741*: Scudder, in Winsor, *Mem. Hist. Boston*, II, 459; 16,382 souls, of which 1,374 are Negroes, according to census of *1742*: *Boston Recds.*, XV, 369; Hutchinson Papers, in MHSC, 3d Series, I, 152; 15,731 population, of whom 14,190 were white and 1,541 colored in *1752*; and 15,631, of whom 14,390 were white and 1,241 colored in *1760*: Shattuck, *Rept. to City Council*, 4-5. Burnaby for same year estimates 3,000 houses and 18,000 to 20,000 inhabitants: Burnaby, *Travels*, 102.

d Dorchester in *1727* had 276 polls: 252 ratable polls, 24 non-ratable; 117 houses; male slaves, 10; female slaves, 7: *Hist. of Town of Dorchester, Mass.*, 293-94.

LOCAL   23

B. Number of Houses, Families, and Inhabitants by County and
                        Town — *Continued*

County	Houses	Families	Total Inhabitants
Suffolk — Continued			
Hull	31	33	170
Stoughton	265	424	2,340
Dedham e	239	309	1,929
Medfield	113	121	639
Wrentham	293	347	2,030
Medway	123	138	793
Bellingham	72	82	462
Needham	129	168	945
Brookline	53	53	338
Chelsea	54	70	452
Walpole	100	106	792
	4,593	5,549	36,352 [36,420] f
2. *Essex*			
Salem g	509	923	4,254
Danvers	288	381	2,061
Ipswich h	531	670	3,642
Newbury i	401	489	2,918
Newburyport	357	546	2,882
Marblehead j	519	935	4,954
Lynn	275	388	2,208
Andover	360	438	2,462
Beverly k	307	404	2,171

e Dedham in *1736* had 259 taxables: Worthington, *Hist. of Dedham*, 59.

f All totals in this census and following tables for Mass. are given as found in the source quoted. Whenever such totals are incorrect, the correct figures are inserted in brackets. When no totals were given in the original, they have been computed and placed at the bottom of the columns in brackets.

g Salem in *1701* had 500 or 600 inhabitants: "Projects vs. New Eng.," in NYCD, IX, 726; in *1732*, 520 houses, 5,000 inhabitants, 1,200 polls: Bentley, "Desc. of Salem," in MHSC, 1st Series, VI, 223; in *1750*, 450 houses: Extracts from Journal of Capt. F. Goelet, in *N.E. Hist. Gen. Reg.*, XXIV, 58.

h Ipswich in *1748* had 161 freemen: List in *N.E. Hist. Gen. Reg.*, II, 50-52.

i Newbury in *1711* had 200 ratables: List from Coffin Papers, I, 41, in *Essex Inst. Hist. Colls.*, XXXV, 133-38; in *1712*, 584 ratable polls; in *1713*, 613 ratable polls; in *1716*, 685 ratable polls: Coffin, *Hist. of Newbury*, 188; in *1724*, 30 families: Rev. Mr. Plant to S.P.G., in Perry, *Hist. Colls. Re. Am. Col. Church*, III, 151; in *1729*, 184 houses, 183 families: (From map of John Brown, Esq.) Coffin, *Hist. of Newbury*, 200.

j Marblehead in *1724* had 300 families: Morrison to S.P.G., in Perry, *Hist. Colls. Re. Am. Col. Church*, III, 149; in *1748*, 730 polls in tax list: List, in *Essex Inst. Hist. Colls.*, XLIII, 209-22; in *1768*, 1,300 ratable polls, or about 6,500 inhabitants: Mr. Weeks to S.P.G., in Perry, *Hist. Colls. Re. Am. Col. Church*, III, 539.

k Beverly in *1708* had 1,680 inhabitants; and 2,023 in *1753*: Stone, *Hist. of Beverly*, 197.

B. NUMBER OF HOUSES, FAMILIES, AND INHABITANTS BY COUNTY AND
TOWN — *Continued*

County	Houses	Families	Total Inhabitants
Essex —Continued			
Rowley	239	290	1,481
Salisbury	201	240	1,344
Haverhill	304	350	1,992
Gloucester	404	677	3,772
Topsfield	105	130	719
Boxford	128	149	841
Almsbury	242	264	1,550
Bradford	173	192	1,166
Wenham	72	95	564
Middleton	83	97	581
Manchester	103	155	739
Methuen	158	158	930
	[5,759]	[7,971]	[43,231]
3. *Middlesex*			
Cambridge [1]	237	257	1,582
Charleston [m]	289	375	2,048
Watertown [n]	103	117	693 [s]
Woburn	228	287	1,517
Concord [o]	244	265	1,564 [s]
Newton	174	222	1,308 [s]
Sudbury	263	316	1,773 [s]
Marlboro	183	213	1,287
Billerica	189	223	1,334
Farmingham	205	234	1,313
Lexington	126	142	912
Chelmsford	133	176	1,012
Sherborn	106	113	643
Reading	224	296	1,537
Malden	144	174	992
Weston [p]	105	126	768

[1] Cambridge in *1708* had 260 polls: Woburn Town Recds., V, 82, in Sewall, *Hist. of Woburn*, 240. In *1750* had 100 houses: Journal of Capt. Goelet, in *N.E. Hist. Gen. Reg.*, XXIV, 58.

[m] Charlestown had about 400 houses in *1775*: *British Annual Reg.*, 1775 (History of Europe), 136.

[n] Watertown had 250 polls in *1708*: Woburn Town Recds., V, 82, in Sewall, *Hist. of Woburn*, 241.

[o] Concord had 223 polls in *1708*: Sewall, *Hist. of Woburn*, 241; 65 ratables in *1734*: List, in *N.E. Hist. Gen. Reg.*, XII, 20-21.

[p] Weston in *1757* had 159 taxables; in *1758*, 127 taxables; in *1759*, 138 taxables; in *1760*, 146 taxables; in *1761*, 198 polls; in *1762*, 198 polls; in *1763*, 124 taxables;

LOCAL   25

B. NUMBER OF HOUSES, FAMILIES, AND INHABITANTS BY COUNTY AND
TOWN — *Continued*

County	Houses	Families	Total Inhabitants
Middlesex — Continued			
Medford	104	147	790
Littleton	122	143	773
Hopkinston	135	154	1,027 ˢ
Westford	143	169	962 ˢ
Waltham	94	107	663
Wilmington	94	97	673 ˢ
Groton q	174	242	1,443 ˢ
Shirley	41	72	430 ˢ
Stow	121	135	794
Townsend	94	97	598 ˢ
Stoneham	54	59	340
Natick	71	91	511 ˢ
Dracut			
Bedford	67	72	457
Lincoln	84	99	646
Tewksbury	103	147	781 ˢ
Holliston r	103	115	705 ˢ
Acton	96	100	611 ˢ
Dunstable	90	98	559 ˢ
Pepperell	117	130	758 ˢ
	[4,860]	[5,810]	[33,804]
4. Worcester			
Worcester	204	229	1,478
Lancaster	301	328	1,999
Sutton	294	370	2,137
Mendon	284	336	1,843
Brookfield t	267	283	1,811
Shrewsbury	199	223	1,401
Uxbridge	186	211	1,213
Westborough	163	181	1,110

in *1764*, 207 polls; in *1765*, 225 polls; in *1766*, 228 polls; in *1767*, 222 polls; in *1768*, 218 polls; in *1769*, 206 polls. The taxables indicate all persons taxed, whether resident, subject to poll tax, or otherwise. The polls indicate those subject to poll tax, i.e., males 16 and above. *Weston Tax Lists*, 1-75.

q Groton had 46 ratables in *1701*: List in *N.E. Hist. Gen. Reg.*, XLI, 263; 67 polls or about 300 inhabitants in *1707-8*: Green, "Pop. of Groton," in MHSP, 2d Series, IV, 136-38.

r Holliston had 24 families in *1724*; 80 families and about 400 souls in *1754*: "Desc. of Holliston," in MHSC, 1st Series, III, 19-20.

s This total was not computed in the original manuscript.

t Brookfield in *1717* had 93 taxable polls: Temple, *Hist. of N. Brookfield*, 194-95.

B. NUMBER OF HOUSES, FAMILIES, AND INHABITANTS BY COUNTY AND
TOWN — *Continued*

County	Houses	Families	Total Inhabitants
Worcester — Continued			
Southboro	110	126	731
Rutland	166	182	1,090
Rutland District	118	118	734
Oxford	128	148	890
Charlton	114	124	741
Leicester	119	146	770
Spencer	100	111	664
New Braintree	94	98	594
Oakham	41	41	270
Lunenburg	145	175	821
Bolton	145	155	993
Sturbridge	136	136	899
Hardwick	153	161	1,010
Grafton	109	109	760
Upton	94	104	614
Leominster	104	107	743
Holden	62	75	495
Western	92	100	583
Douglass	90	97	521
Harvard u	153	173	1,126 w
Dudley v			
Petersham	100	115	707 w
Templeton	65	64	348
Westminster	86	86	468
Athol	41	60	357
Princetown	57	55	284
Fitchburg	43	43	259 w
	[4,563]	[5,070]	[30,464]

5. *Hampshire*

Springfield	404	477	2,755
Northampton	188	203	1,289
Southampton	66	76	437
Southadley	133	142	817
Hadley	89	99	573
Amherst	96	104	645

u Harvard had 60 families in *1732*; and 200 families in *1767*, including 195 communicants of the Church of Eng.: Wheeler, "Acct. of Harvard," in MHSC, 1st Series, X, 88.

v In the Felt version Dudley has 107 houses, 119 families, 733 inhabitants.

w These totals are not computed in the originals.

LOCAL 27

B. Number of Houses, Families, and Inhabitants by County and
Town — Continued

County	Houses	Families	Total Inhabitants
Hampshire — Continued			
Hatfield	126	132	815
Westfield	191	195	1,324
Deerfield	85	123	737
Greenfield	45	58	368
Montague	49	64	392
Northfield	60	60	415
Brimfield	121	130	773
South Brimfield	90	91	624
Monson	68	69	389
Pelham	57	57	371
New Salem	62	69	375
Blanford	68	68	406
Palmer	74	88	508
Granville	100	123	682
Belchertown	61	68	418
Colrain	45	48	297
Ware	74	76	485
Chesterfield	30	30	161
Bernardston	38	40	230
Roxbury Canady x	36	36	191
Shutesbury	56	59	330
Wilbraham	74	82	491
Sunderland			
Greenwich y			
Huntstown			
	[2,586]	[2,867]	[17,298]
6. Lincoln z			
Pownalboro	161	175	899
Georgetown	180	184	1,329
Newcastle	69	69	454
Topsham aa	54	52	327
Woolwich	64	63	415
Bowdoinham	38	37	200
	[566]	[580]	[3,624]

x Or Warwick.
y In the Felt version Greenwich has 70 houses, 70 families, 434 inhabitants.
z Lincoln County in 1761 was supposed to contain about 1,900 families: Rev. Mr.
Bailey to S.P.G., in Hawkins, Hist. Notices, 230.
aa Topsham had 25 inhabitants in 1746: Brunswick Recds., in Wheeler, Hist. Bruns-

B. NUMBER OF HOUSES, FAMILIES, AND INHABITANTS BY COUNTY AND
TOWN — *Continued*

County	Houses	Families	Total Inhabitants
7. *Duke's*			
Edgartown	128	150	1,030
Chilmark	90	114	851
Tisbury	110	100	838
	[328]	[364]	[2,719]
8. *Nantucket*			
Sherburne	413	602	3,526
9. *Berks*			
Great Barrington	87	91	550
Sheffield	126	172	1,073
Sandisfield	66	69	409
Tyringham	51	55	325
Pittsfield	39	70	428
Egremont			
Stockbridge	34	34	244
New Marlboro			
No. 4			
	[403]	[491]	[3,029]
10. *Plymouth*			
Plymouth ab	256	373	2,246
Bridgewater	571	630	3,990
Middleboro	498	577	3,438
Scituate	348	431	2,501
Rochester	272	326	1,985
Pembroke	210	233	1,446
Duxbury	154	197	1,061
Marshfield	150	168	1,159
Plimpton	186	232	1,417
Kingston ac	110	131	774
Abington	174	217	1,263
Halifax	85	97	557
Wareham	57	81	519
Hanover			
	[3,071]	[3,693]	[22,356]

wick, Topsham, and Harpswell, 43; 18 families in *1750*: Ellis, "Desc. Topsham," in
MHSC, 1st Series, III, 142; 28 polls in *1752*; 49 polls in *1757*; and 44 taxables in
1758: Wheeler, *Hist. Brunswick, Topsham, and Harpswell,* 43.

ab Plymouth in *1708* was estimated at 300 or 400 families: Oldmixon, *British Empire*, I, 87.

ac Kingston in *1717* had 48 families: "Desc. of Kingston," in MHSC, 2d Series,
III, 208.

B. NUMBER OF HOUSES, FAMILIES, AND INHABITANTS BY COUNTY AND
TOWN — Continued

County	Houses	Families	Total Inhabitants	
11. *Barnstable*				
Barnstable	325	361	2,146	
Yarmouth	255	295	1,780	
Sandwich	200	245	1,449	
Harwich	235	283	1,772	
Eastham	182	237	1,331	
Wellfleet	129	157	928	
Falmouth	145	182	1,125	
Truro	107	134	925	
Chatham	105	127	678	
Mashpee	82	85	338	
	[1,765]	[2,106]	12,471	[12,472]
12. *Bristol*				
Taunton	397	493	2,744	
Dartmouth	679	790	4,581	
Rehoboth	498	617	3,690	
Swanzey				
Attleboro	266	301	1,739	
Norton	295	343	1,942	
Dighton	148	198	1,177	
Easton	134	154	842	
Raynham ad	100	109	694	
Berkeley	94	110	661	
Freeton				
	[2,611]	[3,115]	[18,070]	
13. *York*				
York	272	397	2,298	
Kittery ae	288	372	2,368	
Berwick	222	364	2,374	
Wells af	219	251	1,569	
Arundel	124	138	837	
Biddeford	87	116	753	
Pepperellboro	66	96	540	
Naragansett No. 1				
	[1,278]	[1,734]	[10,739]	

ad Raynham in *1746* had 96 taxables: List, in *Me. Hist. and Gen. Recorder*, VII,
44-45.

ae Kittery had 500 polls in *1745*: Bourne, *Hist. Wells and Kennebunk*, 405-6; 284
families in *1751*: Me. HSC, 1st Series, IV, 200; 128 taxables in *1756*; 124 taxables in
1758: Lists, in *N.E. Hist. Gen. Reg.*, LV, 249-51; 566 polls in *1760*: Lists, in Me. HSC,
3d Series, II, 205-20; 87 polls in *1770*: List, in *N.E. Hist. Gen. Reg.*, LV, 254-55.

af Wells had 91 heads of families in *1726*: Bourne, *Hist. of Wells*, 330-31; 221 polls
in *1745*: Bourne, *Hist. Wells and Kennebunk*, 405; 1,000 inhabitants in *1751*: Sullivan,
Hist. Me., 235.

B. Number of Houses, Families, and Inhabitants by County and Town — *Continued*

County	Houses	Families	Total Inhabitants
14. *Cumberland*			
Falmouth ag	160	585	3,783
N. Yarmouth	154	188	1,079
Scarborough ah	200	210	1,272
Harpswell	55	110	836
Brunswick ai	73	73	504
Gorham aj			
Windham			
Pearsontown			
	[642]	[1,166]	[7,474]

III. Polls in 1772 a

County	
Suffolk	8,440
Essex	11,457
Middlesex	8,987
Hampshire	6,746
Plymouth	6,163
Barnstable	3,587
Bristol	5,843
York	3,268
Worcester	8,896
Berkshire	2,693
Cumberland	2,473
Lincoln	1,354
Dukes	692
Nantucket	1,180

Ratable polls	71,779
Non-Rat. polls	1,699
	73,478

IV. Negroes in 1776 b

County	
Suffolk	682
Essex	1,049
Middlesex	702
Hampshire	245
Plymouth	487
Barnstable	171
Bristol	585
York	241
Worcester	432
Berkshire	216
Cumberland	162
Lincoln	85
Dukes	59
Nantucket	133
	5,249

V. White Population in March, 1777 c

County	
Essex	50,903
Middlesex	40,119
Suffolk	27,450
Norfolk	
Part of Suffolk	
Plymouth	26,906
Barnstable	15,344
Dukes and Nantucket	7,234
Bristol	26,656
Worcester	46,331
Hampshire	34,315
Franklin) Parts of	
Hampden (Hampshire	
Berkshire	18,552
Maine Counties	50,066

Total white population 343,876

ag Falmouth, or Portland, had 2,346 population in the district in *1749*, about 700 being in Portland proper: Willis, *Journal of Rev. T. Smith*, 37n. The town had 15 men in *1716*; 20 families in *1718*; 64 families in Oct., *1726*; 168 families in *1759*: Willis, *Journal of Rev. T. Smith and S. Deane*, 10, 49, 51, 181. There were 165 families in *1761*: Willis, *Hist. Portland*, 372.

ah Scarborough had 310 taxable polls in *1761*: Southgate, "Hist. Scarborough," in Me. HSC, 1st Series, III, 177.

ai Brunswick had 20 dwelling houses in *1752* and 92 polls in *1757*: Wheeler, *Hist. Brunswick, Topsham, and Harpswell*, 39-41, 118.

aj Gorham had 60 families in *1759* and 80 families in *1762*: Baxter MSS., in *Me. Doc. Hist.*, XIII, 306.

a Felt, 132, 157.   b Felt, 213.   c Cited from *Mass. Archs.*, 332: 99, by Morison, "Mass. Const. Conventions," in MHSP, L, 248.

LOCAL   31

VI. CENSUSES FOR 1776, 1777, 1778, AND 1781 [a]

PLACE	1776	1777		1778	1781
	Whites	Males over 16	Strangers	Quakers	Polls	Polls

1. *Suffolk County*						
Boston [b]	2,719 [c]	2,664	..	11	2,248	2,260
Roxbury	1,433	356	..	..	372	330
Dorchester	1,513	373	6	..	342	368
Milton	1,213	259	13	..	234	243
Braintree	2,871	610	4	..	599	592
Weymouth	1,471	342	..	..	324	332
Hingham	2,087	504	12	..	538	515
Dedham	1,937	495	10	..	528	560
Medfield	775	188	3	..	184	192
Wrentham	2,879	710	3	3	368	376
Franklin	.....	....	..	..	246	235
Foxboro	.....	....	..	..	113	133
Brookline	502	115	..	..	98	104
Needham	912	287	2	1	284	268
Stoughtonham	1,261	300	3	..	209	217
Stoughton	2,097	532	7	..	504	508
Medway	912	206	6	..	210	227
Bellingham	627	136	..	9	126	123
Hull	.....	32	..	..	25	32
Walpole	967	260	..	3	220	230
Chelsea	489	76	18	..	95	94
Cohasset	754	66	2	..	156	158
	27,419	8,511	89	27	8,023	8,097
2. *Essex County*						
Salem	5,337	1,193	16	24	1,032	1,002
Danvers	2,284	519	2	30	500	417
Ipswich	4,508	1,016	15	1	823	887
Newbury	3,239	704	..	25	722	770
Newburyport	3,681	858	..	..	805	816
Marblehead [d]	4,386	1,047	..	2	793	728
Lynn and Lynnfield	2,755	431	..	..	517	517
Andover	2,953	670	22	..	558	610
Beverly	2,754	596	44	..	502	519

a Figures for *1776, 1777, 1778,* and *1781* are from Felt, 158-65.
b Boston is frequently estimated at 30,000 inhabitants between *1776* and *1781*: Anon.,
Hist. North Am., 88; *North Am. and W. Ind. Gazeteer,* under "Boston"; Abbé Robin,
New Travels, 13.
c When Boston was shut up in *1776* the population was very small.
d Marblehead had 1,203 ratable polls in *1772*: Eliot, "Acct. of Marblehead," in
MHSC, 1st Series, VIII, 60; 4,142 inhabitants by town census of *1780*: Orne, "Hist.
of Marblehead," in *Hist. of Essex Co.,* 283.

VI. Censuses for 1776, 1777, 1778, and 1781 —*Continued*

PLACE	1776	1777			1778	1781
	Whites	Males over 16	Strangers	Quakers	Polls	Polls
Essex — Continued						
Rowley	1,678	421	13	..	408	390
Salisbury	1,666	375	13	..	379	387
Haverhill	2,810	552	17	4	462	501
Gloucester	4,512	939	..	..	754	704
Topsfield	773	205	7	..	186	185
Boxford	989	248	1	..	230	235
Amesbury	1,795	422	3	23	386	396
Bradford	1,240	304	4	..	267	279
Wenham	638	143	6	..	96	115
Middleton	650	159	..	..	142	136
Manchester	949	220	..	..	146	112
Methuen	1,326	306	..	..	275	293
	50,923	11,328	163	109	9,983	9,999
3. *Middlesex County*						
Cambridge	1,586	333	44	..	411	411
Charlestown	360	144	17	..	133	145
Watertown	1,057	185	21	..	210	222
Woburn	1,691	417	12	..	413	394
Concord	1,927	391	18	..	312	316
Newton	1,625	348	5	..	322	339
Reading	1,984	402	10	..	382	369
Marlboro	1,554	391	15	..	352	370
Billerica	1,500	348	10	..	286	276
Framingham	1,574	384	..	..	337	370
Lexington	1,088	213	5	..	172	196
Chelmsford	1,341	319	5	..	255	240
Sherburne	699	187	4	..	179	200
Sudbury	2,160	522	7	..	464	280
East Sudbury	.....	.....	..	..	....	207
Malden	1,030	221	5	..	224	202
Weston e	1,027	222	8	..	203	194
Medford	967	190	27	..	198	210
Littleton	1,047	209	6	..	175	193
Hopkinton	1,134	286	..	1	211	267
Westford	1,193	283	1	..	231	268
Waltham	870	174	6	..	192	187
Stow	915	215	2	..	195	204

e Weston had 209 polls in *1771*; 228 in *1772*; 217 in *1773*; 159 taxables in *1774*; 151 polls in *1775*; 113 taxables and 209 polls in *1777*; 285 taxables in *1779*; and 111 polls on the north side, and 128 voters in *1782*: *Weston Tax Lists*, 75-112.

VI. Censuses for 1776, 1777, 1778, and 1781 —*Continued*

PLACE	1776	1777			1778	1781
	Whites	Males over 16	Strangers	Quakers	Polls	Polls
Middlesex — Continued						
Groton	1,639	398	..	..	362	395
Shirley	704	144	3	..	147	152
Pepperell	1,034	221	..	..	201	221
Townsend	794	177	..	..	178	190
Ashby	422	98	..	..	99	116
Stoneham	319	73	7	..	75	75
Natick	535	126	1	1	120	141
Dracut	1,173	225	4	..	206	209
Bedford	482	121	..	..	125	127
Holliston	909	216	3	..	196	213
Tewksbury	821	222	2	..	205	222
Acton	769	195	..	..	167	167
Dunstable	679	166	3	..	164	180
Lincoln	775	187	2	..	172	171
Wilmington	737	187	6	..	194	176
Carlisle	.....	.....	..	..	....	129
	40,121	9,140	259	2	8,468	8,944
4. *Hampshire County*						
Springfield	1,974	452	..	..	404	444
Wilbraham	1,057	260	1	..	278	273
Northampton	1,790	451	..	..	368	415
Westhampton	.....	....	..	..	72	72
Southampton	740	199	..	..	207	191
Hadley *t*	681	201	..	..	210	189
South Hadley	584	161	..	..	142	161
Amherst	915	238	..	..	248	251
Granby	491	116	..	6	123	141
Hatfield	582	190	..	..	190	189
Whately	410	106	..	2	113	128
Williamsburg	534	123	..	..	130	148
Westfield	1,488	373	..	..	355	286
Deerfield	836	241	..	..	213	225
Greenfield	735	148	..	..	170	132
Shelburne	575	154	..	..	169	179
Conway	897	203	..	..	217	265
Sunderland	409	116	..	..	120	114
Montague	575	163	..	..	153	175

t Hadley had 149 taxables in *1770*; 147 ratable polls and 10 unratable in *1771*: Judd, *Hist. of Hadley*, 393, 421-22.

VI. Censuses for 1776, 1777, 1778, and 1781 —*Continued*

PLACE	1776	1777			1778	1781
	Whites	Males over 16	Strangers	Quakers	Polls	Polls
Hampshire — Continued						
Northfield	580	148	..	..	174	147
Brimfield	1,064	251	..	..	209	257
South Brimfield	850	220	..	..	178	199
Monson	813	197	..	..	182	196
Pelham	729	201	..	..	199	199
Greenwich	890	206	..	..	208	214
Blandford	772	187	..	..	199	220
Leverett	293	79	..	..	75	87
Palmer	727	....	..	..	168	180
Granville	1,126	268	..	..	276	302
New Salem	910	226	..	..	134	261
Belchertown	972	225	..	..	310	276
Colerain	566	144	..	..	133	172
Ware	.....	150	..	..	135	147
Warwick	766	166	..	..	176	236
Bernardston	607	138	..	..	150	172
Murrayfield	405	98	..	..	100	127
Charlemont	.....	94	..	..	110	103
Ashfield	628	193	..	..	203	210
Worthington	639	166	..	..	151	222
Shutesbury	598	147	..	..	147	167
Chesterfield	1,092	221	41	1	237	227
Chesterfield Gore	.....	....	..	..	....	54
Southwick	.....	123	..	·..	107	109
W. Springfield	1,744	....	..	..	406	437
Ludlow	413	96	..	..	104	105
No. 5	.....	....	..	..	95	
Norwich	.....	62	..	2	71	91
No. 7	244	56	..	..	60	70
Lee	.....	....	..	..	145	
Montgomery	.....	....	..	..	....	74
Buckland	.....	....	..	..	....	69
	32,701	7,957	42	11	8,724	9,308
5. *Plymouth County*						
Plymouth	2,655	643	6	8	546	520
Scituate	2,672	663	..	..	616	607
Duxbury	1,254	316	..	..	309	296
Marshfield	1,157	289	..	7	279	219
Bridgewater	4,364	1,130	13	2	1,125	1,087
Middleboro g	4,119	1,045	8	5	913	948

g Middleboro according to another estimate had 1,066 males in *1777*, of whom there

VI. Censuses for 1776, 1777, 1778, and 1781 —*Continued*

PLACE	1776	1777		1778	1781
	Whites	Males over 16	Strangers	Quakers	Polls	Polls

PLACE	Whites	Males over 16	Strangers	Quakers	Polls	Polls
Plymouth — Continued						
Rochester	2,449	569	..	39	523	545
Plimpton	1,707	436	6	..	374	362
Pembroke	1,768	418	5	15	426	416
Kingston	980	229	..	..	210	207
Hanòver	1,105	253	1	19	256	224
Abington	1,293	324	..	..	331	338
Halifax	672	148	..	..	155	165
Wareham	711	151	..	..	151	152
	26,906	6,614	39	95	6,214	6,086
6. *Barnstable County*						
Barnstable	.....	554	5	12	596	484
Sandwich	1,912	362	..	66	428	404
Yarmouth	2,227	514	..	30	529	496
Eastham	1,899	458	..	..	370	317
Harwich	1,865	451	..	..	404	382
Wellfleet	1,235	307	..	2	179	149
Chatham	929	210	..	4	191	190
Truro	1,227	292	..	..	199	222
Falmouth	1,355	223	..	55	351	331
Marshpee	82					
Provincetown	205					
	12,936	3,371	5	169	3,247	2,975
7. *Bristol County*						
Taunton	3,259	794	..	..	733	761
Rehoboth	4,191	970	..	5	883	863
Swanzey	.....	447	..	..	497	530
Dartmouth	6,773	1,067	4	340	1,555	1,342
Norton	1,329	330	..	..	296	347
Mansfield	944	247	..	..	212	209
Attleboro	2,200	501	1	1	476	476
Dighton	1,420	317	29	14	288	275
Freetown	1,901	414	15	18	370	376
Raynham	940	223	..	..	211	215
Easton	1,172	293	1	1	262	273
Berkley	787	191	..	6	169	164
	24,916	5,794	50	385	5,952	5,831

were but 5 Indians and 8 Negroes: Backus, "Acct. of Middleboro," in MHSC, 1st Series, III, 152.

VI. Censuses for 1776, 1777, 1778, and 1781 —*Continued*

PLACE	1776	1777			1778	1781
	Whites	Males over 16	Strangers	Quakers	Polls	Polls
8. York County						
York	2,742	607	23	2	527	567
Kittery	2,991	645	..	22	561	574
Wells	2,595	570	..	9	611	591
Berwick	3,315	671	..	..	748	756
Arundel	1,144	251	..	..	207	246
Biddeford	1,006	216	..	..	192	215
Pepperelboro	815	192	..	..	177	188
Lebanon	570	126	..	..	141	161
Sandford	810	158	..	..	185	209
Buxton	698	157	..	..	168	183
Settlements adjacent to Sanford	225					
Fryeburg h	414	102	..	..	120	93
Brownstown	48	19	..	..	....	33
Great Falls	10					
Little Ossipee	240					
Massabeseek	....	99	..	..	84	105
Little Falls	....	72	..	..	....	64
Brownfield	....	19				
Coxhall	....	....	..	..	60	104
	17,623	3,904	23	33	3,781	4,089
9. Duke's County						
Edgartown	1,020	....	..	..	320	
Chilmark	769	....	..	..	200	
Tisbury l	1,033	....	..	..	250	
	2,822	....	..	..	770	
10. Nantucket County						
Sherburn	4,412	....	..	..	1,001	
11. Worcester County						
Worcester	1,925	438	29	..	440	389
Lancaster	2,746	672	..	..	654	646
Mendon	2,322	524	6	50	479	296
Milford	....	....	..	..	....	183
Brookfield	2,649	655	1	..	580	615
Oxford	1,112	275	2	..	214	219
Charlton	1,310	308	..	..	323	340
Sutton	2,644	651	..	..	588	625

h Fryeburg had 74 taxables in *1779*: Baxter MSS., in *Me. Doc. Hist.*, XVI, 175-76.
l Tisbury in *1777* had 106 polls: *Tisbury Town Recds.*, 219-21.

VI. Censuses for 1776, 1777, 1778, and 1781 —*Continued*

PLACE	1776	1777			1778	1781
	Whites	Males over 16	Strangers	Quakers	Polls	Polls
Worcester — Continued						
Leicester	1,005	212	1	7	240	229
Spencer	1,042	257	1	1	267	297
Paxton	. . . . .	116	. .	2	128	133
Rutland	1,006	254	. .	. .	214	254
Oakham	598	135	. .	. .	132	137
Barre	1,329	325	. .	. .	293	323
Hubbardston	488	130	. .	. .	120	132
New Braintree	798	185	. .	. .	184	199
Southboro	753	176	6	. .	161	165
Westboro	900	220	. .	. .	191	221
Northboro	562	127	. .	. .	120	133
Shrewsbury	1,475	384	3	2	342	390
Fitchburg	643	168	. .	. .	166	170
Uxbridge	1,110	235	. .	39	263	250
Harvard	1,315	338	1	. .	275	295
Dudley	875	228	. .	2	230	244
Bolton	1,210	284	4	16	272	297
Sturbridge	1,374	338	. .	. .	311	325
Leominster	978	216	. .	1	217	230
Hardwick	1,393	346	. .	. .	343	363
Holden	749	180	. .	. .	167	199
Western	827	206	. .	. .	212	199
Douglass	800	194	. .	. .	215	212
Grafton	861	213	. .	. .	128	222
Petersham	1,235	289	. .	. .	275	313
Royalston	617	113	. .	. .	151	177
Westminster	1,145	248	1	. .	234	256
Athol	. . . . .	191	. .	. .	201	236
Templeton	1,016	235	. .	. .	209	257
Princeton	701	153	. .	. .	142	182
Ashburnham	551	122	1	. .	119	158
Winchendon	519	119	. .	. .	125	161
Northbridge	481	90	. .	. .	95	106
Ward	. . . . .	. . . .	. .	. .	89	111
Lunenburg	1,265	284	4	. .	245	269
Upton	702	171	. .	2	179	185
	45,031	11,005	60	122	10,533	11,343
12. *Cumberland County*						
Falmouth	3,026	709	. .	64	669	556
Cape Elizabeth	1,469	357	4	1	402	292

VI. Censuses for 1776, 1777, 1778, and 1781 — *Continued*

PLACE	1776	1777			1778	1781
	Whites	Males over 16	Strangers	Quakers	Polls	Polls
Cumberland —Continued						
N. Yarmouth	1,716	398	2	..	386	380
Scarborough	1,817	454	6	..	372	414
Brunswick	867	194	4	..	192	206
Harpswell	977	193	1	11	188	223
Gorham	1,471	302	11	3	321	363
Windham	550	92	8	12	104	158
New Gloucester	773	166	5	..	134	156
Piersontown	551	69	9	..	70	143
Gray	318	72	..	..	64	105
Royalboro	301	57	..	..	50	105
Bakerstown	58	....	..	..	....	40
Sylvester	35	....	..	..	....	40
Bridgetown	68	....	..	..	....	50
Raymondtown ⅃	113	....	..	..	....	50
	14,110	3,063	50	91	2,952	3,281
13. *Berkshire County*						
Sheffield	1,722	338	..	..	383	404
Great Barrington	961	231	..	..	206	217
Stockbridge	907	....	..	..	218	266
Pittsfield	1,132	244	..	..	249	279
New Marlboro	1,087	253	..	..	256	269
Egremont	671	150	..	..	139	155
Richmond	921	....	..	..	246	256
Lennox	931	178	..	..	220	214
Tyringham	809	....	..	..	193	241
W. Stockbridge	370	....	..	..	113	143
Lowden	200	....	..	..	50	50
Alford	298	....	..	..	70	99
Lanesboro	1,434	354	..	..	436	402
Sandisfield	1,044	....	..	..	235	259
Williamstown	1,083	257	..	1	233	273
Becket	414	106	..	..	97	118
Windsor	459	....	..	..	152	199
Partridgefield	376	....	..	..	100	147
Adams	932	150	..	36	215	333
Hancock	977	127	..	4	195	209
No. 7	.....	....	..	..	50	
Washington	750	146	..	..	130	88
New Ashford	215	....	..	..	50	60

⅃ Raymond had 20 families in *1778*: Baxter MSS., in *Me. Doc. Hist.*, XV, 375.

VI. Censuses for 1776, 1777, 1778, and 1781 —*Continued*

| PLACE | 1776 | 1777 | | | 1778 | 1781 |
	Whites	Males over 16	Strangers	Quakers	Polls	Polls
Berkshire — *Continued*						
Mt. Washington	259	....	..	..	....	54
Ashuelot Equiv't.	.....	....	..	..	60	90
	17,952	2,534	..	41	4,296	4,825
14. *Lincoln County*						
Pownalboro	1,424	294	2	..	292	300
Georgetown	.....	424	5	6	386	255
Woolwich	695	167	1	..	91	148
Newcastle	656	159	..	..	132	140
Topsham	657	155	..	..	111	113
Townshend	763	167	..	..	179	179
Bristol	1,214	299	2	..	234	240
Bowdoinham	298	92	..	3	60	67
Meduncook	247	....	..	..	52	70
Hallowell	554	134	3	..	110	130
Waldoboro	.....	....	..	..	120	135
Vassalboro [k]	.....	99	..	..	116	136
Warren	272	73	..	..	70	80
Thomastown	346	....	..	..	70	80
Winthrop and Readfield	307	93	..	2	108	137
Pittstown	.....	98	3	3	100	100
Edgecomb	677	153	..	..	127	132
Pleasant River	238					
Winslow [l]	294	61	..	..	68	68
Belfast [m]	229	....	..	..	25	
Lower St. George's	.....	....	..	..	60	100
Plantation above						
Winslow	390					
Sterlington	474					
Jones Plantation	49					
Settlements adjacent						
to Newcastle	582					
Narrow Gaugus	263					
Machias [n]	626					
No. 4	117					
Frenchman Bay	345					
Union River	233					
Passamaquoddy	206					

k Vassalboro had 10 families in *1768*: Williamson, *Hist. Me.*, II, 391.
l Winslow had 44 families in *1775*: Baxter MSS., in *Me. Doc. Hist.*, XIV, 265.
m Belfast had 109 persons and 18 families in *1779*: Williamson, *Hist. of Belfast*, 121.
n Machias had 150 males over 16, and 60 families, in *1771*: Baxter MSS., in *Me. Doc. Hist.*, XIV, 139.

VI. Censuses for 1776, 1777, 1778, and 1781 —*Continued*

PLACE	1776	1777			1778	1781
	Whites	Males over 16	Strangers	Quakers	Polls	Polls
Lincoln — Continued						
Mt. Desert, etc.	235					
Gouldsboro	293					
Camden	245					
Frankfort o	493					
Deer Island	348					
Bald Hill	165					
Nos. 1 and 2	193					
Fox Island	241					
Naakeag	404					
No. 6	202					
Penobscot	439					
Blue Hill	132					
	15,546	2,468	16	14	2,511	2,610

VII. Account of Male Polls in 1784 [a]

Place	Ratable and Not Ratable	Supported by Town	Place	Ratable and Not Ratable	Supported by Town
1. *Suffolk County*			*Suffolk — Continued*		
Boston b	3,174	50	Walpole	234	
Roxbury c	430	27	Sharon	245	3
Dorchester	412	6	Cohasset	174	
Milton	261	6	Franklin	253	
Braintree	665	4	Medway	241	1
Weymouth	337	3	Bellingham	157	3
Hingham	539	6	Hull	23	2
Brookline	110	1	Chelsea	102	
Dover	107	1	Foxborough	139	1
Dedham	444	4		——	——
Needham	274	2		9,367	139
Medfield	175	3	2. *Essex County*		
Stoughton	492		Salem d	1,043	10
Wrentham	379	16	Danvers	474	8

o Frankfort had 100 families in *1759*: Baxter MSS., in *Me. Doc. Hist.*, XIII, 186.
a Felt, 166-70.

b Boston in *1786* had 2,200 houses: Webster, in *N.Y. Directory for 1786*, 22. In *1789* had 2,235 dwelling houses: Table in MHSC, 2d Series, IX, 204-22.

c Roxbury in *1783* had 213 dwelling houses: Drake, "Roxbury in the Last 100 Years," in Winsor, *Mem. Hist. Boston*, III, 571.

d Salem in *1785* had 730 houses: Webster, in *N.Y. Directory for 1786*, 22.

VII. Account of Male Polls in 1784 — *Continued*

Place	Ratable and Not Ratable	Sup- ported by Town	Place	Ratable and Not Ratable	Sup- ported by Town
Essex — Continued			*Middlesex — Continued*		
Newbury e	825	10	Malden	203	
Newburyport	926	7	Weston g	201	3
Beverly	592	3	Medford	223	4
Ipswich	933	13	Hopkinton	272	3
Marblehead f	932	6	Westford	266	
Gloucester	762	21	Stow	182	3
Lynn	552	5	Groton	418	3
Lynnfield	100	1	Shirley	141	
Andover	680		Pepperell	233	1
Rowley	396	6	Waltham	208	2
Topsfield	189		Townsend	212	2
Haverhill	506	11	Dracut	265	
Salisbury	404	2	Bedford	130	
Amesbury	441	1	Holliston	194	6
Boxford	218	2	Acton	192	2
Bradford	312	1	Dunstable	196	
Methuen	321		Lincoln	169	3
Wenham	109	4	Wilmington	177	
Manchester	158	3	Tewksbury	279	3
Middleton	150	1	Littleton	181	
			Ashby	136	2
	11,023	115	Natick	140	
3. *Middlesex County*			Carlisle	128	
Cambridge	457	10	Stoneham	96	2
Charlestown	268	2	East Sudbury	206	2
Watertown	256	3	Boxboro	88	
Woburn	395	2			
Concord	360	3		9,691	76
Newton	328	3	4. *Hampshire County*		
Reading	399	2	Springfield	324	1
Marlboro	370	2	Long Meadow	171	1
Billerica	317	1	West Springfield	503	4
Framingham	389		Wilbraham	319	
Lexington	216	2	Northampton	441	1
Chelmsford	279	2	Southampton	214	1
Sherburne	210		Hadley	203	3
Sudbury	311	3	South Hadley	184	1

e Newbury in *1785* had 510 houses: *Ibid.*
f Marblehead in *1783* had 873 ratable polls; 4,443 inhabitants: Eliot, "Acct. of Marblehead," in MHSC, 1st Series, VIII, 60.
g Weston in *1789* had 128 taxables: *Weston Tax Lists*, 113.

VII. Account of Male Polls in 1784 — *Continued*

Place	Ratable and Not Ratable	Supported by Town	Place	Ratable and Not Ratable	Supported by Town
Hampshire — Continued			*Hampshire — Continued*		
Amherst	276	1	Westhampton	109	
Granby	135		Leyden	136	
Hatfield	187		Rowe	88	
Williamsbury	189		Cummington	233	
Whately	141		Montgomery	83	
Westfield	390	2	Middlefield	111	
Deerfield	288	1	Buckland	105	
Conway	369		Charlemont	105	
Sunderland	126		Heath	56	
Brimfield	266	1			
S. Brimfield	124	1		11,497	34
Holland	85		*5. Plymouth County*		
New Salem	285	1	Plymouth	611	5
Ashfield	254		Marshfield	299	1
Worthington	238		Bridgewater	1,123	2
Chesterfield	240		Scituate	608	11
Goshen	126		Duxbury	307	4
Monson	195	4	Plympton	371	2
Pelham	217		Pembroke	398	2
Palmer	176		Kingston	211	1
Montague	183	1	Hanover	250	3
Northfield	156		Abington	364	1
Belchertown	316		Halifax	150	
Colerain	234		Wareham	155	1
Shelburne	217	1	Middleboro	970	12
Southwick	153		Rochester	608	2
Granville	375	6			
Warwick	211			6,425	47
Orange	108		*6. Barnstable County*		
No. 7	50		Barnstable	520	15
Greenfield	280		Harwich	424	27
Greenwich	221	2	Sandwich	372	1
Blandford	277		Falmouth	334	5
Ware	162	1	Chatham	222	8
Leverett	96		Yarmouth	498	7
Chester	172		Wellfleet	223	12
Bernardston	136		Truro	182	
Shutesbury	124		Eastham	293	13
Wendell	96		Provincetown	80	
Ludlow	124				
Norwich	114			3,148	88

VII. ACCOUNT OF MALE POLLS IN 1784 — *Continued*

Place	Ratable and Not Ratable	Supported by Town	Place	Ratable and Not Ratable	Supported by Town
7. *Duke's County* h			*York — Continued*		
Edgartown	315		Coxhall	124	
Chilmark	165	4	Fryeburgh	110	
Tisbury ¹	238		Brownfield j	30	
			Limerick k	50	
	718	4	Littlefalls	70	
8. *Nantucket County*			Shapleigh	173	
Sherburn	813	21	Lemington	100	
9. *Bristol County*			Parsonsfield ¹	160	
Taunton	791	4	Washington Plan.	45	
Rehoboth	920	12	Francisboro Pl.	45	
Swanzey	536	6			
Dartmouth	1,408	33		4,944	46
Norton	313	7	11. *Worcester County*		
Mansfield	227	2	Worcester	357	13
Attleboro	517	2	Lancaster	304	3
Dighton	350	8	Mendon	310	7
Freetown	413	3	Brookfield	666	1
Raynham	229	1	Oxford	228	3
Easton	292		Charlton	392	
Berkley	201	5	Sutton	640	5
			Leicester	240	
	6,197	83	Spencer	308	1
10. *York County*			Rutland	268	
York	520	7	Paxton	145	
Kittery	632	6	Oakham	171	
Wells	604	24	Barre	373	3
Berwick	830	3	Hubbardston	163	2
Arundel	296	2	New Braintree	203	6
Biddeford	225		Southboro	186	4
Pepperelboro	235		Westboro	222	1
Waterboro	110		Northboro	156	
Lebanon	192	4	Shrewsbury	421	5
Sanford	162		Lunenburgh	297	1
Buxton	231		Fitchburgh	207	

h Duke's County in *1783* had 3,056 white inhabitants and 522 families: "Desc. of Duke's Co.," in MHSC, 2d Series, III, 89.

¹ Tisbury in *1787* had 71 polls and 241 persons on the tax list: *Tisbury Town Recds.*, 262-66.

j Brownfield had 35 ratable polls in *1787*: List, in *Me. Doc. Hist.*, XXI, 327-29.

k Limerick had 22 families in *1779*: *Me. Doc. Hist.*, XVII, 154.

¹ Parsonsfield had 86 ratable polls in *1786* and *1787*: *Me. Doc. Hist.*, XXI, 252, 382.

VII. Account of Male Polls in 1784 — *Continued*

Place	Ratable and Not Ratable	Supported by Town	Place	Ratable and Not Ratable	Supported by Town
Worcester — Continued			*Cumberland — Continued*		
Uxbridge	281		Standish	124	
Harvard	306		Royalsboro	93	
Dudley	220	3	Raymondtown m	40	
Bolton	216	2	Bakerston	65	
Upton	184		Sylvester	60	
Sturbridge	347		Bridgeton	39	
Leominster	259		Sheppardstown	50	
Hardwick	340		Otisfield Plan.n	37	
Holden	233	3			
Western	192			3,708	
Douglass	231	3			
Grafton	225	2	13. *Berkshire County*		
Petersham	349	4	Sheffield	448	1
Royalston	196		Great Barrington	263	
Westminster	291		Stockbridge	282	
Templeton	274		Pittsfield	419	
Princeton	198	2	Richmond	307	
Ashburnham	197		Lenox	272	
Northbridge	95		Landsborough	405	1
Ward	108	8	Williamstown	339	
Athòl	193		Adams	405	
Milford	195	2	Egremont	171	4
Sterling	339	1	Becket	129	
Berlin	118	1	W. Stockbridge	207	
Winchendon	231		Dalton	103	
Boylston	188		Alford	109	
			New Ashford	61	
	12,263	86	New Marlboro	307	
12. *Cumberland County*			Tyringham	278	1
Falmouth	774		Louden	67	
N. Yarmouth	498		Windsor	235	
Scarboro	454		Partridgefield	190	
Harpswell	199		Hancock	194	8
Brunswick	219		Lee	220	
Cape Elizabeth	262		Washington	106	
Gorham	368		Sandisfield	339	
Windham	163		Mt. Washington	36	
New Gloucester	186				
Gray	77			5,892	15

m Raymond had 200 inhabitants in *1787: Me. Doc. Hist.*, XXI, 320.
n Otisfield had 22 families in *1787:* Ibid., 323.

VII. ACCOUNT OF MALE POLLS IN 1784 — *Continued*

Place	Ratable and Not Ratable	Supported by Town	Place	Ratable and Not Ratable	Supported by Town
14. *Lincoln County*			*Lincoln — Continued*		
Pownalboro	333		Camden	46	
Georgetown	244	1	Hancock	80	2
Newcastle	148	1	Mt. Desart Plan.	85	
Woolwich	161		No. 1 Plan.○	40	
Waldoboro	184		No. 2 Plan.○	38	
Topsham	146		Penobscot ○	150	
Winslow	71		Sedgwick ○	90	
Bowdoinham	111		No. 5 Plan.	69	
Boothbay	173		No. 6 Plan.	69	
Bristol	268	14	Trenton ○	80	
Vassalboro	185		No. 2	80	
Edegcomb	142	1	No. 3	60	
Hallowell	189		No. 4	30	
St. Georges	77		No. 5	70	
Warren	89	2	No. 6	50	
Thomastown	79	1	No. 22	25	
Bath	173	2	Frankfort ○	70	
Winthrop	130	2	Bangor ○	60	
Lewistown	78	1	Deer Island ○	150	
Balltown	72	5	Vinalhaven ○	75	
Walpole	71		Isleboro ○	40	
Wales	33				
Canaan	85	3		5,071	35
Pittston	85				
Meduncook	70		Total No. of Polls:		90,757
Norridgewock	50		Maintained by Towns:		789
Sterlington	30				
Belfast	27				91,546
Machias	110		× 4 = 366,184 population ᴾ		

○ These towns were still plantations, but became incorporated shortly after *1784*: Penobscot in *1787*; Sedgwick in *1789*; Deer Island in *1789*; Isleboro, called Penobscot, Long Island, in *1789*. Vinalhaven was called Fox Island plantation, but no dates are given for the incorporation of it, or of Trenton, Frankfort, and Bangor. The plantations No. 1 and No. 2 are on the east side of the Penobscot River; the plantations listed after Trenton are on the east side of Union River.

ᴾ Felt multiplies the number of polls by 4 to estimate the total population. For other methods of computation see note on p. 000.

VIII. Census of 1784 [a]

Counties	Inhabitants	Counties	Inhabitants
Suffolk	36,783	Nantucket	4,269
Essex	48,723	Bristol	25,640
Middlesex	34,823	York	20,509
Hampshire	43,143	Worcester	47,614
Plymouth	25,016	Cumberland	14,714
Barnstable	13,353	Lincoln	15,270
Dukes	3,110	Berkshire	24,544

357,511

IX. Census of 1790 [b]

COUNTY	No. of Families	FREE WHITE Males Over 16	Under 16	Females	OTHER FREE	TOTAL
Barnstable	2,889	4,200	4,097	8,685	372	17,354
Berkshire	4,899	7,366	7,993	14,809	323	30,291 [30,491]
Bristol	5,541	7,964	6,942	16,074	729	31,709
Dukes	558	822	714	1,696	33	3,265
Essex	10,883	14,263	12,562	30,208	880	57,913
Hampshire	9,617	15,119	15,012	29,099	451	59,681
Middlesex	7,580	11,040	9,606	21,494	597	42,737
Nantucket	872	1,193	1,016	2,301	110	4,620
Plymouth	5,173	7,500	6,534	14,998	503	29,535
Suffolk	8,038	11,371	9,334	23,114	1,056	44,875
Worcester	9,729	14,615	13,679	28,104	409	56,807
Total	65,779	95,453	87,289 [87,489]	190,582	5,463	378,787 [378,987]
MAINE COUNTIES						
Cumberland	4,342	6,214	6,633	12,557	156	25,560
Hancock	1,796	2,436	2,531	4,544	38	9,549
Lincoln	5,309	7,769	7,751	14,052	151	29,723
Washington	564	754	708	1,277	20	2,759
York	5,087	7,299	7,219	14,505	155	29,178
Total	[17,098]	[24,472]	[24,842]	[46,935]	[520]	[96,769]

a Morse, *American Geography* (ed. 1792), 172, reproduces this table together with similar tables for Conn., R.I., N.Y., N.J., Pa., and Md. The figures for N.Y., N.J., and Pa. are available in official publications, and comparison indicates that Morse was generally accurate. It has not been practicable to check those for Mass., Conn., and Md., though further search in state archives might well bring such material to light. For action by the Cont. Congress calling for state enumerations, see *Journals* for Dec. 11, 1781, and April 18, 1783. Cf., for state action, N.C. CR, XVII, 512-13; also *R.I. State Records*, IX, 521; *Laws of State of N.Y., 1777-84*, Chap. XVIII; *N.J. Acts of Council and Assembly, 1776-83*, 273-77; *Pa. Statutes at Large*, XI, 90; *Laws of Md., 1692-1799*, I, Chap. VI; *Va. Statuates at Large*, XI, 40-41; Ga. CR, XIX, Pt. ii, 525-28.

b U.S. Bureau of the Census, *Heads of Families, Mass.*, 8-10; Maine, 9.

CONNECTICUT

GENERAL

1636   800 persons, or 160 to 170 families; 250 men in the 3 towns on the river, and 20 men in the garrison at the entrance of it. Trumbull, *Hist. Conn.*, I, 68.

200 fighting men, less than. Bancroft, I, 265.

1637   800 population, including 250 adult men, in the 3 lower towns on the Connecticut. Palfrey, I, 455.

1642   2,000 English, and no more than 5 or 6 Dutch, on the Connecticut River. Letter from Lord Saye, in NYCD, I, 128.

1643   3,000 in population, and 2,500 in New Haven.[1] Palfrey, II, 5-6.

1649   5,000 persons capable of bearing arms in the 30 villages settled by the English within the Dutch limits including New Haven. Remonstrance of Deputies from New Netherland," in NYCD, I, 288.

1654   777 taxables.[2] See page 52. Conn. CR, I, 265.

3,186 people, on basis of 775 ratable polls times 4½. Felt, 140.

1655   669 taxables. See page 52. Conn. CR, I, 279.

1665   1,700 families, or 8-9,000 inhabitants. Trumbull, *Hist. Conn.*, I, 287.

4,300 fighting men. *See* Thirteen Colonies: General, 1665.

1669   773 freemen. (Middletown, Lyme, and Rye are omitted.[3]) See page 52. Conn. CR, II, 518-26.

1671   2,050 men. Gov. Leete, Ans. Quer., July 1680, in CSPC, 1677-80, 577, No. 1447.

14,000 total forces by land. *See* Thirteen Colonies: General, 1671.

1674   2,070 men in the militia. Trumbull, *Hist. Conn.*, I, 325.

1675   3,120 houses in list of houses for 25 towns. See page 51. "Acct. of New Eng.," in *N.E. Hist. Gen. Reg.*, XXXVIII, 380.

1,400 inhabitants. Bancroft, I, 383.

1676   2,303 men. Gov. Leete, Ans. Quer., July, 1680, in CSPC, 1677-80, 577, No. 1447. See also table of ratables by counties, page 52. Conn. CR, II, 290.

1677   2,362 men. Gov. Leete, Ans. Quer., July, 1680, in CSPC, 1677-80, 577, No. 1447.

2,355 ratables. See page 52. Conn. CR, II, 320.

1678   3,000 freemen able to bear arms. E. Andros, Ans. Quer., Apr. 16, 1678, in NYCD, III, 262-63, and in CSPC, 1677-80, 237-38, No. 660.

2,490 men. Gov. Leete, Ans. Quer., July, 1680, in CSPC, 1677-80, 577, No. 1447.

[1] Bases figures on military levy of New Eng. Confed., which called for 30 men from Conn.

[2] Dexter quotes this, and estimates 4,000 to 4,500 population.

[3] Palfrey, III, 37n., estimates 50 freemen for these towns.

2,435 ratables. See page 52. Conn. CR, III, 17.

1679   2,507 men. Gov. Leete, Ans. Quer., July, 1680, in CSPC, 1677-80, 577, No. 1447.

2,522 ratables. See page 52. Conn. CR, III, 36.

12,535 inhabitants, including Negroes. Warden, *Statist. Polit. and Hist. Acct. of the U.S.*, II, 9.

1680   2,574 ratables; 500 fighting men among the Indians; 30 slaves at the most. See page 53. Conn. CR, III, 66-67, 296-98.

1681   2,640 ratables. See page 53. *Ibid.*, III, 86-87.

1682   2,619 ratables. See page 53. *Ibid.*, III, 106-7.

1683   2,735 taxables. See page 53. *Ibid.*, III, 126.

1684   2,551 taxables. See page 53. *Ibid.*, III, 156-57.

1685   2,956 taxables. See pages 53-4. *Ibid.*, III, 181.

1686   2,840 taxables. See pages 53-4. *Ibid.*, III, 215.

1687   3,000 men able to bear arms. Gov. Dongan, Ans. Quer., Feb. 22, 1687, in NYCD, I, 159.

3,053 taxables. See pages 53-4. Conn. CR, III, 239.

1688   17-20,000 inhabitants. *See* Thirteen Colonies: General, 1688.

1689   2,971 taxables. See pages 53-4. Conn. CR, IV, 9-10.[4]

1690   3,185 taxables. See pages 53-4. *Ibid.*, IV, 33.

3,061 militia. See page 51. Gov. Andros to Sec'y of State, May 13, 1690, in CO 5: 855, Bb, P: 23, pp. 202-5.

1691   3,109 taxables. See page 54. Conn. CR, IV, 56.

1692   3,069 taxables. See page 54. *Ibid.*, IV, 79.

1693   3,092 taxables. See page 54. *Ibid.*, IV, 106.

3,000 men able to bear arms. *See* Thirteen Colonies: General, 1693.

1694   3,238 taxables. See page 54. Conn. CR, IV, 131.

1695   3,321 taxables. See page 54. *Ibid.*, IV, 149-50.

1696   5,000 families. Rept. of Rev. Mr. Miller, in NYCD, IV, 183.

3,000 militia. Proc. BT, in NYCD, IV, 185.

3,370 taxables. See page 55. Conn. CR, IV, 175.

1697   3,430 taxables. See page 55. *Ibid.*, IV, 222.

1698   3,572 taxables. See page 55. *Ibid.*, IV, 265.

1699   3,705 taxables. See page 55. *Ibid.*, IV, 297.

1700   3,606 taxables. See page 55. Conn. CR, IV, 329.

120 fighting men in the Moheagans. Gov. Bellomont to BT, July 15, 1700, in CSPC, 1700, 418, No. 641.

1701   30,000 souls, of whom about 150 are Anglicans. Humphreys, S.P.G., 42.

3,695 taxables. See page 56. Conn. CR, IV, 360.

30,000 total population. *See* Thirteen colonies: General, 1701.

1702   3,912 taxables. See page 56. Conn. CR, IV, 405.

---

[4] Dexter quotes Bancroft, 17,000 to 20,000 for this year.

1703 4,050 taxables. See page 56. *Ibid.*, IV, 441.

1704 4,022 taxables. See page 56. *Ibid.*, IV, 489-80.

3,200 men, "They (Conn.) alledged that they had but. . . ." "Rept. of Commissioners for assistance to Gov. Dudley, Dec. 28, 1704," in CSPC, 1704-5, 668, No. 1424, xlvi. Cf. preceding figure of 4,022 tithables.

1705 3,909 taxables. See page 56. Conn. CR, IV, 521-22.

150 fighting men in the Moheagans. Rept. of Com. of Inquiry to BT, Aug. 25, 1705, in CSPC, 1704-5, 608, No. 1312, i (a).

1706 4,144 taxables. See page 57. Conn. CR, V, 6-7.

1707 4,480 taxables. See page 57. *Ibid.*, V, 31.

1708 4,668 taxables (males). See page 57. *Ibid.*, V, 71.

1709 4,000 inhabitants; 2,000 freemen; 100 servants, white and black; 3,500 militia. Gov. and Council to BT, Ans. Quer., Jan. 24, 1708-9, in CSPC, 1708-9, 206, No. 323.

3,688 taxables. See page 57. Conn. CR, V, 115.

1713 17,000 inhabitants; nearly 4,000 militia. Trumbull, *Hist. Conn.*, I, 451.

25-30,000 inhabitants. Palfrey, IV, 372-73.[5]

1714- 46,750 population, supposing, according to Douglass, that Conn.
1715 was nearly half as populous as Mass. *Chalmers Coll.*, RI, 27. NYPL.

47,500 total population: 46,000 white; 1,500 Negroes. See Thirteen Colonies: General, 1715.

1725 1,500 or 1,600 Indians living in the colony. Gov. Talcott to Col. Winthrop, "Talcott Papers," in Conn. HSC, V, 397-98, 401-2.

1726 20,000 inhabitants. See Thirteen Colonies: General, 1726.

1730 38,000 inhabitants; 700 Indian and Negro slaves; 8,500 militia; 1,600 Indians of all ages and sexes. Sec. Wyllys, Ans. Quer., Sept. 9, 1730, in Conn. CR, VII, 384.[6]

1740 8,000 militia in Conn. and RI. See Thirteen Colonies: General, 1740.

1742 100,000 population. Douglass, *Summary*, II, 180.

1746 80-100,000 inhabitants. "The number of your inhabitants being generally estimated at more than one-half of our [Mass.] number. . . ."[7] Gov. Shirley to Gov. Law, in Conn. HSC, XIII, 224, 229.

1749 70,000 whites and 1,000 blacks; 10,000 militia; 500 Indians. Ans. Quer., in Conn. CR, IX, 596.

[5] Palfrey bases this estimate on tax lists of 1708, 1709 (q.v.), counting the proportion of taxables to the whole population as one to five.

[6] Dexter thinks the inhabitants numbered a third again as many. Rossiter says 51,600.

[7] Gov. Shirley does not give any definite number. See Massachusetts: General, 1742 and 1747.

50 CONNECTICUT

100,000 inhabitants. *See* Thirteen Colonies: General, 1749.

16,000 militia. Anon., *State of British and French Colonies in North Am.*, 1755, 133-34.

1754　130,000 inhabitants. Gov. Shirley to Earl of Holdernesse, *Correspondence*, II, 21.

135,000 white inhabitants; 3,500 black. Bancroft, II, 389-91.

1755　100,000 white inhabitants.[8] Rept. of BT, in NYCD, VI, 993.

100,000 inhabitants. *See* Thirteen Colonies: General, 1755.

1756　129,994 population. Pownall, *Memorial*, 58.

128,212 whites; 3,587 blacks; and 1,000 Indians.[9] Gov. Fitch, Ans. Quer., Apr. 15, 1756, in Conn. CR, X, 623-24.

126,975 whites; 3,109 Negroes; 617 Indians, according to census. See page 58. *Ibid.*, X, 617-18.

1762　141,000 whites; 4,590 blacks, or thereabouts; 930 Indians; 20,264 militia. Gov Fitch, Ans. Quer., Sept. 7, 1762, in Conn. CR, XI, 630; and also in *Kings MS.*, 205, fol. 221, p. 449; 222, p. 450, in LCT.

1765　180,000 inhabitants; 45,000 men. *See* Thirteen Colonies: General, 1765.

1774　191,342 whites;[10] 6,464 blacks; 1,363 Indians; 26,260 militia, on an exact census. Gov. Trumbull, Ans. Quer., Nov. 23, 1774, in CO 5: 1285, fol. 242-43, in LCT; also dated Oct., 1774 in MHSC, 1st Series, VII, 236-37.

For census, see page 58. Conn. CR, XIV, 483-92.

192,000 population; or 200,000; or 191,392. *See* Thirteen Colonies: General, 1774.

257,356 population. Pownall, *Memorial*, 58.

1775　262,000 population. De Witt, *Abstract of Census of Mass.*, 1855, 195.

200,000 total population. *See* Thirteen Colonies: General, 1775.

1782　202,597 whites; 6,273 Indians and Negroes. Holmes, *Annals*, II, 343. Cf. Webster, in *NY Directory for 1786*, 20; Morse, *Amer. Geography*, 218. See page 61.

1783　206,000 population. *See* Thirteen Colonies: General, 1783.

1786　192,000 total inhabitants. *See* Thirteen Colonies: General, 1786.

1787　202,000 total population. *See* Thirteen Colonies: General, 1787.

1790　237,946 total inhabitants: free white males over 16, 60,523; free white males under 16, 54,403; free white females, 117,448; other free persons, 2,808; slaves, 2,764. See page 61. U.S. Bureau of Census, *Heads of Families*, Conn., 9.

[8] The same estimate is found in Anon., *State of British and French Colonies in North Am.*, *1755*, 133-34.

[9] Cf. Census of Indians, taken by Dr. Ezra Stiles in 1761, MHSC, 1st Series, X, 103-105, 112.

[10] Cf. Mandrillon, *Le Spectateur américain*, 253.

LOCAL

I. TRADING TOWNS AND PORTS IN CONN., 1675 [a]

Rye	30	houses	Hommonossett	40	houses
Greenwich	40	Do.	W. Saybrook	100	Do.
Stamford	100	Do.	Lyme	60	Do.
Narwassett	50	Do.	Shirly Mile Island	140	Do.
Fairfield	300	Do.	Middletown	60	Do.
Stratfield	200	Do.	Weathersfield	150	Do.
Milford	200	Do.	Hartford	500	Do.
New Haven	500	Do.	Windsor	400	Do.
Brandford	50	Do.	Farmington	100	Do.
Guilford	100	Do.			
				3,120	

II. ABSTRACT OF MILITIA FOR 1690 [b]

New London County			Hartford — Continued		
New London	243		Windsor	110	
Seabrooke	84		Windsor	120	
Preston	34		Middleton	130	
Norwich	106		Symsbury	61	
Stonington	98		Waterbury	43	
Killingsworth	46		Haddum	51	
Lyme	71				1,055
		682	Hartford, horse		55
New Haven County					1,110
New Haven	246				
Guilford	100		Fairfield County		
Derby	35		Fairfield	96	
Wallingford	71		Stratford	116	
Milford	142		Danbury	22	
Branford	48		Norwalk	80	
		642	Stamford	104	
Hartford County			Woodbury	53	
Hartford	128		Greenwich	55	
Hartford	126		Fayrfield 2d	98	
Wethersfield	191				624
Farmington	95				

Total militia: 3,061 [3,058] [c]

a "Acct. of New Eng.," in *N.E. Hist. Gen. Reg.*, XXXVIII, 380.

b Gov. Andros to Sec'y of State, May 13, 1690, in CO 5: 855, Bb, P: 23, pp. 202-5.

c In this and the following tables for Conn., totals of columns are given as found in the source cited; whenever such figures are incorrect, the true total is, in addition, given in brackets. When no total was given in the source, it has been computed and placed in brackets at the foot of the column, as on page 53.

III. Lists of Taxables

A. Taxables from 1654 to 1679 [a]

Towns	1654	1655	1669	1676	1677	1678	1679
Brandford	...	...	8	48	45	49	53
Fairfield [c]	94	90	44	152	157	177	171
Farmington [d]	46	52	43	102	106	... [b]	95
Greenwich	...	...	...	36	40	38	39
Guilford [e]	...	...	36	98	100	96	94
Haddum	...	...	7	29	29	32	36
Hartford [f]	177	176	117	241	226	227	239
Killingworth	...	...	19	38	33	41	41
Lyme	...	...	... [b]	45	50	60	53
Middleton [g]	31	32	... [b]	94	96	102	110
Milford [h]	...	...	46	151	163	163	160
New Haven [i]	...	...	91	237	214	294	265
New London [j]	...	...	21	153	147	162	171
Norwalk [k]	24	... [b]	33	65	68	70	78
Norwich	...	...	25	71	70	78	85
Rye	...	...	... [b]	32	38	44	48
Saybrook	53	... [b]	23	85	85	90	91
Stamford	...	...	8	81	90	88	105
Stonington	...	...	17	79	87	89	68
Stratford	74	65	64	78	84	100	99
Wallingford	...	...	...	43	48	49	51
Wethersfield [l]	113	102	58	141	160	170	180

a Estimates for *1654* found in Conn. CR, I, 265; for *1655*, *ibid.*, I, 279; for *1669*, *ibid.*, II, 518-26; for *1676*, *ibid.*, II, 290; for *1677*, *ibid.*, II, 320; for *1678*, *ibid.*, III, 17; for *1679*, *ibid.*, III, 36.

b This town is included in the list for this year, but no figure is given.

c Fairfield had 44 freemen in *1669*: Schenk, *Hist. Fairfield*, I, 328.

d Farmington had 339 inhabitants in *1670*: Wyllys Papers, in Conn. HSC, XXI, 191, 197.

e Guilford had 28 freemen and 20 planters not admitted as freemen in *1652*; 46 freemen in *1657*: Rockey, *Hist. New Haven County*, II, 117.

f Hartford in *1639* had 150 settlers: Walker, *Hist. First Church in Hartford*, 419-21; in *1659*, 156 ratables: Conn. HSC, XIV, 494-98; in *1670*, 721 inhabitants: Wyllys Papers, in Conn. HSC, XXI, 191, 195-97.

g Middleton in *1669* had 38 freemen: *Ibid.*, XXI, 190.

h Milford in *1639* had 44 freemen; 10 planters not admitted as freemen: Rockey, *Hist. New Haven County*, II, 215-16; in *1646*, 58 heads of families: Atwater, *Hist. Col. of New Haven*, 639-40.

i New Haven in *1637* had 157 inhabitants: Peters, *Hist. Conn.*, 264; in *1639*, 70 freemen: *New Haven Recds.*, I, 9-10; in *1643*. 420 members in families of planters, 460 souls with hired and indentured servants, 500 with other non-landed persons: *Ibid.*, I, 91-93.

j New London in *1653* had 53 inhabitants: Conn. HSC, III, 284.

k Norwalk in *1651* had 20 families: Trumbull, *Hist. Conn.*, I, 195; 31 taxables in *1655* and 64 in *1673*: Hall, *Ancient Recds. of Norwalk*, 46, 61.

l Wethersfield in *1670* had 349 inhabitants: Wyllys Papers, in Conn. HSC, XXI, 191, 197-99.

III. Lists of Taxables — *Continued*

Windsor m	165	152	113	204	219	216	220
	[777]	[669]	[773]	[2,303]	[2,355]	[2,435]	[2,552]

B. Taxables from 1680 to 1684 n

Towns	1680	1681	1682	1683	1684
Brandford	60	63	51	50	50
Fairfield	177	184	172	181	184
Farmington	95	96	97	101	96
Greenwich	33	52	48	55	50
Guilford	96	100	100	100	96
Haddum	40	37	40	36	43
Killingworth	44	48	44	44	43
Hartford	247	250	243	246	250
Lyme	62	66	55	64	53
Middleton	112	117	117	126	130
Milford	147	150	160	147	150
New Haven	268	240	238	248	268
New London	175	174	174	201	
Norwalk	82	85	92	92	88
Norwich	90	105	98	111	115
Rye	49	50	50	47	
Saybrook	91	96	97	80	86
Stamford	105	110	94	90	97
Stonington	60	57	59	76	65
Stratford	94	101	102	122	120
Wallingford	50	52	55	52	61
Wethersfield	181	189	190	205	204
Windsor	216	218	233	240	240
Woodbury	...	...	...	62	62
	2,574	2,640	2,619 [2,609]	2,735 [2,776]	[2,551]

C. Taxables from 1685 to 1690 o

Towns	1685	1686	1687	1689	1690
Brandford	50	46	52	69	64
Derby	39	39	41	38	39
Fairfield p	192	205	218	168	222
Farmington	100	108	111	81	93

m Windsor in *1670* had 754 inhabitants: *Ibid.*, XXI, 191-95, 197; 147 taxables in *1675*: Stiles, *Hist. and Geneal. Ancient Windsor*, I, 88-89.

n Figures for *1680*, in Conn. CR, III, 66-67, 296-98; *1681, ibid.*, III, 86-87; *1682, ibid.*, III, 106-7; *1683, ibid.*, III, 126; *1684, ibid.*, III, 156-57.

o Figures for *1685* in Conn. CR, III, 181; *1686, ibid.*, III, 215; *1687, ibid.*, III, 239; *1689, ibid.*, IV, 9-10; *1690, ibid.*, IV, 33.

p Fairfield in *1689* had 114 freemen: Schenck, *Hist. Fairfield*, I, 346.

III. Lists of Taxables — *Continued*

Greenwich q	55	65	62	59	62
Guilford	100	107	104	110	108
Haddum	44	43	52	63	69
Hartford	255	269	273	298	307
Killingworth	42	36	43	45	
Lyme	64	62	65	63	74
Middleton	130	130	130	124	120
Milford	158	160	160	155	170
New Haven	302	303	323	317	322
New London	164	189	156	172	182
Norwalk	77	85	93	55	93
Norwich	113	...	103	82	109
Rye					
Saybrook	90	83	89	83	95
Simsbury	...	...	...	70	59
Stamford	99	104	102	113	111
Stonington	74	80	80	83	89
Stratford	134	110	140	110	127
Wallingford	63	69	72	73	76
Waterbury	...	...	...	...	37
Wethersfield	207	213	215	228	232
Windsor	260	270	278	259	279
Woodbury	74	64	91	53	46
	2,956 [2,886]	[2,840]	3,053	2,971	3,185

D. Taxables from 1691 to 1695 r

Towns	1691	1692	1693	1694	1695
Brandford	53	65	58	72	67
Derby	41	37	34	...	42
Fairfield	208	173	175	180	192
Farmington	109	104	106	109	112
Glassenbury	...	...	...	44	44
Greenwich	66	65	60	59	78
Guilford	120	120	115	120	120
Haddum	65	63	66	76	87
Hartford	253	274	267	275	285
Killingworth	43	45	46	48	53
Lyme	66	75	81	79	74
Middleton	110	110	120	120	120
Milford	144	160	155	171	157
New Haven	321	316	262	256	282

q Greenwich in *1688* had 49 freemen: Mead, *Hist. Greenwich*, 71.
r Figures for *1691* in Conn. CR, IV, 56; *1692*, *ibid.*, IV, 79; *1693*, *ibid.*, IV, 106; *1694*, *ibid.*, IV, 131; *1695*, *ibid.*, IV, 149-50.

III. LISTS OF TAXABLES — *Continued*

New London	190	180	182	203	216
Norwalk s	88	90	65	85	74
Norwich	116	102	112	108	106
Preston	...	...	30	...	35
Saybrook	90	98	102	102	104
Simsbury	66	...	78	72	
Stamford	109	108	80	112	90
Stonington	97	88	92	122	102
Stratford	124	130	130	130	
Wallingford	76	80	83	60	95
Waterbury	43	43	46	43	
Wethersfield	234	201	196	212	218
Windsor	285	290	290	319	300
Woodbury t	52	52	61	61	62
	3,109	3,069	3,092	3,238	3,321
	[3,169]				[3,115]

E. TAXABLES FROM 1696 TO 1700 u

Towns	1696	1697	1698	1699	1700
Bedford	...	...	28	26	
Brandford	69	76	73	80	80
Danbury v	...	...	...	...	48
Derby	42	...	40	44	51
Fairfield	170	150	150	150	140
Farmington	115	112	114	116	115
Glassenbury	50	53	58	61	64
Greenwich	70	76	80	78	86
Guilford	125	125	130	136	136
Haddum	88	84	90	92	100
Hartford	285	302	293	300	307
Kenilworth	45	45	50	52	48
Lyme	99	86	72	93	111
Middleton	125	140	161	150	182
Milford	160	162	175	178	180
New Haven	290	300	310	315	330
New London	220	220	190	208	
Norwalk	76	110	100	120	120
Norwich	110	130	117	125	117
Preston	42	42	58	61	62

s Norwalk in *1694* had 101 freemen: Hall, *Anc. Hist. Recds. of Norwalk*, 86-87.
t Woodbury in *1694* had 43 families: "Jour. of Rev. Benj. Wadsworth," in MHSC, 4th Series, I, 109.
u Figures for *1696* in Conn. CR, IV, 175; *1697*, *ibid.*, IV, 222; *1698*, *ibid.*, IV, 265; *1699*, *ibid.*, IV, 297; *1700*, *ibid.*, IV, 329.
v Danbury in *1697* had 24 families: Letter to Rev. T. Prince, in Conn. HSC, III, 315.

III. Lists of Taxables — *Continued*

Rye	...	...	56	60	
Saybrook	112	113	132	134	124
Simsbury	70	70	76	90	83
Stamford	90	90	90	90	100
Stonington	86	103	96	108	128
Stratford	140	140	130	130	130
Wallingford	75	75	80	88	120
Waterbury	40	42	49	47	48
Wethersfield	213	220	212	218	240
Windsor	300	300	290	290	290
Woodbury	63	64	72	65	66
	3,370	3,430	3,572	3,705	3,606

F. Taxables from 1701 to 1705 w

Towns	1701	1702	1703	1704	1705
Brandford	80	86	80	84	82
Danbury	...	...	58	54	61
Derby	47	53	60	56	65
Fairfield	150	150	150	153	175
Farmington	115	118	120	124	127
Glassenbury	71	74	76	60	70
Greenwich	82	90	82	64	64
Groton x	...	...	...	...	120
Guilford	137	150	140	150	160
Haddum	101	95	104	97	112
Hartford	307	310	302	305	313
Killingworth	52	54	56	60	60
Lebanon	...	...	...	...	90
Lyme	123	117	115	120	110
Middleton	177	173	180	180	197
Milford	181	180	160	150	152
New Haven	332	350	355	360	276
New London	210	220	289	326	217
Norwalk	110	110	113	94	100
Norwich	122	111	120	120	163
Preston	68	69	78	70	69
Saybrook	126	134	126	97	109
Simsbury	67	70	92	93	76
Stamford	95	100	100	110	100
Stonington	136	147	138	135	119
Stratford	130	140	120	132	130
Wallingford	100	122	118	120	100
Waterbury	50	52	57	52	52

w Figures for *1701* in Conn. CR, IV, 360; *1702, ibid.*, IV, 405; *1703, ibid.*, IV, 441; *1704, ibid.*, IV, 489-90; *1705, ibid.*, IV, 521-22.
x Groton in *1705* had 70 families: Conn. HSC, III, 293.

III. LISTS OF TAXABLES — *Continued*

Wethersfield	252	257	262	239	200
Windham	59	50	63	62	56
Windsor	250	250	250	275	300
Woodbury	65	80	86	80	84
	3,695	3,912	4,050	4,022	3,909
	[3,795]				[4,109]

G. TAXABLES FROM 1706 TO 1709 [y]

Towns	1706	1707	1708	1709
Brandford	83	90	104	80
Canterbury	...	...	...	35
Colchester	...	...	81	
Danbury	...	62	63	57
Derby	57	53	50	49
Durham [z]	...	...	...	47
Easthaven	...	44	43	40
Fairfield	170	171	160	
Farmington	128	130	150	
Glassenbury	78	82	83	61
Greenwich	60	84	70	64
Groton	117	125	140	105
Guilford	160	165	170	170
Haddum East	72	70	69	60
Haddum West	40	48	55	54
Hartford	290	310	300	230
Killingworth	63	70	63	
Lebanon	105	135	140	112
Lyme	131	133	140	131
Mansfield [aa]	...	...	...	37
Middleton	202	180	172	190
Milford	171	170	180	170
New Haven	276	280	220	260
New London	134	226	249	188
Norwalk	110	130	115	100
Norwich	143	168	174	155
Plainfield	...	...	55	55
Preston	80	77	80	74
Saybrook	92	147	147	
Simsbury [ab]	73	80	74	55

[y] Figures for *1706* in Conn. CR, V, 6-7; *1707, ibid.,* V, 31; *1708, ibid.,* V, 71; *1709, ibid.,* V, 115.
[z] Durham in *1707* had 15 families: Chauncey and Wadsworth to Rev. T. Prince, in Conn. HSC, III, 309.
[aa] Mansfield in *1729* had 88 families: Letter to T. Prince, *ibid.,* III, 297.
[ab] Simsbury in *1730* had 28 families: Clarke, "East Granby" (from a map in State Library in Hartford), in Trumbull, *Mem. Hist. Hartford County,* II, 78.

III. Lists of Taxables — *Continued*

Stamford	110	100	110	110
Stonington	150	117	172	135
Stratford	135	140	134	
Wallingford	120	130	132	122
Waterbury	55	49	50	43
Wethersfield	281	250	250	240
Windham ac	68	69	72	83
Windsor ad	300	315	315	297
Woodbury ae	90	80	86	79
	4,144	4,480	4,668	3,688

IV. Censuses

A. Censuses of 1756 and 1774

Counties	1756 a		1774 b	
	Whites	Blacks	Whites	Blacks
Hartford				
Bolton	755	11	994	7
Chatham	...	...	2,369	28
Colchester	2,228	84	3,057	201
E. Haddam	1,913	65	2,743	65
E. Windsor	...	...	2,961	38
Enfield	1,050	...	1,353	7
Farmington	3,595	112	5,963	106
Glastenbury	1,091	24	1,992	79
Haddam	1,223	18	1,713	13
Hartford c	2,926	101	4,881	150
Hebron	1,855	...	2,285	52
Middletown	5,446	218	4,680	198
Symsbury	2,222	23	3,671	29
Somers	900	...	1,024	3
Stafford d	1,000	...	1,333	1
Suffield	1,414	24	1,980	37
Tolland e	902	15	1,247	15
Wethersfield	2,374	109	3,347	142
Willington	650	...	1,000	1

ac Windham in *1729* had 150 families: Letter to Rev. T. Prince, in Conn. HSC, III, 294.

ad Windsor in *1732* had 136 taxables: Orcutt, *Hist. Torrington*, 8-9.

ae Woodbury in *1712* had 122 taxables: Cothren, *Hist. Ancient Woodbury*, 80-81.

a Conn. CR, X, 617-18.

b *Ibid.*, XIV, 483-92.

c Hartford in *1761* had 3,786 whites and 152 blacks: Conn. CR, XI, 574-75n.

d Stafford in *1723* had 35 families: Letter to Rev. T. Prince, in Conn. HSC, III, 316.

e Tolland in *1720* had 28 families: Trumbull, *Hist. Conn.*, II, 85.

LOCAL 59

IV. Censuses — *Continued*

	1756		1774	
Counties	Whites	Blacks	Whites	Blacks
Hartford —Continued				
Windsor t	4,170	50	2,082	43
Total	35,714	854	50,675	1,215
New Haven				
Branford	1,694	106	1,938	113
Derby	1,000	...	1,819	70
Durham	765	34	1,031	45
Guilford	2,263	59	2,846	84
Milford	1,633	...	1,965	162
New Haven	5,085	...	8,022	273
Wallingford	3,713	...	4,777	138
Waterbury	1,802	27	3,498	38
Total	17,955	226	25,896	925 [923]

New London					*Indians 1756*
Groton	2,532	179	3,488	360	158
Lyme	2,762	100	3,860	228	94
Killingworth	1,442	16	1,957	33	
New London g	3,171	...	5,366	522	
Norwich	5,317	223	7,032	295	
Preston	1,940	78	2,255	83	
Saybrook	1,898	33	2,628	59	
Stonington	2,953	200	4,956	456	365
Total	22,015	829	31,542	2,036	617

Fairfield				
Danbury	1,509	18	2,473	53
Fairfield h	4,195	260	4,544	319
Greenwich i	2,021	...	2,654	122
New Fairfield	713	...	1,288	20
Newtown	1,230	23	2,168	61
Norwalk	2,956	94	4,243	145
Reading	....	...	1,189	45
Ridgfield	1,069	46	1,673	35
Stamford j	2,648	120	3,503	60
Stratford	3,508	150	5,201	354
Total	19,849	711	28,936	1,214

t Windsor in *1732* had 136 taxables: Orcutt, *Hist. Torrington,* 8-9.

g New London in *1730* had 600 inhabitants, of whom 100 belonged to the Anglican Church; 1,000 inhabitants in *1742,* of whom 228 were churchmen: Hawkins, *Hist. Notices,* 294-95.

IV. Censuses — *Continued*

Counties	1756 Whites	1756 Blacks	1774 Whites	1774 Blacks
Windham				
Canterbury	1,240	20	2,392	52
Coventry	1,617	18	2,032	24
Pomfret k	1,677	50	2,241	65
Killingly	2,100	...	3,439	47
Lebanon l	3,171	103	3,841	119
Mansfield	1,598	16	2,443	23
Plainfield	1,751	49	1,479	83
Ashford	1,245	...	2,228	13
Voluntown	1,029	19	1,476	35
Union	500	...	512	2
Windham	2,406	40	3,437	91
Woodstock	1,336	30	1,974	80
Total m	19,669 [19,670]	345	27,494	634
Litchfield				
Barkhamsted	18	...	250	
Canaan	1,100	...	1,573	62
Colebrook	....	...	150	
Cornwall	500	...	957	17
Goshen	610	...	1,098	13
Hartland	12	...	500	
Harwinton	250	...	1,015	3
Kent	1,000	...	1,922	74
Litchfield n	1,366	...	2,509	45
New Hartford o	260	...	985	16
New Milford p	1,121	16	2,742	34
Norfolk q	84	...	966	3
Salisbury	1,100	...	1,936	44
Sharon	1,198	7	1,986	26
Torrington	250	...	843	2

h Fairfield in *1736* had 450 families: Hobart to Prince, in Conn. HSC, III, 310.

i Greenwich in *1762* had 2,021 whites and 52 blacks: Letter of Rev. E. Dibblee, in Conn. CR, XI, 575n.

j Stamford in *1762* had 2,746 whites and 86 blacks: *Ibid.*, XI, 575n.

k Pomfret in *1729* had 100 families: Rev. E. Williams to Rev. T. Prince, in Conn. HSC, III, 296.

l Lebanon in *1741* had 157 ratables in the parish: *N.E. Hist. Gen. Reg.*, XX, 45.

m Windham County in *1736* had 1,737 militiamen: Talcott Papers, in Conn. HSC, IV, 357-58.

n Litchfield in *1729* had 50 families: Letter to Prince, Conn. HSC, III, 316.

o New Hartford in *1761* had 110 families and 674 souls: Rev. J. Marsh, in Conn. CR, XI, 575n.

p New Milford in *1712* had 12 families: Trumbull, *Hist. Conn.*, II, 84.

q Norfolk in *1758* had 27 families: *Ibid.*, II, 113.

IV. Censuses — *Continued*

Counties	1756		1774	
	Whites	Blacks	Whites	Blacks
Litchfield —Continued				
Westmoreland	....	...	1,922	
Winchester	24	...	327	12
Woodbury	2,880	31	5,224	89
Total	11,773	54	26,845 [26,905]	440

B. Census of 1782 [r]

Counties	Whites	Blacks (Indians and Negroes)
Hartford	55,647	1,320
New Haven	25,092	885
New London	31,131	1,920
Fairfield	29,722	1,134
Windham	28,185	485
Litchfield	33,127	529
	202,877 [202,904]	6,273

C. Census of 1790 [s]

COUNTY	FREE WHITES			OTHER FREE PERSONS	SLAVES	TOTAL	
	Males over 16	Males under 16	Females				
Fairfield	9,187	8,398	17,541	327	795	36,248	
Hartford	9,782	8,840	18,814	430	263	38,129	
Litchfield	10,041	9,249	18,909	323	233	38,755	
Middlesex	4,735	4,212	9,631	144	216	18,938	
New Haven	7,856	6,858	15,258	425	433	30,830	
New London	8,224	7,183	16,478	729	586	33,200	
Tolland	3,263	3,192	6,510	94	47	13,106	
Windham	7,440	6,551	14,406	340	184	23,921	[28,921]
Total	60,523 [60,528]	54,403 [54,483]	117,448 [117,547]	2,808 [2,812]	2,764 [2,757]	233,946 [238,127]	

RHODE ISLAND

GENERAL

1655 258 freemen in the four settlements of Providence, Portsmouth, Newport, and Warwick. R.I. CR, I, 299-302.

1,200 population, estimated on basis of above figure. Palfrey, II, 362.

r Morse, *American Geography*, 218. See note a p. 46.
s U.S. Bureau of Census, *Heads of Families*, Conn., 9.

1658 200 families or fewer in the colony. Callender, "Historical Discourse," in R.I. HSC, IV, 149.

1663 3-4,000 population.[1] Durfee, *Historical Discourse*, 16.
2,500 inhabitants. Bancroft, I, 363-64.

1665 3,000 inhabitants. Palfrey, III, 35.

1675 950 houses in the trading towns and ports. See page 64, "An Acct. of New Eng.," in *N.E. Hist. Gen. Reg.*, XXXVIII, 380.

1678 1,000 to 1,200 men able to bear arms.[2] Gov. Andros, Ans. Quer., April, 1678, in NYCD, III, 262; also in CSPC, 1677-80, 237-38, No. 660.

1680 500 planters, above, and about 500 men besides. There may be about 200 whites and blacks born in a year. Gov. Sanford, Ans. Quer., May 8, 1680, in CSPC, 1677-80, 524, No. 1352.

1688 6,000 inhabitants. *See* Thirteen Colonies: General, 1688.

1690 792 militia. See page 64. Gov. Andros to BT, May 13, 1690, in CO 5: 855, Bb, P: 23, pp. 202-5.

1693 1,200 men able to bear arms. *See* Thirteen Colonies: General, 1693.

1696 300 families, capable of furnishing 40 or 50 men. Proc. BT, in NYCD, IV, 185.

1699 16,000 freemen in New Eng., Conn., and R.I. *See* Thirteen Colonies: General, 1699.

1701 10,000 souls, of whom about 150 are Anglicans. Humphreys, S.P.G., 42.
10,000 or 5,000 souls. *See* Thirteen Colonies: General, 1700.

1702 2,000 men fit to bear arms. Repr. BT on Gov. Dudley's letter, *Acts of Privy Council*, Unbound Papers, 16, (75), II, 421.

1704 1,200 men. Rept. of Commissioners to Gov. Dudley, Dec. 28, 1703, in CSPC, 1704-5, 668, No. 1424, xlvi.

1708 1,015 freemen; 1,362 militia; 56 white servants; 426 black servants; total inhabitants 7,181. By census of Dec. 5. Gov. Cranston to BT, in CSPC, 1708-9, 175, No. 230, I; also in R.I. CR, IV, 59. See page 65.

1714-1715 8,550 population. Abstracts of records in State Paper Office. *Chalmers Coll.*, R.I., 27. NYPL.

1715 9,000 total population: 8,500 whites and 500 blacks. *See* Thirteen Colonies: General, 1715.

1721 9,302 whites. See 1731 below.

1726 10,000 inhabitants. *See* Thirteen Colonies: General, 1726.

1730 15,302 whites, and 2,633 blacks, according to an account taken by order of the BT. "Acct. of People in Colony of R.I.," encl. with

[1] Dexter quotes this but thinks population probably less than 2,000. Rossiter gives 2,000 for 1663.

[2] Rossiter gives 3,000 population for 1675.

Gov. Hopkins's letter of Dec. 24, 1755, *Proprieties* V. 159 (iv), in HSPT. Cf. Pownall, *Memorial*, 60.

17,935 total inhabitants: 15,302 whites; 1,648 blacks; 985 Indians. See page 66, "R.I. State Papers," in MHSC, 2d Series, VII, 113.

1731 15,302 whites; 1,648 blacks; 1,889 militia; 985 Indians. Increased about 6,000 in past 10 years. Gov. of R.I., Ans. Quer., 1731,[3] *Kings Ms.*, 205, fol. 227, p. 462, in LCT; *Proprieties S*: 16, Nov. 9, 1731, in HSPT; *Chalmers Coll.*, R.I., 35. NYPL.

1740 8,000 militia in Conn. and R.I. *See* Thirteen Colonies: General, 1740.

1748 29,755 whites; 4,373 blacks, according to census.[4] "Acct. of People in Colony of R.I.," with Gov. Hopkins's Letter, Dec. 24, 1755, *Proprieties V*; 159 (iv), in HSPT.

34,128 total inhabitants: 29,755 whites; 3,101 blacks; 1,272 Indians. Cf. above. Census in "R.I. State Papers," in MHSC, 2d Series, VII, 113.

28,439 whites; 3,077 Negroes; 1,257 Indians. R.I. CR, V, 270; Douglass, *Summary*, II, 89; also in Anon., *State of British and French Colonies in North Am., 1755*, 133; Cf. Pownall, *Memorial*, 60. See page 66-67.

1749 35,000 inhabitants. *See* Thirteen Colonies: General, 1749.

1755 35,000 white inhabitants. Anon., *State of British and French Colonies in North Am., 1755*, 133.

40,636 total inhabitants: 35,939 whites; 4,697 blacks and Indians, chiefly Negroes.[5] See page 67. "Acct. of the People in the Colony of R.I.," with Gov. Hopkins's letter, Dec. 24, 1755, *Proprieties V*: 159 (iv), in HSPT; also in LC *Md. Recds.*, Miscel., 1755-75; *Force Transcripts*, 12 (No. 300), citing Dr. Ezra Stiles MSS.; also in "R.I. State Papers," in MHSC, 2d Series, VII, 113, which gives a total of 46,636.

30,000 whites; or 35,000 total population including Providence. *See* Thirteen Colonies: General, 1755.

1765 15,000 men and 60,000 inhabitants. *See* Thirteen Colonies: General, 1765.

1767 8,952 ratable estates and polls. See page 68. R.I. CR, VI, 576. Also given as of 1769 in *Chalmers Coll.*, 45. NYPL.

1770 59,678 inhabitants, according to census. See page 68. Potter, "Early Hist. Narragansett," in R.I. HSC, III, 174.

1774 59,678 total inhabitants: 54,435 whites; 3,761 blacks; 1,482 Indians. See page 68. "R.I. State Papers," in MHSC, 2d Series, VII,

---

[3] The Governor was J. Jenckes.

[4] Includes Indians under blacks. Cf. census of 1748 below. Cf. also Brissot de Warville, *New Travels*, 367; Douglass, *Summary*, II, 180.

[5] Cf. also Bancroft, II, 389-91; Winsor, *Narr. Crit. Hist.*, V, 151; Burnaby, *Travels*, 93; Brissot de Warville, *New Travels*, 367.

113; R.I. CR, VII, 299, citing *Providence Gazette*, July 2, 1774; Bartlett, *Census of R.I., 1774,* 238.[6]

59,678 inhabitants; or 50,000; or 35,939. *See* Thirteen Colonies: General, 1774.

1775   58,000 total population. *See* Thirteen Colonies: General, 1775.

1776   54,715 inhabitants. See page 68. "List of proportion of salt," in R.I. CR, VII, 616-17.

1780   7,467 ratable polls, and 518 slaves from 10 to 20 years. See page 68. Official Estimate in R.I. CR, IX, 169.

1783   51,869 total inhabitants: 48,538 whites; 2,342 blacks; 989 Indians. See page 69. Census in "R.I. State Papers," in MHSC, 2d Series, VII, 113; also in R.I. CR, IX, 653.

50,400 population. *See* Thirteen Colonies: General, 1783.

1786   59,670 inhabitants. *See* Thirteen Colonies: General, 1786.

1787   58,000 total population. *See* Thirteen Colonies: General, 1787.

1790   68,825 total inhabitants: free white males over 16, 16,019; free white males under 16, 15,799; free white females, 32,652; other free persons, 3,407; slaves, 948. See page 70. U.S. Bureau of Census, *Heads of Families,* R.I., 8.

LOCAL

I. TOWNS IN 1675 [a]

Wickford	50	houses
Warwick	50	Do.
Patuxett	50	Do.
Providence [b]	200	Do.
Newport [c]	400	Do.
Portsmouth	200	Do.
	[950]	houses [d]

II. ABSTRACT OF MILITIA, 1690 [e]

Newport	104	
	85	
Portsmouth	105	
Jamestown	34	
	328	328

a "An Acct. of New Eng.," in *N.E. Hist. Gen. Reg.,* XXXVIII, 380.

b Providence in *1650* had 51 taxables; in *1671,* 85 taxables: *Providence Early Recds.,* XV, 33, 135-36. In *1676* it was estimated at 500 souls: letter of Wm. Harris, quoted in Dow, "Proprietors of Providence," in R.I. HSC, IX, 56n.

c Newport in *1639* had 96 inhabitants according to a census: Arnold, *Hist. of R.I.,* I, 142.

d Block Island in *1684* had 60 freemen: Champlin, "Early Settlers of Block Island," in *N.E. Hist. Gen. Reg.,* XIII, 37.

e Gov. Andros to BT, in CO 5: 855, Bb, P: 23, pp. 202-5.

6 Gives most complete reprint of census by sexes, ages, etc.

II. ABSTRACT OF MILITIA, 1690 — *Continued*

Providence Plantation

Providence f	175	
Rochester	136	
Warwick	60	
Forsham	56	
Deptford	37	
	464	464
Total militia		792

III. CENSUSES

A. CENSUS OF 1708 a

Towns	Freemen	Militia	White Servants	Blacks	Total Inhabitants
Newport b	190	358	20	220	2,203
Providence c	241	283	6	7	1,446
Portsmouth	98	104	8	40	628
Warwick	80	95	4	10	480
Westerly	95	100	5	20	570
New Shoreham	38	47	..	6	208
Kingstown d	200	282	..	85	1,200
Jamestown	33	28	9	32	206
Greenwich	40	65	3	6	240
	1,015	1,362 e	56 [55] f	426	7,181

f Providence had 123 taxables in *1679*; 129 in *1680*; 100 in *1681*; 122 in *1684*; 146 in *1687*; 172 in *1688*; 104 in *1698*: *Providence Early Recds.*, XV, 185-91, 207-14, 223-25; XVII, 44-52, 98-103; Field, *Tax Lists of Providence*, 37-40; *Providence Early Recds.*, XVII, 165-68.

a R.I. CR, IV, 59.

b Militia in and about Newport was estimated at 400 in *1701*: "Projects vs. New Eng.," in NYCD, IX, 726.

c Providence in *1705* had 129 taxables: *Providence Early Recds.*, XVII, 209-13.

d Kingston in *1687* had 138 taxables: "Jeffries Family Papers," in *N.E. Hist. Gen. Reg.*, XXXV, 124-27.

e Militia has increased by 287 since *1704-5*, being then 1,075.

f In this and the following tables for R.I., totals are given as found in the sources cited. Where such figures are incorrect, the true totals are given, in addition in brackets. When a column has only one total and that is in brackets, it signifies that the figure has been computed because the column had not been footed in the original source.

66 RHODE ISLAND

III. Censuses — *Continued*

B. Census of 1730 g

Counties	Whites	Blacks	Indians	Total
Newport h	4,958			
Providence ᵗ	5,884			
Kings	4,460			
Total	[15,302]	1,648	985	17,935

C. Census of 1748-49 ʲ

Towns	Whites	Negroes	Indians
Newport	5,335	110	68
Providence k	3,177	225	50
Portsmouth	807	134	51
Warwick	1,513	176	93
Westerly	1,701	59	49
New Shoreham	260	20	20
North Kingstown	1,665	184	86
South Kingstown	1,405	380	193
Greenwich	956	61	27
Jamestown	284	110	26
Smithfield	400	30	20
Scituate	1,210	16	6
Gloucester	1,194	8	
Charlestown	641	58	303
West Greenwich	757	8	1
Coventry	769	16	7
Exeter	1,103	63	8
Middletown	586	76	18
Bristol ˡ	928	128	13
Tiverton	842	99	99
Little Compton	1,004	62	86
Warren	600	50	30
Cumberland	802	4	
Richmond	500	5	3
	28,439	3,077 [2,082]	1,257

g "R.I. State Papers" in MHSC, 2d Series, VII, 113.

h Newport was estimated at 6,000 in *1729* by Dean Berkeley, quoted in Vinton, *Annals of R.I.*, 24; and at 400 houses in *1731*: Gov. and Assembly, Ans. Quer., 1731, *Proprieties S*: 16 (Vol. 13), in HSPT.

i Providence was estimated at 10,000 souls in *1724*: Bernon to S.P.G., in Updike, *Hist. Episcopal Church in Narragansett*, I, 57.   ʲ R.I. CR, V, 270.

k Providence Parish, which seemed to include more than the town, was estimated to contain from 14,000 to 18,000 people between *1741* and *1747*: Rev. J. Checkley to S.P.G., in *Prince Soc. Pub.*, XXIII, 197, 206, 212-14.

l Bristol had 70 families and 423 souls in *1689* according to census: "Orig. Recds. of First Congr. Church," in *N.E. Hist. Gen. Reg.*, XXXIV, 404-5. In *1738*, Rev. Mr. Usher estimated the town to have 150 families: Updike, *Hist. Episcopal Church in Narragansett*, III, 71.

III. Censuses — *Continued*

D. Census of 1755 m

Towns	WHITES				BLACKS			
	Men	Women	Boys	Girls	Men	Women	Boys	Girls
Newport	1,696	1,633	1,099	1,091	400	341	248	245
Providence	747	741	655	754	72	75	51	64
Portsmouth	243	228	261	440	51	60	50	30
Warwick	426	422	413	423	48	62	61	56
Westerly	523	551	541	562	34	28	24	28
New Shoreham	83	77	52	52	29	41	22	22
North Kingstown	544	465	408	403	70	87	72	60
South Kingstown	366	321	342	368	137	109	145	125
East Greenwich	319	238	212	271	33	33	38	23
Jamestown	86	100	103	72	42	41	36	37
Smithfield	448	454	466	486	16	17	21	13
Scituate	392	403	540	460	4	4	7	3
Gloucester	332	327	437	408	4	0	1	2
Charlestown	171	187	195	159	100	112	101	105
West Greenwich	275	292	316	321	12	10	8	12
Coventry	298	232	309	323	4	2	4	6
Exeter	347	236	367	371	16	20	23	24
Middletown	153	206	157	165	29	26	19	23
Bristol	210	252	251	253	44	35	34	21
Tiverton	277	217	278	323	44	67	58	61
Little Compton	244	342	261	295	28	43	29	30
Warren	193	217	214	203	26	23	25	24
Cumberland	230	254	267	319	4	2	4	3
Richmond	199	195	202	207	9	5	2	10
Cranston	375	354	337	306	21	22	27	18
25 Towns:	9,177	8,944	8,783 [8,683]	9,035	1,277	1,265	1,110	1,045

E. Censuses of 1767, 1774, and 1783

COUNTIES	1767 n	1774 n	1783 n			
	Ratable Polls	Census Inhabs.	Whites	Blacks	Indians	Total
Newport	2,194	15,929	10,194	837	168	11,199
Providence	2,838	19,206	16,962	428	150	17,540
Kings	2,318	13,866	11,835	782	516	13,133 o
Bristol	406	2,789	2,309	119	43	2,471
Kent	1,196	7,888	7,238	176	112	7,526
Total	[8,952]	59,678 p	[48,538]	[2,342]	[989]	[51,869]

m Gov. Hopkins to B.T., Dec. 1755, *Proprieties V*: 159 (iv), in HSPT.
FOR NOTES TO TABLE E, SEE PAGE 68.

III. Censuses — *Continued*

F. Ratable Polls, and Inhabitants, 1767 to 1780[q]

Towns	1767 Ratable Polls	1770 Census Inhabs.	1774 Census Inhabs.	1776 Census Inhabs.	1780 Ratable Polls	Slaves
Newport [r]	1,114	9,209	9,208	5,299		
Portsmouth	233	1,512	1,512	1,347		
New Shoreham	100	575	575	478		
Jamestown	101	563	563	322		
Middletown	160	881	881	860		
Tiverton	258	1,957	1,956	2,091	304	8
Little Compton	228	1,232	1,232	1,302	250	6
Providence [s]	453	4,321	4,321	4,355	509	40
Smithfield	458	2,888	2,888	2,781	425	3
Scituate	564	3,601	3,601	3,289	605	1
Gloucester	488	2,945	2,945	2,832	555	5
Cumberland	287	1,756	1,756	1,686	292	2
Cranston	313	1,834	1,861	1,701	297	12
Johnston	152	1,031	1,031	1,022	183	1
N. Providence	123	830	830	813	127	3
Westerly	369	1,812	1,812	1,824	317	13
N. Kingstown	481	2,472	2,472	2,761	394	78
S. Kingstown	428	2,835	2,835	2,779	398	156
Charlestown	204	1,821	1,821	1,835	232	16
Richmond	208	1,257	1,257	1,204	216	4
Hopkinton	299	1,805	1,808	1,845	315	15
Exeter	329	1,864	1,864	1,982	360	45
Bristol [t]	180	1,209	1,209	1,067	171	16
Warren	226	979	979	1,005	168	14
Warwick	355	2,438	2,438	2,376	324	41

n For *1767*, in R.I. CR, VI, 576; for *1774*, ibid., VII, 299; for *1783*, "R.I. State Papers," in MHSC, 2d Series, VII, 113.

o Kings County was changed to Washington.

p Divided as follows:　Whites 54,435
　　　　　　　　　　　Indians　1,482
　　　　　　　　　　　Blacks　_3,761

　　　　　　　　　　　　59,678

q Census for *1767* in R.I. CR, VI, 576; *1770*, R.I. HSC, III, 174; *1774*, Bartlett, *Census of R.I.*, *1774*, 239; *1776*, R.I. CR, VII, 616-17; *1780*, *ibid.*, IX, 169.

r Newport in *1760* had 800 to 1,000 houses and 6,000 or 7,000 inhabitants: Burnaby, *Travels*, 90.

s Providence in *1768* had 2,958 inhabitants, of which 2,619 were white and 339 black: Arnold, *Hist. of R.I.*, II, 280n; quoting *Providence Gazette*, Jan. 2, 1768.

t Bristol had 150 families in *1763*: Rev. Mr. Usher to S.P.G., in Updike, *Hist. Episcopal Church in Narragansett*, III, 87.

III. CENSUSES — *Continued*

Towns	1767 Ratable Polls	1770 Census Inhabs.	1774 Census Inhabs.	1776 Census Inhabs.	1780 Ratable Polls	1780 Slaves
Barrington	...	601	601	538	92	6
E. Greenwich	262	1,663	1,663	1,664	273	18
W. Greenwich	250	1,764	1,764	1,653	317	12
Coventry	329	2,023	2,023	2,300	343	3
	[8,952]	59,678	59,707 u [59,706]	54,715 [55,011]	7,467	518

G. CENSUS OF 1783 v

Towns	Whites	Indians	Mulattoes	Blacks	Total	
Newport w	4,914	17	51	549	5,530	[5,531]
Providence x	4,015	6	33	252	4,310	[4,306]
Portsmouth	1,266	7	11	67	1,350	[1,351]
Warwick	1,951	37	36	100	2,112	[2,124]
Westerly	1,667	9	36	28	1,720	[1,740]
N. Kingstown	2,110	8	22	188	2,328	
S. Kingstown	2,190	32	38	415	2,675	
E. Greenwich	1,529	10	17	53	1,609	
Jamestown	270	...	...	65	345	[335]
Smithfield	2,158	12	7	40	2,217	
Scituate	1,613	...	19	3	1,628	[1,635]
Gloucester	2,769	...	...	22	2,791	
Charlestown	1,204	280	9	30	1,523	
W. Greenwich	1,677	...	7	14	1,698	
Coventry	2,093	2	3	9	2,107	
Exeter	1,946	18	7	87	2,058	
Middletown	646	...	4	29	674	[679]
Bristol	954	2	13	63	1,032	
Tiverton	1,792	21	44	93	1,959	[1,950]
Little Compton	1,294	13	...	34	1,341	
Warren	867	3	5	30	905	
Cumberland	1,537	...	2	9	1,548	
Richmond	1,061	1	15	17	1,094	
Cranston	1,508	9	17	50	1,589	[1,584]
Hopkinton	1,677	30	11	17	1,735	

u The *1774* census given in R.I. CR, VII, 299, has a total of 59,678. The difference in the two totals is accounted for by the fact that in the R.I. CR table Newport is listed as having 9,209 inhabitants; Tiverton, 1,957; Cranston, 1,834; and Hopkinton, 1,805.

v R.I. CR, IX, 653.

w Newport had 790 houses in *1786*: Webster in *N.Y. Directory for 1786*, 22.

x Providence had 560 houses in *1786*: Ibid., 22.

III. Censuses — *Continued*

Towns	Whites	Indians	Mulattoes	Blacks	Total
Johnston	928	3	37	28	996
N. Providence	676	5	...	17	698
Barrington	488	...	20	26	534
Foster	1,756	...	..⸗	7	1,763
Total	[48,556]	[525]	[464]	[2,342]	51,869 [51,887]

H. Census of 1790 y

COUNTY	FREE WHITES		Females	OTHER FREE PERSONS	SLAVES	TOTAL
	Males					
	Over 16	Under 16				
Bristol	781	678	1,562	92	98	3,211
Kent	2,157	2,128	4,149	351	63	8,848
Newport	3,231	2,842	7,047	814	366	14,300
Providence	6,154	5,500	11,877	778	82	24,391
Washington	3,696	4,651	8,017	1,372	339	18,075
Total	16,019	15,799	32,652	3,407	948	68,825

NEW HAMPSHIRE

General

1639 1,000 souls. Hoyt, "Hist. and Bibliog. Notes on Laws of N.H.," in *Amer. Antiq. Soc. Proc.*, Apr., 1876, 91.

1671 1,800 total forces by land. *See* Thirteen Colonies: General, 1671.

1675 800 houses. "An Acct. of New Eng.," in *N.E. Hist. Gen. Reg.*, XXXVIII, 381.

4,000 inhabitants, and 3,000 Indians at most. Bancroft, I, 383 [1]

1680 445 taxables in towns. See page 73. *N.H. Prov. Papers*, I, 424-28.

1682 450 militia, of which 60 are horse, the rest foot. Gov. Cranfield to Lds. of Trade, Oct. 23, 1682, in CSPC, 1681-85, 312, No. 756.

1684 4,000 inhabitants. Gov. Cranfield to Lds. of Trade, Jan. 16, 1684, in CSPC, 1681-85, 576, No. 1508.

1688 6,000 inhabitants. *See* Thirteen Colonies: General, 1688.

1692 754 men between 16 and 60. Lt. Gov. Usher to Lds. of Trade, Oct. 29, 1692, in CSPC, 1689-92, 728, No. 2586.

1701 10,000 total population; or 3,000. *See* Thirteen Colonies: General, 1701.

y U.S. Bureau of Census, *Heads of Families, R.I.*, 8.

[1] Dexter and Rossiter quote Bancroft, but Dexter thinks this figure too high.

1702 700-800 effective men. "Memorial of Lt. Gov., Counc., and Reps. of
      N.H. to the King, May 29, 1702," in CSPC, 1702, 358, No. 544.
1708 1,000 men, "and that number daily lessening." Mr. Vaughn, Agent
      for N.H., to BT, July 6, 1708, in CSPC, 1708-9, 21, No. 19.
1709 5,150 souls. Estimated as follows: on basis of muster rolls there
      were 5,000 in 1702; plus an increase of 150; result 5,150. Gov.
      Dudley, Ans. Quer., March 1, 1709, in CSPC, 1708-9, 243, No.
      392.
1712 6,642 population; militia 1,107, being 1/6 of total. Gov. Dudley to
      BT, Apr. 8, 1712, in CSPC, 1712, 260, No. 375, 1 (e).
1715 9,650 total population: 9,500 whites; 150 Negroes. See Thirteen
      Colonies: General, 1715.
1716 9,000 people, of which 1,500 men, very few white servants, and 150
      blacks. Repr. BT to King, Sept. 8, 1721, Kings MS., 205, fol.
      7, p. 10, in LCT; also, NYCD, V, 595.
1721 9,500 people, the increase for the last 4 years being 500. Repr. of
      BT to King, Kings MS., 205, fol. 7, p. 10, in LCT; also NYCD,
      V, 595.
      9,000 inhabitants, of which about 150 are blacks; 1,500 militia; no
      Indians. Henry Newman to Wm. Popple, Apr. 12, 1721, in
      CO 5: 868, X: 35, p. 113.
1726 7,000 inhabitants. See Thirteen Colonies: General, 1726.
1730 10,000 white inhabitants, and 200 blacks; 1,800 militia; no Indians;
      increase about 4,000 in 10 years past, of which 1,000 are Irish.
      Gov. Belcher, Ans. Quer., March 25, 1731, in CO 5: 872, Z:
      191,192, p. 427;N.H. Prov. Papers, IV, 532-33; N.H. HSC, I,
      229.
1732 2,946 ratable inhabitants; 25 incorporated townships; ² 1,316 two-
      story and 606 one-story dwelling houses. Holmes, Annals, II, 539,
      from Docs. in Sec'y's office.
1737 11,000 inhabitants, men, women, and children; blacks, about 200;
      no Indians; militia, 1,900 men. Increase about 1/10 in last 4
      years. Gov. Belcher, Ans. Quer., Apr. 4, 1737, in CO 5: 880, Cc.
      54.
1741 20,000 planters. Chalmers, Revolt, II, 249.
1742 5,172 ratable polls, excluding Nottingham, Barrington, and Gos-
      port, from which no returns.³ N.H. Prov. Papers, VII, 723.

² "This view of the province embraced the towns of Portsmouth, Greenland, Hampton,
Hampton-Fall, Dover, Durham, Somersworth, Exeter, Newmarket, Newcastle, Stratham,
Kingston, Newington, and Londonderry. The remaining ten townships had been granted
but a few years and some of them had not been settled." Holmes, Annals, II, 539.
³ Report furnished by Sec. of State J. Pearson in 1792. He is not sure whether 5 or
6 times the number of ratable polls will give the number of people with any degree of
certainty.

72 NEW HAMPSHIRE

24,000 inhabitants; 6,000 ratable whites; 500 Negroes. Douglass, *Summary*, II, 48, 180.

26,000 whites; 500 Negroes. Anon., *State of British and French Colonies in North Am.*, *1755*, 131.

1745 7,000 ratable polls.[4] Rob't Hale to Gov. Shirley, Mar. 14, 1755, in *Amer. Antiq. Soc. Proc.*, XIX, 263.

1749 30,000 inhabitants. *See* Thirteen Colonies: General, 1749.

1753 6,392 ratable polls. *N.H. Prov. Papers*, VII, 723.

1754 80,000 inhabitants, of which 550 may be blacks. Gov. B. Wentworth, Ans. Quer., Sept. 2, 1754, *Kings MS.*, 205, fol. 214, p. 435, in LCT.

50,000 white inhabitants. Bancroft, II, 389.

7,000 ratable polls. Stone, *Hist. of Beverly*, 48n.

1755 30,000 souls must be the utmost of its inhabitants. Anon., *State of British and French Colonies in North Am.*, *1755*, 131.

75,000 white inhabitants, with 6,000 militia. Rept. of BT, in NYCD, VI, 993.

75,000 white inhabitants; or 30,000 total population. *See* Thirteen Colonies: General, 1755.

34,000 inhabitants. Stiles, *Christian Union*, 142.

1760 40,000 inhabitants. Burnaby, *Travels*, 115.

1761 9,146 ratable polls;[5] 8,868 white polls; 278 black polls. Holmes, *Annals*, II, 540, from Stiles MS.

1765 80,000 inhabitants; 20,000 men. *See* Thirteen Colonies: General, 1765.

1767 52,700 total inhabitants, of which 633 were slaves, according to census. See page 74. *N.H. Prov. Papers*, VII, 168-70, citing MS. Vol. in Sec'y's Office labeled "Census of N.H., 1767 & 75."

11,964 ratable polls. *N.H. Prov. Papers*, VII, 166-67, 723. Citing Belknap Papers, 320. See page 74.

1773 15,108 ratable polls. *Ibid.*, VII, 326-29. See page 74.

72,092 white inhabitants; 379 male slaves; 295 female slaves, by census. *Ibid.*, X, 621-36. See pages 73, 74.

1774 150,000 total population; 80,000; or 100,000. *See* Thirteen Colonies: General, 1774.

1775 81,050 inhabitants, including 656 Negroes. N.H. HSC, I, 231-35; and *N.H. Prov. Papers*, VII, 724-81. See page 74.

100,000 total population. *See* Thirteen Colonies: General, 1775.

1777 15,746 ratable polls. *N.H. Prov. Papers*, VIII, 687-89.

1780 100,000 inhabitants. John Sullivan to M. Marbois, Dec. 10, 1780, *Correspondence of Henry Laurens*, 194.

[4] Dexter and Rossiter give 30,000 for 1749.
[5] Dexter quotes this; Rossiter estimates 38,000 for this year.

1783 82,200 population. *See* Thirteen Colonies: General, 1783.
1785 102,000 population. Webster, in *N.Y. Directory for 1786*, 21.
1786 95,452 free inhabitants; 46 slaves; 303 others. See pages 74, 79-85. Census in *N.H. Prov. Papers*, X, 637-89. 150,000 total inhabitants. *See* Thirteen Colonies: General, 1786.
1787 102,000 total population; or 82,000 white inhabitants. *See* Thirteen Colonies: General, 1787.
1790 141,885 total inhabitants: free white males over 16, 36,086; free white males under 16, 34,851; free white females, 70,160; other free persons, 630; slaves, 158. U.S. Bureau of Census, *Heads of Families*, N.H., 9-10. See page 85.

LOCAL

I. TAXABLES IN 1680 a

Hampton	126
Exeter	66
Cocheco	66
Dover Neck	30
Bloody Point	24
Portsmouth b	133

[445] c Total Taxables in towns.

II. CENSUSES

A. CENSUS OF 1773 BY COUNTIES a

County	White Inhabs.	Male Slaves	Female Slaves	Polls
Rockingham	34,707	260	206	7,170
Strafford	10,826	64	38	2,292
Hillsborough	13,514	39	38	2,946
Cheshire	9,496	7	2	2,052
Grafton	3,549	9	11	648
	72,092	[379]	[295]	[15,108]

a *N.H. Prov. Papers*, I, 424-28.
b Portsmouth figure for 1681.
c Throughout these tables for N.H., totals of columns are given as found in the source cited. When the source gives no total, it has been computed and placed in brackets, as here. When the total given is incorrect, the sum is presented in brackets beside that found in the source used. See page 79.
a FOR NOTES TO II, TABLE A, SEE PAGE 74.

II. Censuses — *Continued*

B. Censuses of 1775 and 1786 by Counties [b]

County	1775 Total Inhabs.	1775 Negroes	1786 Free Inhabs.	1786 Slaves	1786 Others
Rockingham	37,850	435	32,138	21	185
Strafford	12,713	103	13,877	9	8
Hillsborough	15,948	87	25,933	9	48
Cheshire	10,659	7	15,160	7	6 [54]
Grafton	3,880	24	8,344	0	56
	[81,050]	[656]	95,452	46	303 [351]

C. Censuses by Towns, 1767 to 1775 [c]

Towns	1767 Inhabs.	1767 Polls	1773 Inhabs.	1773 Polls	1775 Inhabs.
Acworth	....	....	....	28	
Alexandria	....	....	....	11	137
Allenstown	....	....	143	40	149
Alstead	130	....	232	46	317
Alton	....	....	....	....	100
Amherst [d]	858	203	1,370	287	1,428 (estimated)
Andover	....	....	....	....	179
Atkinson	476	118	535	112	575
Barnstead	....	....	152	33	252 (46 families)
Barrington	1,001	209	1,341	226	1,655
Bath [e]	....	....	150	27	144
Bedford	362	86	388	105	495
Boscawen	285	66	504	102	585
Bow [f]	187	48	308	64	350
Brentwood [g]	1,064	221	1,089	208	1,100
Compton	....	....	139	18	190
Canaan	19	....	62	19	67
Candia	363	94	663	144	744
Canterbury [h]	503	122	600	133	723
Charlestown [i]	334	100	590	128	594

a "Census of Inhabitants," *N.H. Prov. Papers*, X, 621-36. Polls, *ibid.*, VII, 326-29.
b Census of *1775* in N.H. HSC, I, 231-35; for *1786*, in *N.H. Prov. Papers*, X, 637-89.
c Figures for *1767*, Inhabitants, from *N.H. Prov. Papers*, VII, 168-70; *1767*, Polls, *ibid.*, VII, 166-67; *1773*, ibid., VII, 326-29, and X, 621-36; *1775*, *ibid.*, VII, 780-81.
d 15 families in *1740*: Farmer, "Sketch of Amherst," in MHSC, 2d Series, II, 250; 35 families, including 58 men over 16 in *1747:N.H. Prov. Papers*. IX, 8; 160 families in *1767*: Letter of Rev. Daniel Wilkins, *ibid.*. IX, 15.
e 8 families and 6 single men in *1768: Ibid.*, XI, 165-66.
f 154 polls, 91 houses and 6 Negroes in *1761: Ibid.*, IX, 73.
g 36 ratable polls in *1743: Ibid.*, XI, 223-24.
h 30 families in *1741*; 57 polls, 33 houses and 1 Negro in *1761: Ibid.*, IX, 87, 73.
i 26 families in *1756*: "N.H. Towns on Conn. River, Jan. 1756," *N.H. Miscellaneous*, 1752-64, in LO MS.

II. CENSUSES — *Continued*

Towns	1767 Inhabs.	1767 Polls	1773 Inhabs.	1773 Polls	1775 Inhabs.
Chester J	1,189	320	1,552	358	1,599
Chesterfield	365	....	747	146	874
Chichester	....	....	273	53	418
Claremont	157	50	423	80	523
Colebrook (Coleburne)	....	....	....	....	4
Columbia (Cockburne)	..	....	....	....	14
Concord	752	179	1,003	205	1,052
Conway	....	....	203	20	273
Cornish	133	30	213	41	309
Croyden	51	....	91	25	143
Dalton(Apthorpe)	....	....	14	....	50
Deerfield	...	141	911	199	929
Derryfield	230	47	279	50	
Dorchester	....	....	121		
Dover k	1,614	384	1,665	338	1,666
Dublin	....	40	255	{ 55	305
	....	....	....	} 61	
Dunbarton	271	61	464	88	497
Dunstable (Nashua) l	520	104	610	112	705
Durham	1,232	249	1,149	231	1,214
East Kingston	451	111	402	93	428
Effingham m	....	....	111	24	83
Enfield (Relham)	....	....	....	....	50
Epping	1,410	317	1,648	311	1,569
Epsom	239	47	327	65	387 (estimated)
Exeter	1,690	390	1,714	359	1,741
Fisherfield (now Newbury)	....	....	....	....	130
Fitzwilliam	....	....	214	61	
Francestown	....	....	....	43	200
Franconia	....	....	....	....	29
Gilmantown n	250	65	635	133	774
Gilsum	128	31	139	37	178

j 148 taxables in *1741: N.H. Prov. Papers*, XI, 309-10.

k In *1648* there were 57 taxpayers: "Extracts from Old Town Recds. of Dover," in *N.E. Hist. Gen. Reg.*, IV, 31; 92 taxpayers in *1657*: Quint, "Extracts from Dover Town Recds.," *ibid.*, 247-48; 353 taxed for parish rates in *1753: N.H. Prov. Papers*, XI, 518-22.

l There were 35 families in *1680: N.H. Prov. Papers*, XII, 625; 42 freemen in *1746: Ibid.*, IX, 211.

m There were 15 polls in *1775: Ibid.*, XI, 608.

n 400 ratable polls in *1770: N.H. Prov. Papers*, XII, 4.

II. Censuses — *Continued*

Towns	1767 Inhabs.	1767 Polls	1773 Inhabs.	1773 Polls	1775 Inhabs.
Goffstown	....	83	732	149	831
Gosport	284	60	....	....	44
Grantham o	....	....	60	....	74
Greenland p	805	169	731	137	759
Groton (Cockermouth)	....	....	107 q	20	118
Hampstead	644	140	728	139	768
Hampton	866	199	917	192	862
Hampton-Falls r	1,381	312	648	119	645
Hanover s	92	....	342	77	434
Haverhill	172	53	387	76	365
Hawke (now Danville)	488	98	478	87	504
Henniker	....	....	338	68	347
Hillsborough	64	26	153	43	
Hinsdale t	158	38	220	45	
Holderness	....	....	147 u	35	172
Hollis v	809	203	1,162	251	1,255
Hopkinton	473	122	943	175	1,085
Jaffrey	....	....	303	....	351
Keene w	430	106	645	150	758
Kensington	755	182	822	163	797
Kingston x	999	213	989	208	961
Lancaster	....	....	37	12	61
Landoff	....	....	....	....	40
Lebanon	162	....	295	70	347
Lee	861	169	960	177	954
Lemster	....	....	66	10	128
Lisbon	....	....	....	10	47
Litchfield	234	60	299	63	284
Londonderry	2,389	455	2,471	475	2,590
Loudon	....	....	204	42	349

o 14 polls in *1775*: *Ibid.*, XII, 59.

p 320 inhabitants in *1705*: *Ibid.*, XII, 59; 70 ratable polls in *1711*, and 62 in *1723*: *N.E. Hist. Gen. Reg.*, XXII, 451-54; 92 ratable polls in *1727*: *N.H. Prov. Papers*, IX, 691.

q As Cockermouth.

r 122 taxables in *1709*: *N.E. Hist. Gen. Reg.*, XXVIII, 373-75.

s 110 male inhabitants in *1772*: *N.H. Prov. Papers*, XII, 160.

t 64 taxable polls in *1764*: *N.H. Prov. Papers*, IX, 388-89.

u 20 families: *Ibid.*, IX, 396.

v 9 families in *1736*; 20 in *1739*; 29 taxables in *1740*; 78 in *1745*: Worcester, "Hist. of Hollis," in *N.E. Hist. Gen. Reg.*, XXVIII, 53, 56, 262.

w 22 families in *1756*: "N.H. Towns on Conn. River, Jan., 1756," *N.H. Miscellaneous* in LC MS.

x 81 families in *1725* and 164 inhabitants in *1732*: Belknap, *Hist. N.H.*, 171n.

II. Censuses — *Continued*

Towns	1767 Inhabs.	1767 Polls	1773 Inhabs.	1773 Polls	1775 Inhabs.
Lyman	....	....	....	6	
Lyme y	....	....	241	61	252
Lyndeborough z	272	50	....	108	713
Madbury	695	153	625	147	677
Manchester (Derryfield)	....	....	....	....	285
Marlborough	93	....	275	47	322
Marlow aa	77	....	156	46	207
Mason (No. 1)	278	65	463	103	501
Meredith ab	....	....	218	49	259
Merrimac ac	400	100	552	117	606
Middleton	....	....	....	44	238
Mile-Slip	68	17			
Monson ad	293	50			
Moultonborough ae	....	....	263	50	272
Nelson	93	....	117	28	186
New Almsbury [Warner]	....	....	213	43	
New Boston	296	72	410	77	569
New Britain [Andover]	....	....	135	27	
New Castle af	606	128	601	137	449
New Chester [Hill]	....	....	179	30	196
New Durham	157	....	280	78	286
Newington ag	514	98	548	191	332
New Ipswich (now Hudson)	....	150	882	169	960
New Market ah	1,286	266	1,344	252	1,289
Newport	29	....	156	35	157
Newtown	529	104	572	121	540
Northumberland	....	....	46	12	57
North Hampton	583	139	702	133	652
North-Wood	....	....	250	53	313

y 70 taxables in *1688*: "Jeffries Family Papers," in *N.E. Hist. Gen. Reg.*, XXXIV, 371-82; 59 taxables in *1773*: *N.H. Prov. Papers*, XII, 503.
z 40 families in *1765*: *N.H. Prov. Papers*, XII, 519.
aa 34 polls in *1773*: *Ibid.*, XII, 573.
ab 17 families in *1768*: *Ibid.*, XII, 582.
ac 70 odd families in *1767*: Letter of Rev. Daniel Wilkins, *ibid.*, IX, 14.
ad 36 polls, "several of them transiently hired," in *1753*: *Ibid.*, IX, 11.
ae 44 polls in *1773*: *Ibid.*, XIII, 411.
af 130 taxables in *1728*: *Ibid.*, IV, 503.
ag 92 ratable polls in *1727*: *N.H. Prov. Papers*, IX, 691.
ah 78 ratable polls in *1727*: *Ibid.*, IX, 691.

II. Censuses — *Continued*

Towns	1767 Inhabs.	1767 Polls	1773 Inhabs.	1773 Polls	1775 Inhabs.
Nottingham al	708	152	904	170	999
Nottingham West	583	131	592	123	649
Orford aj	75	....	228	46	222
Ossipee	....	....	....	....	26
Pelham	543	123	684	138	749
Pembroke	557	145	666	155	744
Peterborough	443	100	514	88	546
Peterborough Slip	....	51	81	18	
Perrystown (now Sutton)	....	....	....	12	
Piermont	....	....	....	30	168
Pittsfield					
Plainfield	112	28	275	61	308
Plaistow	576	142	591	111	575
Plymouth	227	60	345	67	382
Poplin	521	104	564	104	552
Portsmouth ak	4,466	910	4,372	682	4,590
Raby	....	....	....	33	
Raymond	455	99	683	122	683
Richmond	333	....	745	138	864
Rindge	298	....	604	157	542
Rochester al	984	225	1,420	301	1,548
Rowley	...	65			
Rumney	...	....	192	36	237
Rye am	736	123	842	153	870
Salem	847	184	....	227	1,084
Salisbury	....	....	416	83	498
Sanbornton an	....	37	352	70	459
Sandown	509	120	590	124	635
Sandwich	....	....	204	30	245
Saville (now Sunapee)	....	....	72		
Seabrook	....	....	596	125	607
Society Land	....	....	....	47	177
Somersworth	1,044	212	1,038	209	965
South Hampton	491	123	473	100	498
Stevens-Town	210	52			
Stewartstown	....	....	88		

al 350 families in *1774*: *Ibid.*, IX, 692.
aj 142 inhabitants in *1772*: *Ibid.*, IX, 648-50.
ak 50 to 60 families in *1653*: Belknap, *Hist. N.H.*, App. 434.
al 60 families in *1737* and 130 families in *1762*: *N.H. Prov. Papers*, XIII, 333-36.
am 240 or 250 souls in *1721*; 60 families or about 400 souls in *1724*; 72 ratable polls in *1727*: *Ibid.*, IX, 734-36, 691.
an 32 families in *1768* and 40 families in *1770*: *Ibid.*, IX, 755-57.

II. Censuses — *Continued*

Towns	1767 Inhabs.	1767 Polls	1773 Inhabs.	1773 Polls	1775 Inhabs.
Stoddard (sometimes Limerick)	....	....	215	36	224
Stratford	....	....	....	....	41
Stratham	916	242	1,068	90	1,137
Surry	....	....	208	47	215
Swanzey	320	74	536	100	647
Tamworth	....	....	....	....	151
Temple	....	....	418	91	491
Thornton	....	....	74	18	117
Town No 6	....	50			
Trecothick	....	....	50		
Unity	....	....	106	25	146
Wakefield	....	....	248	63	320
Walpole [ao]	308	75	549	122	658
Warner	....	....	....	....	262
Washington	....	....	132	40	163
Weare	268	60	884	150	837
Wendall (Saville) [ap]	....	....	....	16	65
Wentworth	....	....	42		
Westmoreland	391	94	698	131	758
Wilton	350	89	580	121	632
Winchester [aq]	428	108	646	130	723
Windham	402	73	502	76	529
Wolfeborough	....	....	165	36	211
	52,700	11,964	72,092 [73,093]	15,108 [15,128]	[80,925]

D. Censuses by Counties and Towns, 1777 to 1786 [ar]

County and Town	1777 Polls	1782-83	1786 Inhabs.[as]
1. *Cheshire County*			
Acworth	40		
Alstead	89		

ao 7 families in *1756*: "N.H. Towns on Conn. River, Jan., 1756," *N.H. Miscellaneous,* 1752-1764, in LC MS.

ap 15 families and 22 men in militia in *1776*: *N.H. Prov. Papers*, XIII, 496.

aq 17 families ·in *1756*: "N.H. Towns on Conn. River, Jan., 1756," *N.H. Miscellaneous*, 1752-64, in LC MS.

ar Figures for *1777* from *N.H. Prov. Papers*, VIII, 687-89; for *1782-83*, see footnotes indicated; for *1786*, *N.H. Prov. Papers*, X, 637-89. Figures for 1786 include all inhabitants except Indians, for many towns did not distinguish whites, blacks and others. Totals given by editor of *Prov. Papers* are thus misleading and occasionally inaccurate.

as In the *1786* Census Acworth, Alstead, Charleston, Chesterfield and Cornish are listed in Hillsborough County.

II. CENSUSES — *Continued*

County and Town	1777 Polls	1782-83	1786 Inhabs.
Cheshire — Continued			
Charleston at	143		
Chesterfield	189	273 male polls au	
Claremont	121	164 ratable polls av	965
Croyden aw	39	. . . .	381
Dublin	62	. . . .	658
Fitzwilliam	81	. . . .	870
Gilsom	51	68 male polls ax	305
Hinsdale	. . .	. . . .	330
Jaffrey	113	190 male polls ay	
Keene	167	228 male polls az	1,122
Lempster	32	53 ratable polls ba	322
Marlborough	76	. . . .	618
Marlow	45	. . . .	252
New Grantham	. . .	. . . .	201
Newport	43	89 male polls bb	554
Packersfield	55	. . . .	567
Plainfield	. . .	. . . .	580
Protectworth	. . .	. . . .	127
Richmond	177	. . . .	1,250
Rindge	162	. . . .	759
Stoddard	53	. . . .	563
Surry	53	82 male polls bc	
Swanzey	132	182 male polls bd	1,000
Unity	41	. . . .	404
Walpole	143	. . . . .,.	
Washington	44	. . . .	474
Wendell	. . .	34 taxable polls be	195
Westmoreland	178	. . . .,.	1,621
Winchester	138	. . . .	1,103
			15,221
2. Grafton County			
Alexandria	36 bf	40 freeholders bf	291
Bath	29 bg	. . . .,. . . .	335

at 26 families and 36 men in *1756*: "N.H. Towns on Conn. River, Jan., 1756," *N.H.*
Miscellaneous, 1752-64, in LC MS.
au *N.H. Prov. Papers*, XI, 342.
av *Ibid.*, XI, 378; 196 polls over 18 and 3 Negroes in *1784*: *Ibid.*, 378.
aw 53 polls over 18 in *1779*: *Ibid.*, XI, 467.
ax *Ibid.*, XII, 23.   ay *Ibid.*, XII, 298.   az *Ibid.*, XII, 321.
ba 101 taxables in *1787*: *Ibid.*, XII, 397-99.
bb *Ibid.*, XIII, 48.
bc *N.H. Prov. Papers*, XIII, 513.   bd *Ibid.*, XIII, 533.
be Being 25 families and 11 single men: *Ibid.*, XIII, 498.
bf *Ibid.*, XI, 12 and 14.
bg For *1779*: *Ibid.*, XI, 167; 8 families and 6 single men in *1768*: *Ibid.*, 165-66.

II. Censuses — *Continued*

County and Town	1777 Polls	1782-83	1786 Inhabs.
Grafton — *Continued*			
Campton	34	60 polls bh	307
Canaan	...	50 polls bi	253
Cardigan	...	....	80
Cockermouth	...	....	281
Concord			
[alias Gunthwaite]	233	....	152
Dorchester bj	9	17 families	116
Enfield [alias Relham]	...	83 male polls bk	484
Grafton	...	....	354
Hanover	...	154 male polls bl	870
Haverhill	66	....	458
Lancaster	...	10 male polls bm	102
Lebanon	....	....	843
Lyman	8 bn	....	116
Lyme	...	....	502
New Chester	34	66 male polls bo	496
New Holdernesse	30	37 male polls bp	267
Northumberland	...	17 male polls bq	
Orange	...	16 families br	
Orford	...	....	376
Piermont	...	50 polls bs	356
Plymouth	74	97 male polls bt	532
Rumney	45	50 male polls bu	359
Stratford	10 bv	13 polls bv	
Thornton	27	47 male polls bw	302
Wentworth	...	27 male polls bx	168
			8,400
3. *Hillsborough County*			
Acworth	...	....	483
Alstead	...	....	943
Amherst	322	309 polls by	1,912
Andover	...	....	410

bh For *1785*: *Ibid.*, XI, 251.   bi *Ibid.*, XI, 258.
bj "Not 10 families" in *1779*: *Ibid.*, 500-503.
bk *N.H. Prov. Papers*, XI, 613.   bl *Ibid.*, XII, 171.   bm *Ibid.*, XII, 352-53.
bn The same number holds for *1776* and *1778*; 18 polls in *1779*: *Ibid.*, XII, 494-95.
bo As Hill: *Ibid.*, XII, 199.   bp *Ibid.*, XII, 228.
bq *Ibid.*, XIII, 89-90.   br *Ibid.*, XIII, 121; 15 families in *1785*: *Ibid.*, 122.
bs In *1781*; 40 polls in *1780*: *Ibid.*, XIII, 193.
bt *Ibid.*, XIII, 228.   bu *Ibid.*, XIII, 357.
bv *Ibid.*, XIII, 474; 10 polls in *1777*; 7 families in *1778*: *Ibid.*, 473-74.
bw *Ibid.*, XIII, 571; 52 polls in *1785*: *Ibid.*, 571.
bx *Ibid.*, XIII, 644.
by *N.H. Prov. Papers*, XI, 90. In *1747* the town had 35 families, and 58 men over 16;
160 families in *1767*; 300 ratable polls in *1782*: *Ibid.*, IX, 8, 15; XI, 83.

II. Censuses — *Continued*

County and Town	1777 Polls	1782-83	1786 Inhabs.
Hillsborough — *Continued*			
Antrim	23	....	289
Bedford	109	....	785
Boscawen	121	128 male polls [bz]	831
Charleston	...	....	968
Chesterfield	...	....	1,535
Cornish	...	....	605
Dearing	49	86 polls [ca]	
Derryfield	53	62 male polls [cb]	338
Dunbarton	93	....	741
Dunstable	103	119 male polls [cc]	554
Duxbury Mile-Slip	20	....	140
Fishersfield	...	....	217
Francestown	...	65 male polls [cd]	
Goffstown	147	168 male polls [ce]	1,063
Hancock	...	....	291
Henniker	101	....	862
Hillsborough	62	98 male polls [cf]	
Hollis	251	....	1,423
Hopkinton	211	....	1,537
Litchfield	58	55 male polls [cg]	
Lyndborough	142	166 ratable polls [ch]	
Mason	111	140 male polls [ci]	866
Merrimac	114	....	701
New Bradford	...	....	130
New Boston	124		
New Britain	47	152 polls [cj]	
New Ipswich	160	189 polls [ck]	1,049
New London	...	....	219
Nottingham West	129	....	1,010
Perrystown	36	....	....
Peterborough	118	133 male polls [cl]	831
(Peterborough Slip)	24	....	175
Raby	30	....	262
Salisbury	109	....	1,045
Society Land	22	....	157

bz *Ibid.*, XI, 204.   ca *Ibid.*, XI, 492.
cb As Manchester: *Ibid.*, XII, 550; 50 families in *1780*: *Ibid.*, 549.
cc *Ibid.*, XII, 634. The town had 35 families in *1680*: *Ibid.*, XII, 625; 54 taxables in *1744*: Nason, "Dunstable," in Drake, *Hist. Middlesex Co.*, I, 422-23; 42 freemen in *1746*: *N.H. Prov. Papers*, IX, 211; 559 inhabitants including 16 colored in *1764*: Nason, "Dunstable," in Drake, *Hist. Middlesex Co.*, I, 422-23.   cd *N.H. Prov. Papers*, XI, 684.
ce *Ibid.*, XII, 40. 150 families in *1779*: *Ibid.*, 33.   cf *Ibid.*, XII, 228.
cg *N.H. Prov. Papers*, XII, 422. 40 families in *1780*: *Ibid.*, 419.
ch *Ibid.*, XII, 521.   ci *Ibid.*, XII, 580.   cj *Ibid.*, XII, 655.
ck Kidder and Gould, *Hist. New Ipswich*, 261. 185 polls in *1779* and 222 polls in *1788*: *Ibid.*   cl *N.H. Prov. Papers*, XIII, 183-84.

LOCAL 83

II. CENSUSES — *Continued*

County and Town	1777 Polls	1782-83	1786 Inhabs.
Hillsborough — Continued			
Sutton	...	....	337
Temple	94	....	701
Warner	56	114 polls cm	
Weare	204	250 polls cn	1,574
Wilton	134	....	1,006

4. *Rockingham County*

[25,990] co

Allenstown	32	30 polls cp	175
Atkinson	91	81 male polls cq	500
Bow cr	72		
Brentwood	194	196 male polls cs	
Candia	143	155 ratable polls ct	982
Canterbury cu	179	....	860
Chester	339	362 male polls cv	1,759
Chichester	119	120 families cw	
Concord	...	....	1,402
Deerfield	219	....	1,283
East Kingston	84	....	420
Epping	258	260 male polls cx	1,347
Epsom	73	99 male polls cy	
Exeter cz	307	....	1,592
Greenland	128	....	655
Hampstead	133		
Hampton	180	....	867
Hampton Falls	115	106 male polls da	569
Hawke	91	70 male polls db	301
Kensington	158	153 male polls dc	798
Kingston	188		

cm *Ibid.*, XIII, 560.   cn *Ibid.*, XIII, 641.
co Includes 4,533 for the towns of Acworth, Alstead, Charleston, Chesterfield, and Cornish, listed in Cheshire County.
cp *N.H. Prov. Papers*, XI, 39.
cq *Ibid.*, XI, 122.
cr 154 polls, 91 houses and 6 Negroes in *1761*: *Ibid.*, IX, 73.
cs *Ibid.*, XI, 236. 36 ratable polls in *1743*: *Ibid.*, 223-24.
ct *Ibid.*, XI, 261.
cu 40 families in *1741*; 57 polls, 33 houses and 1 Negro in *1761*: *Ibid.*, IX, 73, 87.
cv *Ibid.*, XI, 319. 148 taxables in *1741*: *Ibid.*, 309-10.
cw In *1780*: *Ibid.*, XI, 356.
cx *Ibid.*, XI, 625.
cy *Ibid.*, XI, 631.
cz 20 qualified voters in *1680*: Tenney, "Desc. of Exeter," in MHSC, 1st Series, IV, 87.
da *N.H. Prov. Papers*, XII, 149.
db As Danville: *Ibid.*, XI, 481.
dc *N.H. Prov. Papers*, XII, 327-28.

II. Censuses — *Continued*

County and Town	1777 Polls	1782-83	1786 Inhabs.
Rockingham — *Continued*			
Londonderry	514	453 polls dd	
Loudon	93	....	822
Newcastle	87	....	
Newington	108	....	476
Newmarket	238	....	1,174
Newtown	91	....	343
Northampton	127	....	659
Northfield	...	....	349
Northwood	64	....	575
Nottingham	146	....	1,026
Pelham	138	155 polls de	875
Pembroke	143	....	994
Pittsfield	...	120 male polls df	598
Plaistow	99	....	551
Poplin	106	96 male polls dg	500
Portsmouth	717	....	4,222 dh
Raymond	131	117 male polls di	786
Rye	143	....	655
Salem	210	....	1,082
Sandown	121	103 polls dj	521
Seabrook	127	111 polls dk	668
South Hampton	103	86 polls dl	452
Stratham	192	183 ratable polls dm	907
Windham	103	....	592
			[32,337] dn
5. Strafford County			
Barnstead	58	94 ratable polls do	569
Barrington	260	287 ratable polls dp	990
Burton	...	....	74
Conway	52	73 polls dq	
Dover	296	....	1,431
Durham	209	190 polls dr	1,233

dd Polls 18-75 years old, 3 female slaves; in *1783* the polls had fallen to 442: *Ibid.*, XII, 473.

de *Ibid.*, XIII, 150.   df *Ibid.*, XIII, 198.   dg As Fremont: *Ibid.*, XI, 702.

dh 450 houses in *1785*: Webster, *N. Y. Directory for 1786*, 22.

di *N.H. Prov. Papers*, XIII, 311.

dj *Ibid.*, XIII, 406.   dk *Ibid.*, XIII, 423-24.   dl *Ibid.*, XIII, 440.

dm 20 to 75 years old: *Ibid.*, XIII, 487.

dn In *N.H. Prov. Papers*, X, 689, the total of 48,431 for Rockingham County on page 651 is stated to be incorrect.

do *N.H. Prov. Papers*, XI, 139.

dp *Ibid.*, XI, 159.

dq 63 polls in *1779*; 67 in *1780*; 73 in *1781*; 77 in *1782*: *Ibid.*, XI, 419-20.

dr *Ibid.*, XI, 591.

LOCAL

85

II. Censuses — *Continued*

County and Town	1777 Polls	1782-83	1786 Inhabs.
Strafford — Continued			
Eaton	...	....	138
Effingham	...	30 ratable polls ds	122
Gilmanton	186	252 polls dt	1,639
Leavitts-Town	16	....	
Lee	180	224 taxables du	956
Madbury	124	87 polls dv	585
Meredith	68	85 polls dw	572
Middleton	...	90 families dx	
Moultonborough	72	....	400
New Durham	...	70 polls dy	242
New Hampton	...	75 ratable polls dz	
Rochester	341	....	2,456
Sanbornton	101	180 polls ea	1,107
Sandwich	60	101 polls eb	653
Somersworth	186	....	
Tamworth	29	53 polls ec	288
Wakefield	81	....	505
Wolfeborough	44	....	.... ed
	[15,746]		[13,960]

[95,908]

E. Census of 1790 ee

County	Free Whites			Other Free	Slaves	Total
	Males		Females			
	Over 16	Under 16				
Cheshire	7,008	7,567	14,090	70	18	28,753
Grafton	3,768	3,311	6,340	28	21	13,468
Hillsborough	8,145	8,392	16,168	176	..	32,881
Rockingham	11,141	9,668	21,987	292	97	43,185
Strafford	6,012	5,918	11,594	64	21	23,609
Total	36,086	34,851	70,160	630	158	141,885
	[36,074]	[34,856]	[70,179]		[157]	[141,896]

ds *Ibid.*, XI, 608. dt *Ibid.*, XII, 10. du In *1787*: *Ibid.*, XII, 392-93.
dv *Ibid.*, XII, 539. dw *Ibid.*, XIII, 398. dx *Ibid.*, XIII, 735.
dy *Ibid.*, XII, 705. dz *Ibid.*, XIII, 398. ea *Ibid.*, XIII, 398.
eb *Ibid.*, XIII, 417. ec *Ibid.*, XIII, 542.
ed 45 families in *1785*: *Ibid.*, XIII, 735.
ee U.S. Bureau of Census, *Heads of Families, N.H.*, 9-10.

VERMONT [1]

GENERAL

1763   70 families scattered in about a dozen townships on the Conn. River, the chief of them in Brattleborough, Westminster, Pultney, and Rockingham. "Deposition of Simon Stevens," *Controversy between N.Y. and N.H.*, 693.

1767   Not 250 families settled on the west side of the Conn. River. Gov. Moore to the Earl of Shelburne, June 9, 1767, in NYCD, VII, 936.

1768   727 families in Vt., as follows: 8 townships of Pownall, Bennington, Shaftsbury, Arlington, Rupert, Manchester, Sunderland, and Winhall, 251 families; Brattleborough, Putney, Hertford, and Chester, 88 families; Windsor, Fulham, Ware, and Reading, 47 families; 14 townships of Marlborough, Halifax, Guilford, Hinsdale, New Fane, Westminster, Rockingham, Springfield, Wethersfield, Norwich, Thetford, Newberry, Addison, and Whiting, 341 families. Gov. Moore to Lord Hillsborough, July 5, 1768, CO 5: 1099, fol. 363-68, A 34, in LCT. See page 87.

1771   4,669 inhabitants, according to census: Cumberland Co., 3,947; Gloucester Co., 722. Included in Census of N. Y. for 1771; see N. Y., page 102.

      600 to 700 families. Earl of Dunmore to Earl of Hillsborough, March 9, 1771, in NYCD, VIII, 267.

1789   200,000 souls in Vt. "Letter from Levi Allen, May 29, 1789," *Pa. Mag. Hist.*, XI, 169.

1790   85,425 total population, according to Census of 1790. Bureau of Census, *Heads of Families, Vt.*, 9-10. See page 88.

      20,000 fighting men, and about 90,000 to 100,000 inhabitants. W. L. Smith, "Journal," in MHSP, LI, 52.

LOCAL [2]

Bennington

1763   50 families. "Petition to Gov. Wentworth," *N.H. Prov. Papers*, IX, 56.

Castleton

1777   17 miserable houses. *Letters of Brunswick and Hessian Officers*, 85. (Stone, W. L., ed.).

Charlotte County

1772   268 families: Socialborough, 35 families; Durham, Grafton, and Chesterfield, 96 families; Chatham, 15 families; Eugene, 40 fam-

---

[1] See also New York for figures before 1775.
[2] For other estimates of local groups see pages 87-88.

ilies; Princetown, 70 families; W. Camden, 12 families. "Petition
to Gov. Tryon," *Controversy between N.Y. and N.H.*, 774.

Cumberland County

1778   615 families: Hinsdale, 42 families; Guilford, 100; Halifax, 119;
       Brattleboro, 116; Wilmington, 35; Marlborough, Fulham, and
       New Fane, no returns; Putney, 136; Westminster, no returns;
       Springfield, 44; Weathersfield, 23. List in Clinton, *Papers*, III,
       622-24.

Danby

1778   101 freemen. List in Williams, *Hist. and Map of Danby*, 34-35.

Guilford Township

1772   586 inhabitants. List, in *Controversy between N.Y. and N.H.*, 784-
       85.

Shelburn

1787   20 families. Palmer, *Hist. of Lake Champlain*, 158.

I. SURVEY OF SETTLEMENTS . . . LAYING WEST OF CONN. RIVER, 1768 [a]

Pownall	50 families	Fulham	8 families
Bennington	85 Do.	New Fane	2 Do.
Shaftsbury	30 Do.	Townshend	No settlement
Arlington	16 Do.	Putney	5 families
Rupert	10 Do.	Westminster	80 Do.
Manchester	30 Do.	Rockingham	50 Do.
Sunderland	20 Do.	Springfield	8 Do.
Winhall	10 Do.	Wethersfield	2 Do.
Whiting	1 family	Windsor	19 Do.
Bridport	No settlement	Ware, now Hertford	20 Do.
Addison	1 family	Norwich	20 Do.
Weybridge	A number of families	Hartford	18 Do.
Panton	Do.	Thetford	14 Do.
Marlborough	5 families	Fairley	No settlement
Halifax	40 Do.	Newbury	40 families
Guilford	60 Do.	Hamstead	20 Do.
Hinsdale	18 Do.	63 towns	No settlement
Brattleborough	45 Do.		
		96 towns	727 families
		[97 towns]	

[a] Enclosure in Gov. Moore's letter of July 5, 1768, CO 5: 1099, fol. 369-84, in LCT.

II. Census of 1790 [a]

County	Free Whites			Other Free	Slaves	Total
	Males		Females			
	Over 16	Under 16				
Addison	1,768	1,656	2,959	37	....	6,420
Bennington	3,103	3,205	5,865	33	....	12,206
Crittenden	2,251	1,761	3,252	23	....	7,287
Orange	2,873	2,765	4,847	41	....	10,526
Rutland	3,990	4,098	7,470	32	....	15,590
Windham	4,416	4,672	8,426	58	....	17,572
Windsor	4,004	4,148	7,543	45	....	15,740
Total	22,435	22,328	40,505	255	....	85,425
	[22,405]	[22,305]	[40,362]	[269]		[85,341]

NEW YORK [1]

GENERAL

1625 200 souls. Brodhead, *Hist. N.Y.*, I, 159.

1628 270 souls, including men, women, and children. Extracts from Wassemaer, "Historie van Europa," in NYDH, III, 47.

1643 200 freemen, exclusive of the English. "Petition to W. Ind. Co.," [2] in NYCD, I, 190.

3,000 population, estimated on the basis of 500 men in New Amsterdam, and 400 more in Rensselaerswyck and the few towns on Long Island. O'Callaghan, *Hist. New Neth.*, I, 385-86.

1644 400 or 500 men. Jogues, "New Neth. in 1644," in NYDH, IV, 21.

480 available men, including 50 English in the pay of the Dutch. O'Callaghan, *Hist. New Neth.*, I, 312n.

1647 250 to 300 men capable of bearing arms. Gov. Stuyvesant to the States General, in NYDH, I, 689.

1648 100 men left around the Manhattans after the Indian war. O'Callaghan, *Hist. New Neth.*, I, 357, 386n.

1664 10,000 inhabitants. *Ibid.*, II, 540. (Address of Burgomasters and Schepens to Director and Council.) [3]

1667 8,000 souls, consisting of about 1,500 families. "Petition to States General," in NYCD, II, 512 (March 25, 1667).

a U.S. Bureau of Census, *Heads of Families, Vt.*, 9-10.
[1] It should be remembered that during the Dutch period, New Netherland included more territory than the later province of New York.
[2] "Journal of New Netherlands," in NYCD, I, 181, gives 14,000 souls.
[3] Roberts, *N.Y.*, I, 95, attributes this estimate to Stuyvesant, but thinks 8,000 a liberal estimate. Dexter quotes him, but both he and Rossiter prefer 7,000. This last figure is also given by Stevens, "English in N.Y.," in Winsor., *Narr. Crit. Hist.*, III, 385.

1671 1,500 men. *See* Thirteen Colonies: General, 1671.

1672 2,000 militia; 10,000 or 12,000 inhabitants. Dunlap, *Hist. N.Y.*, II, App. CXX, Misc. Matter.

1673 6,000 inhabitants. "Address of Burgomasters to Bencks and Evertsen," in NYDH, I, 689.

6,000 to 7,000 Dutch inhabitants. "Corporation of New Orange to States-General," Sept. 1673, Royal Archs. at the Hague, File W.I., in NYCD, II, 526.[4]

1674 2,000 militia. "Heads of Inquiries and Answers, April 7-8, 1674," in *Chalmers Coll.*, N.Y., I, 10, NYPL.

1678 2,000 militia. Gov. Andros, Ans. Quer., April 16, 1678, in CSPC, 1677-85, 237-38, No. 660.

1687 4,000 foot, 300 horse, and 1 company of dragoons. Gov. Dongan, Ans. Quer., Feb. 22, 1687, in NYDH, I, 149;[5] also in *Chalmers Coll.*, N.Y., I, n.p. NYPL.

1688 8,000 families, and about 12,000 fighting men. Statement of Leisler and Gouverneur as to the state of N.Y. Prov. since 1687, in CSPC, 1696-97, 146, No. 262.

2,000 militia; horse, 300; dragoons, 50. Abeel, "Historical Notes," *N.Y. Holl. Soc. Year Book*, 1916, 71.

20,000 inhabitants. *See* Thirteen Colonies: General, 1688.

1693 3,000 men "cannot be mustered, whereas a few years ago we could muster 5,000." Gov. Fletcher to Blathwayt, Aug. 15, 1693, in CSPC, 1693-96, 141, No. 500.

2,932 militia. See page 92. NYDH, I, 318-19.

3,000 men able to bear arms. *See* Thirteen Colonies: General, 1693.

1695 3,000 families. Brook and Nicoll to Lords Justices, in NYCD, IV, 172.

1697 3,000 families. N.Y. Agents to BT, in CSPC, 1697-98, 353, No. 691.

1698 18,067 total population. Gov. Bellomont to BT, in *Ibid.*, 1697-98, 532, No. 978, vi. See page 92.

1699 4,000 freemen. *See* Thirteen Colonies: General, 1699.

1700 3,182 militia. NYCD, IV, 807. See page 94.

80,000 population in N.Y., the Jerseys, Pa., Del., and Md. *See* Thirteen Colonies: General, 1700.

1701 30,000 souls. Humphreys, S.P.G., 42.

30,000 total population; or 25,000. *See* Thirteen Colonies: General, 1701.

---

[4] Dexter quotes this figure but would add about half as many English and other whites. Rossiter says 10,500 inhabitants. Hough, *Census of the State of N.Y. for 1855*, Intro. IIIn, thinks the estimate of 6,000 as given in the Vanderkemp translation a bit uncertain, as it seems too large for New York City, and too small for the whole province.

[5] Dexter quotes Brodhead for 1686 at about 18,000 people. Cf. Watson, *Annals of N.Y.*, 45, who estimates 20,000 on basis of Dongan's figures.

1703 20,749 inhabitants by census. Gov. Hunter to BT, in NYDH, I,
691; and in CSPC, 1711-12, 301-2, No. 454. See page 94.
20,665 total inhabitants: 18,282 whites, 2,383 Negroes. See page
95. Hough, *Census of State of N.Y. for 1855*, Intro. IV, citing
N.Y. Col. MSS., XLVIII.[6]

1708 4,000 militia. Lord Cornbury to BT, July 1, 1708, in CSPC, 1708-9,
8, No. 10.

1712 12,286 inhabitants, 1,775 slaves, by an incomplete census.[7] See page
94. Gov. Hunter to BT, in NYDH, I, 691; NYCD, V, 339; and
CSPC, 1711-12, 301-2, No. 454.

1715 5,000 militia (computed). Gov. Hunter, Ans. Quer., Nov. 12, 1715,
in NYDC, V, 459.[8]
31,000 total population: 27,000 whites, 4,000 Negroes. *See* Thirteen Colonies: General, 1715.

1716 5,060 militia. Gov. Hunter to BT, in NYDH, I, 692.

1717-
1718(?) 5,685 men. See page 94.[9] "Memorial of Several Aggrievances and
Oppressions of H.M. Subjects in Colony of N.Y. in Amer.,"
in *Amer. Hist. Assoc. Rept.*, 1892, 47, citing Bodleian Library,
Fol. 660, fol. 158-59b.

1718 3,000 families. *N.Y. Eccles. Recds.*, III, 1672-73.

1721 6,000 militia. Gov. Hunter, Ans. Quer., Aug. 1720, in NYDH, I,
692; Repr. of BT to King, Sept. 8, 1721, *Kings MS.*, 205, fol. 14,
p. 23, in LCT; *Chalmers Coll.*, N.Y., I, NYPL; NYCD, V, 602.

1723 40,564 total population, 6,171 Negroes, according to census. See
page 96. NYDH, I, 693.
40,580 total population: 34,375 whites; 6,205 blacks. *Chalmers
Coll.*, N.Y., I. NYPL.

1726 20,000 inhabitants. *See* Thirteen Colonies: General, 1726.

1731 50,289 total population, 7,231 Negroes, according to census. See
page 97. NYDH, I, 694. Cf. Anon., *State of British and French
Colonies in North Am., 1755*, 134.

1737 60,436 total population; 8,941 Negroes, according to census. See
page 98. NYDH, I, 694, citing *Lond. Doc.* XXVI.

1740 10,000 militia in N.Y. and the Jerseys. *See* Thirteen Colonies: General, 1740.

[6] This census differs from that sent by Gov. Hunter. Hough is not sure which is correct, and thinks there is no way of ascertaining. Dexter quotes both. Rossiter says
20,748 inhabitants.
[7] No returns for Queens, Suffolk, Albany, Ulster, and Dutchess Cos. Dexter thinks
28,000 total population is indicated by the above partial returns, and Rossiter also gives
28,000.
[8] Rossiter estimates 31,000 population.
[9] No date is given in this document, but the context indicates that it was written early
in the reign of George I, and probably just after 1716.

GENERAL 91

1746 61,589 total population; 9,107 Negroes, according to census. See page 99. NYDH, I, 695, citing *Lond. Doc.* XXVIII.

1749 73,448 total population: 62,756 whites; 10,692 blacks, according to census. See page 100. NYDH, I, 695, citing *Lond. Doc.* XXIX. 100,000 inhabitants. *See* Thirteen Colonies: General, 1749.

1754 85,000 white inhabitants; 11,000 black. Bancroft, II, 389-91.

1755 55,000 whites; or 100,000 total. *See* Thirteen Colonies: General, 1755. Cf. Anon., *State of British and French Colonies in North Am.*, 1755, 134.

1756 96,775 total population: 83,233 whites; 13,542 blacks, according to census of 1756. Gov. Tryon, Ans. Quer., 1774, in NYDH, I, 763. Census is in *ibid.*, I, 696. See page 101. Cf. Pownall, *Memorial* 60.

1761 80,000 to 100,000 inhabitants. Burke, *European Settlements*, II, 191.

100,000 inhabitants. Burnaby, *Travels*, 84.

1765 100,000 inhabitants; 25,000 men. *See* Thirteen Colonies: General, 1765.

1770 80,000 to 100,000 inhabitants. Wynne, *Hist. Brit. Empire in Amer.*, I, 201.

1771 168,007 total inhabitants: 148,124 whites; 19,883 blacks, according to census. See page 102. NYDH, I, 697; Gov. Tryon, Ans. Quer., 1774, *ibid.*, I, 762.

1773 150,000 inhabitants (white). Estimated on basis of 148,124 people for 1771.[10] Rodgers, "State of Relig. Liberty in N.Y.," in MHSC, 2d Series, I, 147.

1774 182,251 population. Pownall, *Memorial*, 60.

182,247 total population, supposing it to be increased by 12,974 whites and 1,266 blacks over the figures of the census of 1771, according to the rate of increase from 1756 to 1771. Gov. Tryon, *Ans. Quer.*, 1774, in NYDH, I, 763.

250,000 total population according to Congress estimate; or 180,000; or 148,000. *See* Thirteen Colonies: General, 1774.

1775 238,000 population.[11] De Witt, *Abstract of Census of Mass., 1855,* 195.

200,000 total population. *See* Thirteen Colonies: General, 1775.

1776 191,741 total population: 169,148 whites; 21,993 blacks. Estimated on basis of ratio of increase from 1771 to 1774. Northrup, "Slavery in N.Y.," in *N.Y. State Lib. Bull.*, I, 284.[12]

1783 200,000 population. *See* Thirteen Colonies: General, 1783.

[10] Brissot de Warville, *New Travels*, 156, gives 148,124 for 1773. See 1771.
[11] Dexter thinks 190,000 a fair estimate for this year. Rossiter gives the same.
[12] Anon., *Hist. of North Amer.*, 104, gives 100,000 souls, and militia of 18,000 men.

1786   238,897 total inhabitants: 219,996 whites; 18,889 blacks; 12 Indian taxpayers. See page 104. Hough, *Census of State of N.Y., for 1855,* Intro. viii. (Recorded in Sec'y's Office. Deeds XXII, p. 35.) Cf. Brissot de Warville, *New Travels,* 156.

243,566 total population. Same census plus Cumberland Co., 3,947, and Gloucester Co., 722. Webster, in *N.Y. Directory for 1786,* 20.

250,000 inhabitants. See Thirteen Colonies: General, 1786.

1787   280,000 souls, computed on the basis of an increase of 40,000 souls over a total of 190,000 in 1775, and adding 50,000 for Vt. Livingston to Lafayette, April 24, 1787, in Bancroft, *Hist. of the Const.,* II, App. 418.

233,000 population; or 238,000. See Thirteen Colonies: General, 1787.

1790   340,120 total population: free white males over 16, 83,700; free white males under 16, 78,122; free white females, 152,320; other free persons, 4,654; slaves, 21,324. U.S. Bureau of Census, *Heads of Families, N.Y.,* 9-10. See page 105.

LOCAL

I. MILITIA OF 1693 AND CENSUS OF 1698 [a]

COUNTIES	1693	CENSUS OF 1698			
	Militia	*Men*	*Women*	*Children*	*Negroes*
Albany City and Co.[b]	359	380	270	803	23
Ulster [c] and Dutchess	277	248	111	869	156
Orange [d]	...	29	31	140	19
New York City and Co.[e]	477	1,019	1,057	2,161	700
Richmond	104	328	208	118	73
Westchester [f]	283	316	294	307	146
Suffolk [g]	533	973	1,024	124	558
Kings [h]	319	308	332	1,081	296
Queens [i]	580	1,465	1,350	551	199
	2,932	5,066	4,677	6,154	2,170

1698 total population: 18,067.

North Am. and W. Ind. Gazetteer gives 250,000 inhabitants for 1776; and Mandrillon, *Le Spectateur américain,* 256, gives the same figure for 1785.

a Figures for *1693* in NYDH, I, 318-19; and for *1698* in CSPC, 1697-98, 532, 978, vi.

b Albany County in *1686* had 1,986 white inhabitants and 157 Negroes: Hough, *Census of State of N.Y. for 1855,* Intro. iv, citing *N.Y. Col. MSS.,* XXXV. In *1689* according to census it had 2,016 inhabitants: CSPC, 1697-98, 175, No. 381. The town of Albany was variously estimated at 150 houses and 300 inhabitants capable of bearing arms: M. de Collières to M. de Seignelay, in NYCD, IX, 406; and 200 houses: Miller, "Desc. of N.Y.," 29, in Gowan, *Bibliotheca Americana.* Kinderhook in *1694* had about 20 families; Wadsworth, "Journal," in MHSC, 4th Series, I, 104. Schenectady in *1698* had 238 inhabitants according to census: Munsell, *Annals of Albany,* IX, 81-89.

c Ulster County in *1689* had 222 male inhabitants: NYDH, I, 279, 282.

d Orange County was included with N. Y. City and County in *1693*, when it contained about 20 families: NYCD, IV, 28.

e In *1656*, the city, then New Amsterdam, contained 1,000 souls and 120 houses according to a survey by Capt. de Konick: O'Callaghan, *Hist. New Neth.*, II, 540. In *1660*, Skipper Huys informed the commissioners there were 350 houses on Manhattan Island: NYCD, II, 125. In *1664* there were 1,500 inhabitants of whom only 250 were capable of bearing arms: "Remonstrance to Director General and Council," in *ibid.*, II, 248. After it became English, Ogilby, *America*, 169, estimated the town at 400 houses in *1671*. In *1676* there were 303 taxables, and 398 taxables in *1677*: *Common Council Minutes*, I, 29-37, 50-62. The provincial agent, Mr. Weaver, reported 343 houses in *1678*: CSPC, 1697-98, 459, No. 846, xxiv. M. de Collières in *1689* and Lamothe Cadillac in *1692* estimated 400 and 500 men capable of bearing arms: NYCD, IX, 406, 548. Mr. Weaver reported 937 houses in *1696*: CSPC, 1697-98, 458, No. 847, xxii.

f Westchester County in *1675* had 41 persons taxed, of whom 20 persons were in the town of East Chester: NYCD, XIII, 488-89. In *1683* the county had 53 persons taxed: *Ibid.*, XIII, 574. East Chester in *1682* had 19 freeholders: Bolton, *Hist. Westchester Co.*, I, 128-29. Rye in *1683* had 112 freeholders: *Ibid.*, II, 28-29.

g Suffolk County Census for *1786* gives Huntington 386 inhabitants; Southampton 786; Southold 555; total 1709: Hough, *Census of State of N.Y. in 1855*, Intro. iv, citing *N.Y. Col. MSS.*, XXXV. Southampton in *1649* had 25 townsmen, including 16 freemen: *S. Town Recds.*, I, 55-56; in *1657*, 61 freeholders: Howell, *Early Hist. Southampton*, 32; in *1665*, 37 taxables, and in *1696*, 165 taxables: *S. Town Recds.*, II, 250-51, 361-64. In *1696* it had 973 inhabitants according to census: NYDH, I, 665-69. Easthampton had 73 persons taxed in *1678*: NYCD, XIV, 736-37; and 502 inhabitants in *1687*: NYCD, III, 360-61. Southold had 881 inhabitants according to census in *1698*: *Ibid.*, 669-73.

h Brooklyn in *1660* had 134 souls: O'Callaghan, *Hist. New Neth.*, II, 437. Bushwick in *1661* had 23 families; and in *1663*, 40 men able to bear arms: Brodhead, *Hist. N.Y.*, I, 693. New Utrecht in *1664* had 22 to 24 Dutch families: NYCD, XIV, 546. Wiltwick in *1661* had 68 persons taxed: *Ibid.*, XIII, 212. The whole of Kings County in *1676* had 250 taxables: Flatbush, 56; Brooklyn, 71; Bushwick, 43; New Utrecht, 34; Flatlands, 46: NYDH, II, 470-93. In *1687* it contained 293 male inhabitants: *Ibid.*, I, 659-61; and in *1698*, 2,013 inhabitants: Brooklyn, 509; Bushwick, 301; New Utrecht, 259; Flatlands, 256; Gravesend, 215; Flatbush, 476: *Ibid.*, III, 133-38.

i Flushing in *1698* had 530 white inhabitants and 113 Negroes: NYDH, I, 661-65. Hempstead in *1673* had 106 male inhabitants: *Ibid.*, I, 658. Newtown had 125 persons on tax list in *1678*: NYCD, XIV, 738-40; and 125 men, 265 children, 31 servants, and 49 slaves in *1687*: Hough, *Census of State of N.Y. for 1855*, Intro. iv, citing *N.Y. Col. MSS.*, XXXV. Oyster Bay had 21 freeholders in *1671*, 45 in *1677*, and 66 in *1682*: *Oyster Bay Town Recds.*, I, 130, 217-18, 232.

In *1673* there were 645 men in the towns on the west end of Long sland, as follows: Midwout, 73; Amesfort, 48; Breukelen, 81; New Utrecht, 41; Bushwyck, 35; Gravesend, 31; Hemstede, 107; Flushing, 67; Rustdorp, 63; Middleborgh, 99: NYCD, II, 596. In *1675* there were 694 ratable men, including Easthampton, 57; Huntington, 69; Southhould, 107; Flushing, 61; Gravesend, 30; Newtowne, 82; Brookhaven, 31; Boswick, 41; Breucklen, 73; Middlewout, 62; Amesfort, 48; New Utrecht, 33: "List for King's County Towns," in NYCD, III, 139-61; and in NYDH, II, 441-69. In *1683*, 1,240 were on the rate list: Bushwyck, 32; Flatlands, 54; Breucklen, 68; Flatbush, 64; New Utrecht, 33; Gravesend, 33; Newtowne, 104; Flushing, 71; Jamaica, 107; Hempstead, 154; Oyster Bay, 79; Huntington, 70; Smith's Town, 10; Brookhaven, 62; Southold, 98; Southampton, 93; Easthampton, 98: List, in *ibid.*, II, 493-542.

II. Censuses by Counties Only [a]

Counties	Militia 1700	Inhabs. 1703	Inhabs. 1712.	No. of Men. 1717-18
Albany City and Co.[b]	371	2,273	....	540
Ulster [c] and Dutchess [d]	325	1,669	....	620 (U) 60 (D)
Orange [e]	....	268	439	65
Westchester [f]	155	1,946	2,803	630
New York City and Co.[g]	684	4,436	5,840	1,200
Richmond [h]	152	504	1,279	350
Kings [i]	280	1,915	1,925	420
Queens [j]	601	4,392	....	1,000
Suffolk [k]	614	3,346	....	800
	3,182	20,749	12,286	5,685

a Figures for *1700* in NYCD, IV, 807; *1703*, NYDH, I, 691; *1712*, *ibid.*, I, 691 (see also footnote 7, page 90); *1717-18*, *Amer. Hist. Assoc. Rept.*, 1892, 47.

b Albany County in *1714* had 2,871 whites and 458 slaves; total 3,329: NYDH, III, 905. 514 freeholders according to a census of *1720*: *Ibid.*, 370-73. Albany in *1712* was estimated at 4,000 souls, of which 450 were Negroes or Indian slaves; Humphreys, S.P.G., 214. Schenectady in *1710* had about 100 Dutch and 16 English families: Barclay to S.P.G., in NYCD, III, 897.

c Esopus in *1658* had 30 fighting men; by *1701* it had 400 to 600 men capable of bearing arms: NYCD, VIII, 87; IX, 726, 729. Kingston was estimated to have 200 families in *1708*: Oldmixon, *British Empire*, I, 120.

d Dutchess County had 129 taxables in *1717* and 165 in *1718*: *Dutchess Co. Bk. of Supervisors*, I, 1-4, 9-12. Dutchess County in *1714* had 416 whites and 29 slaves according to census: NYDH, I, 368-69.

e Orange County in *1702* had 268 inhabitants according to census: NYDH, I, 366-67.

f Westchester in *1702-3* had about 2,000 souls; Rye had 800 white people: Humphreys, S.P.G., 204, 210. East Chester in *1710* had 314 inhabitants according to census: NYDH, III, 947. New Rochelle had 23 freeholders in *1708*: Bolton, *Hist. Westchester Co.*, I, 393; and 261 inhabitants, of whom 57 were slaves, in *1710*: NYDH, III, 946-47.

g New York City and Co. had 799 males, 16-60; females, 985; male children, 903; female children, 924; male Negroes, 298; female Negroes, 288; male Negro children, 124; female Negro children, 100; all above 60, 55: NYDH, I, 611-24. In *1708* the city was estimated to have 800 to 1000 houses: Oldmixon, *British Empire*, I, 119, 129.

h Richmond was estimated to have 450 effective men in *1701*: D'Iberville, in NYCD, IX, 729.

i King's County had 255 militia in *1715*: NYDH, III, 183-85. Brooklyn in *1706* had 64 freeholders: Furman, *Antiquities of Long Island*, 392.

j Oyster Bay and Huntington were estimated at 50 houses each in *1708*: Oldmixon, *British Empire*, I, 132. Jamaica was estimated at 2,000 souls in *1704*: Onderdonk, *Antiquities of the Parish Church, Jamaica*, 20; and at 8,000 souls in *1712* by Col. Heathcote, *N.Y. Eccles. Recds.*, III, 1903. In *1708-9* it had 189 taxables: list in McDonald, *Two Centuries in Hist. Presby. Church, Jamaica*, 243-45.

k Brookhaven in *1704* had 70 taxables: *Brookhaven Town Recds.*, 97-100. All Long Island in *1701* had about 1,300 families; 800 in the 10 English towns in east end. and 500 in the 9 Dutch towns in the western part: Humphreys, S.P.G., 32, D'Iberville estimated 1,500 men: NYCD, IX, 729.

III. CENSUS BY COUNTIES, SEX, AND RACE

A. CENSUS OF 1703 a

COUNTIES	WHITES			
	Adults		Children	
	Males 16-60	Females	Males	Females
Albany	510	385	515	605
Kings	345	304	433	487
New York	813	1,009	934	989
Orange	49	40	57	84
Queens	952	753	1,093	1,170
Richmond	176	140	42	49
Suffolk	787	756	818	797
Ulster	383	305	436	357
Westchester	472	469	382	386
Total	4,487	4,161	4,710	4,924

	NEGROES				ALL OVER 60	TOTAL
	Adults		Children			
	Males	Females	Males	Females		
Albany	83	53	36	28	58	2,273
Kings	135	75	72	61	...	1,912 b
New York	102	288	131	109	...	4,375 b
Orange	13	7	7	6	5	268
Queens	117	114	98	95	...	4,392
Richmond	60	32	4	1	...	504
Suffolk	60	52	38	38	...	3,346
Ulster	63	36	31	15	23	1,649
Westchester	74	45	50	29	39	1,946
Total	707	702	467	382	125	20,665

a Hough, *Census of State of N.Y. for 1855*, Intro. iv.
b These totals differ from those of the Census of 1703 on the preceding page. *See* New York: General, 1703.

III. Censuses by Counties, Sex, and Race — *Continued*

B. Census of 1723 [c]

COUNTIES	WHITES				
	Adults		Children		Total
	Males	Females	Males	Females	
New York [d]	1,460	1,726	1,352	1,348	5,886
Richmond	335	320	305	291	1,251
Kings	490	476	414	394	1,774
Queens	1,568	1,599	1,530	1,371	6,068
Suffolk	1,441	1,348	1,321	1,156	5,266
Westchester [e]	1,050	951	1,048	912	3,961
Orange	309	245	304	239	1,097
Dutchess [f]	276	237	259	268	1,040
Ulster [g]	642	453	563	699	2,357
Albany	1,512	1,408	1,404	1,369	5,693
	9,083	8,763	8,500	8,047	34,393

	NEGROES AND OTHER SLAVES					GRAND TOTAL
	Adults		Children		Total	
	Males	Females	Males	Females		
New York	408	476	220	258	1,362	7,248
Richmond	101	63	49	42	255	1,506
Kings	171	123	83	67	444	2,218
Queens	393	294	228	208	1,123	7,191
Suffolk	357	367	197	54	975	6,241
Westchester	155	118	92	83	448	4,409
Orange	45	29	42	31	147	1,244
Dutchess	22	14	2	5	43	1,083
Ulster	227	126	119	94	566	2,923
Albany	307	200	146	155	808	6,501
	2,186	1,810	1,178	997	6,171	40,564

c NYDH, I, 693.

d New York City was estimated to have 1,600 families of English, Dutch, and Jews, and 1,362 Indian and Negro slaves in *1722*: Mr. Vesey to Bishop of London, in Dix, *Hist. Trinity Church*, I, 199.

e Rye Parish, which included Rye, Mamaroneck, Scarsdale Manor, White Plains, Bedford, and North Castle, had 340 taxable persons in *1727*, according to Rev. Mr. Wetmore: Luquer, *Centennial Address at St. Matthew's Church*, 14.

f Dutchess County had 149 taxables in *1720*; 183 in *1722*; 195 in *1723*; 218 in *1725*; 262 in *1726*; and 262 in *1727*: list in *Dutchess Co. Book of Supervisors*, I, 24-28, 34-39, 54-60; II, 8-14, 23-29, 49-69, 79-109.

g Ulster County in *1728* had 378 freeholders, of whom 145 were of Kingston: NYDH, III, 969-72; and Schoonmaker, *Hist. of Kingston*, 195.

III. CENSUSES BY COUNTIES, SEX, AND RACE — *Continued*

C. CENSUS OF 1731 h

COUNTIES	WHITES				
	Males over 10	Females over 10	Males under 10	Females under 10	Total Whites
New York i	2,628	2,250	1,143	1,024	
Albany	2,481	1,255	2,352	1,212	
Queens	2,239	2,175	1,178	1,139	
Suffolk	2,144	1,130	2,845	955	
Westchester	1,879	1,701	1,054	707	
Ulster	990	914	577	515	
Kings	629	518	243	268	
Orange	627	534	325	299	
Richmond	423	571	263	256	
Dutchess	570	481	263	298	
	14,613 [14,610] j	11,529	10,243	6,673	43,508 [43,055]

	BLACKS				GRAND TOTAL
	Males over 10	Females over 10	Males under 10	Females under 10	
New York	599	607	186	185	8,622
Albany	568	185	346	174	8,573
Queens	476	363	226	199	7,995
Suffolk	239	83	196	83	7,675
Westchester	269	96	176	151	6,033
Ulster	321	196	124	91	3,728
Kings	205	146	65	76	2,150
Orange	85	47	19	33	1,969
Richmond	111	98	51	44	1,817
Dutchess	59	32	13	8	1,727 [1,724]
	2,932	1,853	1,402	1,044	50,289 [50,286]

Total Blacks   7,231
Total Whites   43,508 [43,055]

50,289 [50,286]

h NYDH, I, 694.

i New York City supposedly had 1,500 houses: Anon, *State of British and French Colonies in North Am., 1755*, 134.

j In this and the following tables for N.Y., totals of columns are given as found in the source cited. When the total is incorrect, the true sum has been presented in brackets beside that found in the source used, as here. When no total is given in the source, it has been computed and placed in brackets, as on page 100.

III. CENSUSES BY COUNTIES, SEX, AND RACE — *Continued*

D. CENSUS OF 1737 k

COUNTIES	WHITES			
	Males over 10	*Females over 10*	*Males under 10*	*Females under 10*
New York	3,253	3,568	1,088	1,036
Albany	3,209	2,995	1,463	1,384
Westchester	2,110	1,890	950	944
Orange	860	753	501	433
Ulster	1,175	1,681	541	601
Dutchess	940	860	710	646
Richmond	488	497	289	266
Kings	654	631	235	264
Queens	2,407	2,290	1,395	1,656
Suffolk	2,297	2,353	1,175	1,008
	17,393	17,518	8,347	8,238

	BLACKS				
	Males over 10	*Females over 10*	*Males under 10*	*Females under 10*	GRAND TOTAL
New York	674	609	229	207	10,664
Albany	714	496	223	197	10,681
Westchester	304	254	153	140	6,745
Orange	125	95	38	35	2,840
Ulster	378	260	124	110	4,870
Dutchess	161	42	37	22	3,418
Richmond	132	112	52	53	1,889
Kings	210	169	84	101	2,348
Queens	460	370	254	227	9,059
Suffolk	393	307	203	187	7,923
	3,551	2,714	1,397	1,279	60,437

k NYDH, I, 694.

III. Censuses by Counties, Sex, and Race — *Continued*

E. Census of 1746 [1]

Counties	WHITES				
	Males			Females	
	Under 16	*16-60*	*Over 60*	*Under 16*	*Over 16*
New York	2,117	2,097	149	2,013	2,897
Kings	350	435	71	366	464
Queens	1,946	1,826	233	2,077	1,914
Dutchess m	2,200	2,056	200	2,100	1,750
Suffolk n	1,887	1,835	226	1,891	2,016
Richmond	445	376	35	421	414
Orange	536	763	67	871	721
Westchester	2,435	2,090	303	2,095	1,640
Ulster	1,022	1,044	116	972	1,000
	12,938	12,522	1,400	12,196 [12,806]	12,816

	BLACKS					
	Males			Females		Grand Total
	Under 16	*16-60*	*Over 60*	*Under 16*	*Over 16*	
New York	419	645	76	735	569	11,717
Kings	140	167	32	154	152	2,331
Queens	365	466	61	391	361	9,640
Dutchess	106	160	26	108	100	8,806
Suffolk	329	393	52	315	310	9,254
Richmond	92	88	13	95	94	2,073
Orange	82	99	34	51	44	3,268
Westchester	187	180	27	138	140	9,235
Ulster	244	331	43	229	264	5,265
	1,964	2,529	364	2,216	2,034	61,589

l Albany not numbered because of the enemy. Census of *1746* in NYDH, I, 695.

m Rhinebeck in *1740* had 77 freeholders: List, in Morse, *Historic Old Rhinebeck*, 422.

n Brookhaven in *1741* had 245 taxables: *Brookhaven Town Recds.*, 152-55.

III. Censuses by Counties, Sex, and Race — *Continued*

F. Census of 1749 o

COUNTIES	WHITES					Total Whites
	Males			Females		
	Under 16	*16-60*	*Over 60*	*Under 16*	*Over 16*	
New York	2,346	2,765	183	2,364	3,268	10,926
Kings	288	437	62	322	391	1,500
Albany p	2,249	2,359	322	2,137	2,087	9,154
Queens	1,630	1,508	151	1,550	1,778	6,617
Dutchess	1,970	1,820	160	1,790	1,751	7,491
Suffolk q	2,058	1,863	248	1,960	1,969	8,098
Richmond	431	420	36	424	434	1,745
Orange	1,061	856	66	992	899	3,874
Westchester	2,511	2,312	228	2,263	2,233	9,547
Ulster	913	992	110	810	979	3,804
	[15,457]	[15,332]	[1,566]	[14,612]	[15,789]	62,756

	BLACKS					Total Blacks
	Males			Females		
	Under 16	*16-60*	*Over 60*	*Under 16*	*Over 16*	
New York	460	610	41	556	701	2,368
Kings	232	244	21	137	149	783
Albany	309	424	48	334	365	1,480
Queens	300	386	43	245	349	1,423 [1,323]
Dutchess	103	155	21	63	79	421
Suffolk	305	355	41	292	293	1,286
Richmond	88	110	20	93	98	409
Orange	62	95	16	84	103	360
Westchester	303	270	66	238	279	1,156
Ulster	217	301	50	198	240	1,006
	[2,379]	[2,950]	[367]	[2,240]	[2,656]	10,692 [10,592]

Total whites   62,756
Total blacks   10,692 [10,592]

Total Inhabs. 73,448
           [73,348]

o NYDH, I, 695.
p Kinderhook in *1744* had 134 taxables: List, in Collier, *Hist. of Old Kinderhook,* 109. Saratoga in *1745* was estimated at 30 families: Gov. Phips to Gov. Law, "Law Papers," in Conn. HSC, XIII, 120.
q Brookhaven had 283 taxables: *Brookhaven Town Recds.,* 161-69.

III. Censuses by Counties, Sex, and Race — *Continued*
G. Census of 1756 [r]

COUNTIES	WHITES					Total Whites
	Males			Females		
	Under 16	16-60	Over 60	Under 16	Over 16	
New York [s]	2,260	2,308	174	2,359	3,667	10,768
Albany [t]	3,474	3,795	456	3,234	3,846	14,805
Ulster	1,655	1,687	156	1,489	1,618	6,605
Dutchess	3,910	2,873	203	3,530	2,782	13,289 [13,298]
Orange	1,213	1,088	74	1,083	998	4,446 [4,456]
Westchester	3,153	2,908	1,039	2,440	2,379	11,919
Kings	417	467	84	358	536	1,862
Queens [u]	1,960	2,147	253	1,892	2,365	8,617
Suffolk [v]	2,283	2,141	221	2,265	2,335	9,245
Richmond	344	411	107	334	471	1,667
	[20,669]	[19,825]	[2,767]	[18,984]	[20,997]	83,223 [83,242]

	BLACKS					Total Blacks
	Males			Females		
	Under 16	16-60	Over 60	Under 16	Over 16	
New York	468	604	68	443	695	2,272 [2,278]
Albany	658	786	76	496	603	2,619
Ulster	328	437	49	326	360	1,500
Dutchess	211	270	53	163	162	859
Orange	103	116	24	93	94	430
Westchester	296	418	77	267	280	1,338
Kings	212	214	21	201	197	845
Queens	581	563	55	500	470	2,169
Suffolk	278	297	40	194	236	1,045
Richmond	145	92	30	97	101	465
	[3,280]	[3,797]	[493]	[2,780]	[3,198]	13,542 [13,548]

Total whites   83,223 [83,242]   Total blacks   13,542 [13,548]
Total Inhabs.   96,765 [96,790]

r NYDH, I, 696.

s In *1761* New York City was estimated to have 2,000 houses by Lt. Gov. Colden. Colden Papers, in NYHSC, IX, 61. Burke, *European Settlements*, II, 190, adds to this 12,000 inhabitants, an estimate repeated as of *1770* by Wynne, *Hist. Brit. Empire in Am.*, I, 201. Burnaby estimates 16,000 to 17,000 inhabitants: Burnaby, *Travels*, 81.

t In the Mohawk Valley in *1758* were 942 or 952 families, 300 houses in Schenectady: Halsey, *Tour of Four Great Rivers*, Intro. i.

u Jamaica in *1761* had 710 ratables, and in *1763* about 720 families: S. Seabury to S.P.G., in Onderdonk, *Antiquities of the Parish Church, Jamaica*, 61; Hawkins, *Missions of Church of England*, 299.

v Hempstead in *1761* had 5,940 inhabitants: Moore, *Hist. St. George's Church of Hempstead, L.I.*, 102.

III. CENSUSES BY COUNTIES, SEX, AND RACE — *Continued*

H. CENSUS OF 1771 w

COUNTIES	WHITES					
	Males			Females		Total
	Under 16	16-60	Over 60	Under 16	Over 16	Whites
New York x	3,720	5,083	280	3,779	5,864	18,726
Albany y	9,740	9,822	1,136	9,086	9,045	38,829
Ulster z	2,835	3,023	262	2,601	3,275	11,996
Dutchess	5,721	4,687	384	5,413	4,839	21,044
Orange	2,651	2,297	167	2,191	2,124	9,430
Westchester	3,813	5,204	549	3,483	5,266	18,315
Kings	548	644	76	513	680	2,461
Queens	1,253	2,083	950	2,126	2,332	8,744
Suffolk aa	2,731	2,834	347	2,658	3,106	11,676
Richmond	616	438	96	508	595	2,253
Cumberland	1,071	1,002	59	941	862	3,935
Gloucester	178	185	8	193	151	715
	34,877	37,302	4,314	33,492	38,139	148,124

	BLACKS					
	Males			Females		Total
	Under 16	16-60	Over 60	Under 16	Over 16	Blacks
New York	568	890	42	552	1,085	3,137
Albany	876	1,100	250	671	980	3,877
Ulster	518	516	57	422	441	1,954
Dutchess	299	417	34	282	328	1,360
Orange	162	184	22	120	174	662
Westchester	793	916	68	766	887	3,430
Kings	297	287	22	261	295	1,162
Queens	374	511	271	546	534	2,236
Suffolk	350	389	59	320	334	1,452
Richmond	177	152	22	106	137	594
Cumberland	...	6	1	3	2	12
Gloucester	2	4	...	1	...	7
	4,416	5,372	848	4,050	5,197	19,883

w Rossiter says this is the only N.Y. census, so far as the evidence shows, which includes Vt. Census given in NYDH, I, 697.

x New York City in *1776* was estimated to have 2,500 or 3,000 buildings: Anon., *Hist. North Am.*, 94, 104; *North Am. and W. Ind. Gazetteer*, under "York, New."

y Albany was estimated at 300 houses in *1765* by Ralph Izard, *Journey to Niagara*, 5; at 500 houses in *1769*: "Journal of Richard Smith," in Halsey, *Tour of Four Great Rivers*, 16; at 350 houses in *1776* by Mandrillon, and the *North Am. and W. Ind. Gazetteer*; at 300 families in *1778* by Alvarez, in Munsell, *Annals of Albany*, X, 397. Schenectady in *1769* had 300 dwelling houses: "Journal of Richard Smith," in Halsey, *Tour of Four Great Rivers*, 22. Sir William Johnson estimated in *1770* that about

III. CENSUSES BY COUNTIES, SEX, AND RACE — *Continued*

Total Number in Each County

New York	21,863
Albany	42,706
Ulster	13,950
Dutchess	22,404
Orange	10,092
Westchester	21,745
Kings	3,623
Queens	10,980
Suffolk	13,128
Richmond	2,847
Cumberland	3,947
Gloucester	722
Total	168,007

I. CENSUS OF SUFFOLK COUNTY, 1776 ab

TOWNSHIPS	WHITES					NEGROES		GRAND TOTAL
	Males			Females		Male and Female		
	Over 50	16-50	Under 16	Over 16	Under 16	Over 16	Under 16	
Shelter Island	11	29	29	40	32	21	12	
St. Geo. Manor and Meritches	19	43	73	76	81	50	34	
Brookhaven Twp.	123	391	498	546	473	68	74	
Southold Twp.	167	549	720	814	696	125	109	
Smithtown	35	109	141	152	118	91	70	
Easthampton	69	249	297	341	294	45	22	
Islip	19	64	84	88	60	33	27	
Southampton W.	95	252	319	396	299	38	23	
Southampton E.	75	290	318	407	340	68	35	
Total	[613]	[1,976]	[2,479]	[2,860]	[2,393]	[539]	[406]	[11,266]

2,000 men lived "between the south bounds of the Patroon's Manor and the north line of Livingston, including Kinderhook, Claverack, etc.," NYDH, II, 965.

z (Ulster) New Paltz in *1765* had 113 taxables: List, in Le Fevre, *Hist. of New Paltz*, 94-96. Kingston in *1776* was supposed to have about 100 houses "in the compact part of town," *North Am. and W. Ind. Gazetteer*, under "Kingston."

aa Shelter Island in *1771* had 140 whites and 27 blacks according to census: Wallmann, *Hist. Papers on Shelter Island*, 62-63. For census of Suffolk County in *1776*, see above.

ab *N.Y. Cal. Hist. MSS., Revolutionary Papers*, I, 378-417.

III. CENSUSES BY COUNTIES, SEX, AND RACE — *Continued*

J. CENSUS OF 1786 ac

COUNTIES	WHITES				
	Males			Females	
	Under 16	16-60	Over 60	Under 16	Over 16
Albany ad	17,703	15,866	1,364	16,644	16,093
Dutchess ae	8,209	6,973	628	7,700	7,481
Kings	542	776	66	519	766
Montgomery	3,564	3,487	342	3,844	3,415
New York af	4,360	5,742	399	4,260	6,746
Orange	3,382	3,182	247	3,206	3,187
Queens	2,441	2,717	295	2,308	3,140
Richmond	616	622	43	540	638
Suffolk	2,917	3,141	334	2,700	3,633
Ulster ag	4,971	4,792	464	4,381	4,865
Washington	1,130	1,152	58	1,118	983
Westchester ah	4,972	4,477	491	4,546	4,818
	54,807	52,927	4,731	51,766	55,765

	SLAVES		INDIAN TAXPAYERS	TOTAL
	Males	Females		
Albany	2,335	2,355	..	72,360
Dutchess	830	815	..	32,636
Kings	695	622	..	3,986
Montgomery	217	188	..	15,057
New York	896	1,207	4	23,614
Orange	442	416	..	14,062
Queens	1,160	1,023	..	13,084
Richmond	369	324	..	3,152
Suffolk	567	501	..	13,793
Ulster	1,353	1,309	8	22,143
Washington	8	7	..	4,456
Westchester	649	601	..	20,554
	9,521	9,368	12	238,897 Total Inhabs.

ac This Census given in Hough, *Census of State of N.Y. for 1855*, Intro. viii. Cumberland Co., 3,947, and Gloucester Co., 722, are given with this census by Webster in *N.Y. Directory for 1786*, 20. These figures are the same as those of 1771.

ad Albany had 550 houses "by actual numeration": Munsell, *Annals of Albany*, I, 85. Schenectady was estimated at 500 houses in *1780* by Chastellux, *Travels*, II, 400; and 450 inhabitants by Peter Sailly, *N.Y. State Lib. Bull.*, XII, 59. Cf. 1790.

ae Fishkill was estimated to have 50 houses in *1778 and 1780*: Anburey *Travels*, II, 234; Chastellux, *Travels*, I, 63.

af New York City had 3,340 houses in *1786*: Webster in *N.Y. Directory for 1786*, 22.

ag According to a census in *1782* Ulster had 15,697 whites; 1,205 refugees: NYDH, III, 996.

ah According to census in *1782* Westchester had 6,278 inhabitants and 1,052 refugees: *Ibid.*, III, 958.

III. Censuses by Counties, Sex, and Race — *Continued*

K. Census for 1790 a1

Counties	Free Whites			All Other Free	Slaves	Total
	Males Over 16	Under 16	Females			
Albany	18,549	18,866	34,407	170	3,929	75,921
Clinton	546	357	678	16	17	1,614
Columbia	6,573	6,737	12,744	55	1,623	27,732
Dutchess	10,968	11,062	20,940	440	1,856	45,266
Kings	903	700	1,414	46	1,432	4,495
Montgomery	7,857	7,201	13,152	41	588	28,839
N. Y. City and Co.	8,500	5,907	15,254	1,101	2,369	33,131
Ontario	524	192	342	6	11	1,075
Orange	4,600	4,340	8,371	201	966	18,478
Queens	3,554	2,863	6,480	808	2,309	16,014
Richmond	749	751	1,449	127	759	3,835
Suffolk	3,756	3,273	7,187	1,126	1,098	16,440
Ulster	7,058	6,791	12,485	157	2,906	29,397
Washington	3,606	3,752	6,625	3	47	14,033
Westchester	5,877	5,330	10,958	357	1,419	23,941
	83,700	78,122	152,320	4,654	21,324	340,120
	[83,620]		[152,486]		[21,329]	[340,211]
Albany City	804	653	1,443	26	572	3,498
Brooklyn	362	257	565	14	405	1,603

NEW JERSEY

General

1665-1668 137 male inhabitants taking oath of allegiance: Bergen (1665), 33; Elizabeth (1665), 65; Woodbridge (1667), 11; Navesink (1667), 24; Others, 4. *N.J. Arch.*, 1st Series, I, 49-51.

1671 1,500 men in N.Y., Long Island, and N.J. *See* Thirteen Colonies: General, 1671.

1673 469 men: Bergen, 69 (9 absent); Elizabeth, 80; New Worck [Newark], 86; Woodbridge, 54; Piscattaway, 43; Middletown, 60; Shrewsbury, 68. *N.J. Archs.*, 1st Series, I, 133; and NYCD, II, 580, 587, 598, 607.[1]

1676 3,500 people. "Gov. Coxe's Narrative," in *N.J. Archs.*, 1st Series, II, 14.

1682 3,450 people: Shrewsbury about 400; Middletown about 500; Piscattaway about 400; Woodbridge about 600; Elizabethtown about

a1 U.S. Bureau of Census, *Heads of Families, N.Y.*, 8.

[1] Dexter quotes Whitehead, E. *Jersey under the Prop. Gov'ts*, 76, who gives 469 male inhabitants from NYCD.

700; Newark about 500; Bergen about 350. Scot, "Model of the Gov't of the Prov. of East N.J., 1685," in Whitehead, *E. Jersey under the Prop. Gov'ts*, 402-9.

700 families in the towns of E. Jersey, which, reckoning 5 to a family, would give 3,500 inhabitants, besides the out plantations, which were thought to contain half as many more. *Ibid.*, 409.

1688   10,000 inhabitants. *See* Thirteen Colonies: General, 1688.

1696   1,000 militia in the two Jerseys. Proc. BT in NYCD, IV, 185.

1698   12,000 families.[2] Att'y Gen'l Graham to Gov. Bellomont, in CSPC, 1697-98, 301, No. 621.

1699   2,000 freemen. *See* Thirteen Colonies: General, 1699.

1700   2,000 males over 16, according to Gov. Hamilton. Parker, *Historical Address*, 37.

8,000 souls. Col. Morris, to Bishop of London, in Morris, *Papers*, 7.

80,000 total population in N.Y., the Jerseys, Pa., Del., and Md. *See* Thirteen Colonies: General, 1700.

1701   15,000 population. Humphreys, S.P.G., 42.[3]

15,000 population; or, by another estimate, E. New Jersey, 6,000, and W. New Jersey, 2,000. *See* Thirteen Colonies: General, 1701.

1702   8,000 inhabitants. Chalmers, *Revolt*, I, 376.[4]

1708   2,300 militia, besides the Quakers. Lord Cornbury to BT, July 1, 1708, in CSPC, 1708-9, 15, No. 11.

20,000 souls; 200 Indians at most. Oldmixon, *British Empire*, I, 141-46.

1715   22,500 total population: 21,000 whites; 1,500 Negroes. *See* Thirteen Colonies: General, 1715.

1721   3,000 militia. Brig. Hunter, Ans. Quer., Aug. 11, 1720, in *N.J. Archs.*, 1st Series, IV, 450-51; Repr. BT, Sept. 8, 1721, *Kings MS.*, 205, fol. 15, p. 26, in LCT; NYCD, V, 603.

1726   32,442 total inhabitants: 29,861 whites; 2,581 blacks. *N.J. Archs.*, 1st Series, V, 164; also Andrews, *Guide to Pub. Rec. Off.*, I, 174, citing CO 5: 980-82. See page 109.

10,000 inhabitants. *See* Thirteen Colonies: General, 1726.

1738   47,369 total population: 43,388 whites; 3,981 blacks. *N.J. Archs.*, 1st Series, VI, 244. Census, see page 110. Cf. Brissot de Warville, *New Travels*, 367.

1740   10,000 militia in N.Y. and the Jerseys. *See* Thirteen Colonies: General, 1740.

1745   61,383 total population: 56,777 whites; 4,606 blacks. See page 111.

[2] The editor puts (?200) after 12,000. Dexter gives 832 freeholders for 1699 for W. Jersey, from *N. J. Archs.*, II, 305, and quotes "near 10,000" from Winsor and Bancroft. Rossiter gives nothing.

[3] Dexter quotes Humphreys, and Rossiter gives an estimate of 15,000 for 1702.

[4] Dexter calls this "a wild guess."

N.J. *Archs.*, 1st Series, VI, 242-43. Cf. Brissot de Warville, *New Travels*, 367.

1747 70,000 people. "Journal of the Prov. Council," in *N.J. Archs.*, 1st Series, XV, 602.

1749 61,383 inhabitants, white and black; 4,500 militia; 60 families of Indians.[5] Gov. Belcher, Ans. Quer., April 21, 1749, in *N.J. Archs.*, 1st Series, VII, 245.

50,000 souls. Anon., *State of British and French Colonies in North Am.*, *1775*, 134.

60,000 inhabitants. *See* Thirteen Colonies: General, 1749.

1750 50,000 inhabitants, of whom 10,000 are available for militia. Douglass, *Summary*, II, 286.

1752 79,000 total population, computing an increase of 18,000 over the census figures of 1745, according to the ratio of increase between the census of 1738 and that of 1745. Article in *N.J. Gazette*, Feb. 22, 1782, from "Newspaper Extracts," in *N.J. Archs.*, 2d Series, V, 389.

1754 80,000 whites; 1,500 blacks, "pretty much conjectural." Gov. Belcher, Ans. Quer., in *N.J. Archs.*, 1st Series, VIII, Pt. 2, 84.

73,000 whites; 5,500 blacks. Bancroft, II, 389-91.[6]

1755 60,000 souls. Anon., *State of British and French Colonies in North Am.*, *1755*, 134-35.

80,000 whites, of which about 16,000 able to bear arms; 1,500 to 1,800 blacks. Gov. Belcher, Ans. Quer., in *N.J. Archs.*, 1st Series, VII, Pt. 2, 186.[7]

75,000 white inhabitants; or 60,000. *See* Thirteen Colonies: General, 1755.

1758 60,000 inhabitants.[8] Anon. article in "Newspaper Extracts," in *N.J. Archs.*, XX, 199.

1759 70,000 to 80,000 people, and 15,000 fencible men. Gov. Bernard to Pitt, in *N.J. Archs.*, 1st Series, IX, 167.

102,000 inhabitants. (Computed as in 1752, q.v.),[9] Article in *N.J. Gazette*, Feb. 22, 1782, from "Newspaper Extracts," in *N.J. Archs.*, 2d Series, V, 389.

1760 70,000 inhabitants. Burnaby, *Travels*, 78.

1762 12,700 militia. Gov. Hardy to BT., in *N.J. Archs.*, 1st Series, IX, 367.

[5] Dexter gives 60,000 whites from Pitkin's *Statist. View.* Rossiter also says 60,000.

[6] Dexter quotes both figures, and Rossiter says 78,500, apparently from Bancroft.

[7] Dexter quotes this, but considers Gov. Belcher's estimate of Negroes an understatement. He also gives 50,000 from Douglass' *Summary.* Rossiter gives no figures for this year.

[8] Also given for 1763 in Holmes, *Annals*, II, 117, from the *Universal History*, XXXIX, 368.

[9] Cf. Smith, *Hist. of N. J.*, 489.

108 NEW JERSEY

1765 80,000 inhabitants; 20,000 men. *See* Thirteen Colonies: General, 1765.

1766 ⸱31,000 inhabitants. (Computed as in 1752, q.v.) Article in *N.J. Gazette*, Feb. 22, 1782, from "Newspaper Extracts," in *N.J. Archs.*, 2d Series, V, 389.

1770 122,806 inhabitants, supposing the population doubles every 25 years, the census of 1745 being 61,403 people. Article in *N.J. Gazette*, Feb. 22, 1782, from "Newspaper Extracts," in *N.J. Archs.*, 2d Series, V, 389.

1772 67,710 whites; 3,313 blacks, according to census. See page 112.[10] *N.J. Archs.*, 1st Series, X, 452.

1773 168,000 inhabitants. (Computed as in 1752, q.v.) Article in *N.J. Gazette*, Feb. 22, 1782, from "Newspaper Extracts," in *N.J. Archs.*, 2d Series, V, 289.

1774 120,000 total inhabitants.[11] Gov. Franklin, Ans. Quer., in *N.J. Archs.*, X, 445-47.

130,000 inhabitants according to Congressional estimate.[12]

130,000 total population; or 77,000. *See* Thirteen Colonies: General, 1774.

1775 130,000 total population. *See* Thirteen Colonies: General, 1775.

1776 150,000 inhabitants estimated by Congress in 1776.[13] Rutherford, "Notes on N.J., 1776," in N.J. HSP, 2d Series, I, 85.

1780 215,000 inhabitants. (Computed as in 1752, q.v.). Article in *N.J. Gazette*, Feb. 22, 1782, from "Newspaper Extracts," in *N.J. Archs.*, 2d Series, V, 389.

1782 175,000 souls. (Estimated on basis of population doubling every 25 years.) *Ibid.*

1783 130,000 population. *See* Thirteen Colonies: General, 1783.

1784 139,934 whites; 10,501 blacks.[14] Brissot de Warville, *New Travels*, 140,435 inhabitants. New Jersey: *Compendium of Censuses, 1726-1905*, 41. Cf. Warden, *Statist. Pol. and Hist. Acct. of U.S.*, II, 38. See page 113.

1786 150,000 inhabitants. *See* Thirteen Colonies: General, 1786.

1787 138,000 total population; or 138,000 to 145,000. *See* Thirteen Colonies: General, 1787.

1790 184,139 inhabitants according to Federal Census. Rossiter, *Cent. of Pop. Growth*, 9; New Jersey: *Compendium of Censuses, 1726-1905*, 41. See page 113.

[10] Incomplete census. Returns missing from Waterford Town, Bergen, Essex, Somerset, Middlesex, and Monmouth.
[11] Dexter quotes both this and Congress estimate. Rossiter says 120,000.
[12] Cf. *North Am. and W. Ind. Gazetteer*, under "Jersey, New"; Mandrillon, *Le Spectateur américain*, 259.
[13] Mellick, *Story of an Old Farm*, 303, says "less than 150,000" and cites no authority.
[14] Dexter quotes this figure as an estimate of the General Assembly. Rossiter gives 149,434 for this year.

LOCAL

I. CENSUS OF 1726 [a]

COUNTIES [b]	WHITES				
	Males Over 16	Females Over 16	Males Under 16	Females Under 16	Total Whites
Middlesex	953	878	1,016	859	3,706
Essex [c]	992	1,021	983	926	3,922
Monmouth	1,234	1,061	1,095	1,056	4,446
Somerset	582	502	403	405	1,892
Bergen	569	509	556	547	2,181
Burlington	1,080	983	965	844	3,872
Hunterdon	892	743	851	750	3,236
Glocester	608	462	526	529	2,125
Salem	1,060	861	1,015	891	3,827
Cape May	209	156	148	141	654
Total	8,179	7,176	7,558	6,948	29,861

	BLACKS					TOTAL BLACKS AND WHITES
	Males Over 16	Females Over 16	Males Under 16	Females Under 16	Total Blacks	
Middlesex	90	73	73	67	303	4,009
Essex	92	78	70	68	308	4,230
Monmouth	170	90	88	85	433	4,879
Somerset	126	96	87	70	379	2,271
Bergen	173	121	100	98	492	2,673
Burlington	86	63	53	55	257	4,129
Hunterdon	43	45	32	21	141	3,377
Glocester	32	21	24	27	104	3,229 [2,229]
Salem	52	38	35	25	150	3,977
Cape May	8	5	1	..	14	668
Total	872	630	563	516	2,581	32,442 [d]

a N.J. Archs., 1st Series, V, 164.

b West Jersey in 1699 had 832 freeholders: Burlington County, 302; Glocester County, 134; Salem County, 326; Cape May County, 70: Extracts from "Daniel Leed's Almanack for 1701," in CSPC, 1704-5, 375, No. 863. Col. Quary estimated East Jersey to contain 1,000 inhabitants and more in 1703: Col. Quary to BT, in N.J. Archs., III, 14.

c Newark in 1708 comprised 100 families: Oldmixon, British Empire, I, 136, Elizabeth in 1692 had 100 houses: Randolph to Blathwayt in Prince Soc. Pub., XXXI, 399; in 1708, 250 families: Oldmixon, British Empire, I, 136; and 300 families in 1728: Humphreys, S.P.G., 188. Newark, Elizabeth, and Woodbridge in 1716 were estimated to contain 1,000 families: Holiday to S.P.G., in Clark, Hist. St. John's Church, Elizabethtown, 44.

d This figure is correct if Glocester is given the correct sum of 2,229; as the column stands, this total should be 33,442. In this and the following tables for N.J., totals of columns are given as found in the source cited. When the total is incorrect, the true sum has been presented in brackets beside that found in the source used, as in the total for

II. Census of 1738 [a]

COUNTIES	WHITES				
	Males over 16	Females over 16	Males under 16	Females under 16	Total Whites
Middlesex [b]	1,134	1,085	1,086	956	4,261
Essex	1,118	1,720	1,619	1,494	6,644 [5,951]
Bergen [c]	939	822	820	708	3,289
Somersett	967	940	999	867	3,773
Monmouth [d]	1,508	1,339	1,289	1,295	5,431
Burlington [e]	1,487	1,222	1,190	996	4,895
Gloucester [f]	930	757	782	676	3,145
Salem [g]	1,669	1,391	1,313	1,327	5,700
Cape May	261	219	271	211	962
Hunterdon	1,618	1,230	1,270	1,170	5,288
	12,334 [11,631]	10,725	10,639	9,700	43,388 [42,695]

	NEGROES AND OTHER SLAVES					
	Males over 16	Females over 16	Males under 16	Females under 16	Total Slaves	TOTAL POPULATION
Middlesex	181	124	91	107	503	4,764
Essex	114	114	84	63	375	7,019 [6,326]
Bergen	256	203	187	160	806	4,095
Somersett	255	175	170	132	732	4,505
Monmouth	233	152	129	141	655	6,086
Burlington	134	87	58	64	343	5,238
Gloucester	42	24	32	24	122	3,267
Salem	57	56	40	31	184	5,884
Cape May	12	10	9	11	42	1,004
Hunterdon	75	53	49	42	219	5,507
	1,359	998	849	775	3,981	47,369 [46,676]

Glocester in this table. When no total is given in the source, it has been computed and placed in brackets, as on page 112.

a N.J. Archs., 1st Series, VI, 244.

b Piscataway was estimated at 80 families in 1708: Oldmixon, British Empire, I, 137; at 100 families in 1714, in "Letters from Piscataway Church to S.P.G.," Dally, Woodbridge and Vicinity, 123. Maidenhead or Princeton, in 1708 had about 40 or 50 families: Oldmixon, British Empire, I, 140. Woodbridge in 1692 contained about 150 houses: Randolph to Blathwayt, in Prince Soc. Pub., XXXI, 399; and about 120 families in 1708: Oldmixon, British Empire, I, 137.

c Bergen (town) had 350 inhabitants, mostly Dutch in 1708: Ibid., I, 136.

d Freehold in 1708 had 40 families, and Shrewsbury 160 families: Oldmixon, British Empire, I, 138.

e Burlington (town) had 200 families in 1708: Ibid., I, 140; 100 houses in 1728, according to Rev. Mr. Coxe, in Hills, Hist. Church in Burlington, 239. Lewiston was supposed to comprise 58 families: Watson, Annals of Philadelphia, II, 569.

f Glocester (town) had 100 houses in 1708: Oldmixon, British Empire, I, 140.

g Salem (town) had 18 heads of families in 1678, according to list, in NYCD, XII, 608; 120 families in 1708: Oldmixon, British Empire, I, 139.

III. Census of 1745 [a]

COUNTIES	WHITES				QUAKERS	SLAVES		COUNTY TOTAL
	Males		Females			Males	Females	
	Over 16	Under 16	Over 16	Under 16				
Western Division								
Morris	1,109	1,190	957	1,087	22	57	36	4,436
Hunterdon	2,302	2,182	2,117	2,090	240	244	216	9,151
Burlington [b]	1,786	1,528	1,605	1,454	3,237	233	197	6,803
Gloucester [c]	913	786	797	808	1,436	121	81	3,506
Salem [d]	1,716	1,746	1,603	1,595	1,090	90	97	6,847
Cape May	306	284	272	274	54	30	22	1,188
	8,132	7,716	7,331 [7,351]	7,308	6,079	775	649	31,911 [31,931]
Eastern Division								
Bergen	721	494	590	585	....	379	237	3,006
Essex [e]	1,694	1,652	1,649	1,548	35	244	201	6,988
Middlesex [f]	1,728	1,651	1,659	1,695	400	483	396	7,612
Monmouth	2,071	1,975	1,783	1,899	3,131	513	386	8,627
Somersett	740	765	672	719	91	194	149	3,239
	6,954	6,537	6,353	6,446	3,557 [3,657]	1,813	1,369	29,472
Total, E. and W.	15,086	14,253	13,684 [13,704]	13,754	9,636 [9,736]	2,588	2,018	61,383 [61,403]

FOR NOTES TO THIS TABLE, SEE PAGE 112.

IV. CENSUS OF 1772 [incomplete]

COUNTIES	White Males	White Females	Total Whites		Negro Males	Negro Females	Total Negroes
Sussex b	4,751	4,193	8,944		154	131	285
Hunterdon	7,369	7,141	14,510		586	509	1,095
Burlington c	6,452	5,941	12,393		411	320	731
Gloucester	4,330	4,108	8,438		178	138	316
Salem	2,909	2,753	5,662		169	129	298
Cumberland	2,615	2,334	4,947	[4,949]	66	44	110
Cape May	886	762	1,648		59	52	111
Morris d	5,944	5,224	11,168		211	156	367
	[35,256]	[32,456]	67,710		[1,834]	[1,479]	[3,313]
			[67,712]		Total Population [71,025]		

NOTES TO TABLE III. CENSUS OF 1745, PAGE 111.
a N.J. Archs., 1st Series, VI, 242-43. The number of Quakers is omitted in the county totals because they are included in the whites.
b Burlington (town) was estimated at 170 houses by Gov. Belcher: MHSP, 2d Series, IX, 16n; at 130 houses by Acrelius, Desc. of Cond. of Swedish Churches, in Pa. HS Mem., XI, 144; at 200 families by Odell, in Hills, Hist. Church in Burlington, 292. Acrelius estimated Bordentown at 60 houses in 1758.
c Gloucester (town) was estimated by Acrelius (see above) at 30 houses in 1758.
d Salem (town) was estimated by Acrelius (see above) at 120 houses in 1758.
e Elizabeth in 1761 had from 200 to 300 houses: Burnaby, Travels, 75. Essex County had 1,122 freeholders in 1755: List taken from Office of Clerk of Supreme Court at Trenton, in N.J. HSP, 2d Series, XIII, 29-34.
f Middlesex County in 1750 had 550 freeholders; and 594 freeholders in 1752: N.J. HSP, 2d Series, XIII, 91-94; 3d Series, I, 105-9. New Brunswick in 1760 had 100 houses; Perth Amboy, 100 houses; Trenton, 100 houses: Burnaby, Travels, 73-75. Acrelius estimated Trenton at 130 houses in 1758: Acrelius, Desc. Of Cond. of Swedish Churches, in Pa. HS Mem., XI, 144.

NOTES TO TABLE IV. CENSUS OF 1772.
a Found in N.J. Archs., 1st Series, X, 452. Returns are missing for Waterford Town, Bergen, Essex, Somerset, Middlesex, and Monmouth counties. Newark in 1777 had about 141 houses: Atkinson, Hist. of Newark, 112; Mellick, Story of an Old Farm, 303. In Middlesex County, Perth Amboy had 200 houses in 1776-77: Anon., Hist. North Am., 116; Journals of Nicholas Cresswell, 242. Princeton had 60 to 80 houses in 1780: Chastellux, Travels, I, 160. Trenton had 185 houses in 1785: Webster, in N.Y. Directory for 1786, 22. Windsor Township had 1,918 persons according to a census of 1772: "Newspaper Extracts," in N.J. Archs., XXVIII, 324-25.
b Sussex County in 1770 was estimated to contain 1,500 families by Dr. Chandler, in Clark, Hist. St. John's Church, Elizabethtown, 143. In 1728 the county had about 1,750 families besides 241 Negroes: Watson, Annals of Philadelphia, II, 569.
c Bordentown in 1774 was estimated at 20 or 25 dwelling houses by Col. Harvey, in Vt. HSP, 1921, 23, 227.
d Ringwood in 1780 contained about 7 or 8 houses "in the hamlet formed by Mrs. Erskine's manor and the iron forges": Chastellux, Travels, I, 346.

V. CENSUS OF 1784 [a]

Counties	Inhabitants	Counties	Inhabitants
Bergen	9,356	Middlesex	12,005
Burlington	15,801	Monmouth	14,708
Cape May	2,231	Morris	13,416
Cumberland	6,300	Salem	8,473
Essex	13,430	Somerset	10,476
Gloucester	10,689	Sussex	14,187
Hunterdon	18,363		
		Total	149,435

VI. CENSUS OF 1790 [b]

Counties	Inhabitants
Bergen	12,601
Burlington	18,095
Cape May	2,571
Cumberland	8,248
Essex	17,785
Gloucester	13,363
Hunterdon	20,153
Middlesex	15,956
Monmouth	16,918
Morris	16,216
Salem	10,437
Somerset	12,296
Sussex	19,500
Total	184,139

PENNSYLVANIA [1]

GENERAL

1681 500 souls. Stone, "Founding of Pa.," in Winsor, *Narr. Crit. Hist.*, III, 480.

1682 3,000 inhabitants. Belknap, *Amer. Biog.*, II, 409.

1683 4,000 souls in the 6 counties: Philadelphia, Buckingham, Chester, New Castle, Kent, and Sussex.[2] Letter from Wm. Penn, Aug. 16, 1683, in Proud, *Hist. of Pa.*, I, 261.

1685 8,200 persons.[3] Penn, "A Further Acct. of the Prov. of Pa.," *Pa. Mag. Hist.*, IX, 65.

a New Jersey: *Compendium of Censuses, 1726-1905*, 41.

b New Jersey: *Compendium of Censuses, 1726-1905*, 41.

[1] In some instances it is uncertain whether estimates for Pennsylvania include the lower counties of Delaware.

[2] Newcastle, Kent, and Sussex are the Del. counties.

[3] Dexter uses this figure from Winsor; Rossiter also uses it.

1688   12,000 inhabitants in Pa. and Del. *See* Thirteen Colonies: General, 1688.

1689   12,000 inhabitants. Bancroft, I, 608.

1693   2,000 men able to bear arms. *See* Thirteen Colonies: General, 1693. See page 117.

1698   20,000 Christians, young and old. Thomas, *Hist. and Geog. Acct. of Pa.*, 37-38.

1699   7,000 men capable to bear arms. Col. Quary to BT in CSPC, 1699, 266, No. 483.

       2,000 freemen. *See* Thirteen Colonies: General, 1699.

1700   80,000 population in N.Y., the Jerseys, Pa., Del., and Md. *See* Thirteen Colonies: General, 1700.

1701   10,000 persons. Humphreys, S.P.G., 31.

       20,000 souls. Quoting Col. Heathcote,[4] *ibid.*, 42.

       20,000 total population; or 15,000. *See* Thirteen Colonies: General, 1701.

1708   10,000 effective men. Col. Quary to BT, Jan. 10, 1708, in CSPC, 1706-8, 636, No. 1273.

       35,000 souls; 6,000 Indians. Oldmixon, *British Empire*, I, 161-80.

1715   45,800 total population: 43,300 whites; 2,500 Negroes. *See* Thirteen Colonies: General, 1715.

1721   60,000 whites and 5,000 blacks. Col. Hart, Ans. Quer., 1720, *Proprieties, R*: 7, Vol. XI, in HSPT; also in Repr. BT to King, Sept. 8, 1721, *Kings MS.*, 205, fol. 17, p. 29, in LCT; and in NYCD, V, 604. Cf. page 117.

1722   40,000 souls with few blacks. Sir Wm. Keith to BT, Dec. 18, 1722, in *Proprieties R*: 42, Vol. XI, in HSPT.

1724   100,000 inhabitants, French, Welsh, Swedes, Dutch, and Germans. Letter by Christopher Sower, in *Pa. Mag. Hist.*, XLV, 249.

1726   15,000 inhabitants. *See* Thirteen Colonies: General, 1726.

1730   45,000 whites and 4,000 blacks.[5] Lt. Gov. Gordon, Ans. Quer., 1731, in *Kings MS.*, 205, fol. 244, pp. 496-97, in LCT.

1731   9-10,000 taxables. Proud, *Hist. of Pa.*, II, 275.

1733   80,000 inhabitants. "Acct. of the Establ't. of Col. of Ga.," in Force, *Tracts*, Vol. I, Tract II, 7.

1740   100,000 population. Stillé, in *Pa. Mag. Hist.*, X, 284-85.

       50,000 militia in Pa. and the lower counties. *See* Thirteen Colonies: General, 1740. Cf. page 117.

1747   120,000 inhabitants of which 3/5 were Germans, acccording to Gov. Thomas. Diffenderffer, *German Immig. into Pa.*, 100.

---

[4] Dexter quotes the Heathcote figure, and Rossiter uses it for 1700.

[5] Chalmers cites this figure for 1732. Dexter gives it also for 1730 from *Brit. Mus. Add. MSS.*, 30,372, but his own estimate for 1730 is 69,000 for Pa. and Del. Rossiter gives 69,000 for 1731, and thinks Gov. Gordon's estimate probably too small.

1749 250,000 in Pa. and Del. *See* Thirteen Colonies: General, 1749.

1751 190,000 total population according to Michael Schlatter, missionary and organizer in the Reformed Church. Diffenderffer, *German Immig. into Pa.*, 101.

200,000 inhabitants. Mittelberger, *Journey to Pa.*, 107.

1752 21,200 taxables. Hazard, *Reg. of Pa.*, IV, 12. Cf. page 117.[6]

1754 195,000 white inhabitants; 11,000 black, including Delaware. Bancroft, II, 389-91.[7]

400,000 to 500,000 inhabitants.[8] Shirley, to Earl of Holderness, Jan. 7, 1754, in *Shirley Corr.*, II, 20-21.

1755 300,000 inhabitants. Gov. Morris to Gen. Braddock, in *Pa.* CR, VI, 336.

220,000 white inhabitants, of whom 100,000 are Germans and other foreign Protestants.[9] Rept. of BT, in NYCD, VI, 993; also in Anon., *State of British and French Colonies in North Am.*, 1755, 135-37.

220,000 whites; or 360,000 including Del. *Sec* Thirteen Colonies: General, 1755.

1757 200,000 inhabitants, of whom 30,000 capable of bearing arms. Rev. Mr. Peters to Lord Loudoun,[10] in *Pa.* CR, VII, 448.

20,000 houses in the province, including those in the towns and on plantations. Rept. of Committee, in *Pa. Votes and Proc.*, IV, 692.

1759 250,000 souls in Pa. Dr. William Smith to the Archbishop of Canterbury, in Rush, *Acct. of Manners of German Inhabs. of Pa.* (ed. T. E. Schmank); also in *Pa. German Soc. Proc.*, XIX, 42; and in NYCD, VII, 407.

1760 31,673 taxables.[11] *Pa. Votes and Proc.*, V, 120; also in *Pa.* CR, XIV, 336. See page 117.

1761 250,000 souls. Burke, *European Settlements*, II, 199.

400,000 to 500,000 inhabitants. Appendix footnote says the population may not have amounted to more than 350,000. Burnaby, *Travels*, 63.

1765 400,000 inhabitants; 100,000 men, in Pa. and Del. *See* Thirteen Colonies: General, 1765.

[6] Dexter quotes Proud, *Hist. of Pa.*, II, 275, and both he and Rossiter estimate 150,000 for 1750.

[7] Dexter thinks Bancroft's figures are too high.

[8] Shirley's estimate of 400,000 to 500,000 is a palpable exaggeration; he was protesting against the military levy which he thought had been made too high for Mass. and too low for Pa.

[9] Fernow, "The Middle Colonies," in Winsor, *Narr. Crit. Hist.*, V, 216.

[10] Mr. Peters also says "The inhabitants have never been numbered, but it is believed by good Judges that they amount to, etc."

[11] Dexter quotes this figure. Rossiter says 220,000 people.

1766 150,000 white people, and 30,000 blacks. Anon., *Hist. of North Am.*, 121.

160,000 white inhabitants, of whom 1/3 are Quakers and perhaps another third Germans.[12] Franklin, "Examination before the House of Commons," in *Writings* (Smyth), IV, 415-16.

1769 230,000 people. D'Auberteuil, *Essais historiques et politiques*, 25.

1770 39,665 taxables. *Pa.* CR, XIV, 336. See page 117. Cf. Proud, *Hist. of Pa.*, II, 276.

250,000 population. Proud, *Hist. of Pa.*, II, 275; Wynne, *Hist. British Empire in Am.*, I, 219.

1774 300,000 inhabitants, of which 1/3 are blacks.[13] Smyth, *Tour of the U.S.*, II, 309.

350,000 population including Del., by a Congressional estimate. 300,000 in Pa.;[14] or 350,000 in Pa. and Del. *See* Thirteen Colonies: General, 1774.

1775 302,000 souls, of whom 300,000 are whites and 2,000 blacks. Gov. Penn, Ans. Quer., Jan. 30, 1775, in *Pa. Archs.*, 1st Series, IV, 597. Cf. *Chalmers Coll., Pa.*, II. NYPL.

300,000 total population. *See* Thirteen Colonies: General, 1775.

1779 54,683 taxables, according to list. See page 117. Hazard, *Reg. of Pa.*, IV, 12. Cf. also Table C, page 119.

1780 300,000 population: "Quotas of several states for 1780," by Congress. *Pa. Archs.*, 1st Series, VIII, 473; Cf. Prince de Broglie, in *Mag. Amer. Hist.*, I, Pt. 1, 231.

375,000 inhabitants, men, women, and children. "The Crisis Extraordinary," by Commonsense, from "Newspaper Extracts," in *N.J. Archs.*, 2d Series, V, 60.

1783 320,000 population. *See* Thirteen Colonies: General, 1783.

1786 66,925 taxables. Brissot de Warville, *New Travels*, 326. See page 117 for list. Hazard, *Reg. of Pa.*, IV, 12.

300,000 total inhabitants. *See* Thirteen Colonies: General, 1786.

1787 360,000 total population; or 341,000. *See* Thirteen Colonies: General, 1787.

1790 434,373 total population: free white males over 16, 110,788; free white males under 16, 106,948; free white females, 206,363; other free persons, 6,537; slaves, 3,737. U.S. Bureau of Census, *Heads of Families, Pa.*, 8-11. See page 120.

---

[12] Dexter thinks Franklin was probably too cautious in his estimate.
[13] Smyth thinks the Congressional estimate overrated about 50,000 or more.
[14] Cf. *North Am. and W. Ind. Gazetteer*, under "Pa."

I. LISTS OF TAXABLES

LOCAL

A. TAXABLES FOR 1693 TO 1751 a

Counties	1693	1720	1740		1749		1751
Philadelphia b	712 b	1,995	4,850		....		7,100
Bucks c	...	....	....		....		3,012
Chester d	...	....	3,007	[1742]	3,444	[1747]	3,951
Lancaster e	...	205 e	2,560	[1738]	4,598		3,977
York f	...	....	....		1,466		2,043
Cumberland	...	....	....		807		1,134

[21,217] g

B. TAXABLES FOR 1760 TO 1786

Counties	1760 h	1770 h	1779 h	1786 h	
Philadelphia	8,321 i	10,455	10,747 p	9,392	
Bucks	3,148 j	3,177	4,067 q	4,273	
Chester	4,761 k	5,483	6,378	6,286	
Lancaster	5,635 l	6,608	8,433 r	5,839	
York	3,302 m	4,426	6,281 s	6,254	
Cumberland	1,501	3,521	5,092	3,939	
Berks	3,016 n	3,302	4,662 t	4,732	
Northampton	1,989 o	2,793	3,600 u	3,967	
Bedford	....	....	1,201	2,632	
Northumberland	....	....	2,111	2,166	
Westmoreland	....	....	2,111	2,653	[1,773]
Washington	....	....	....	3,908	
Fayette	....	....	....	2,041	
Franklin	....	....	....	2,237	
Montgomery	....	....	....	3,725	
Dauphin	....	....	....	2,881	
	[31,673]	39,665 [39,765]	[54,683]	66,925	

a Pa. Votes and Proc., IV, 226.
b Taxables for 1693 are found in Pa. Mag. Hist., VIII, 85-105. The town of Philadelphia was estimated by Penn to have 80 houses and 300 "farmers" in July, 1683; and 150 houses with 500 farmers by the next Dec.: Pa. Archs., I, 69; Pa. HS Mem., I, 446; 300 houses and 2,500 inhabitants in 1684: Proud, Hist. of Pa., I, 288n; 600 houses in 1686: Penn, "Acct. of Province," in Pa. Mag. Hist., IX, 74; 1,400 houses in 1690: Morris, in Pa. Mag. Hist., IV, 200; 12,000 inhabitants in 1697: Journal of BT, Nov., 1, 1697, in HSPT, X, 333; 2,000 houses in 1698: Thomas, Hist. and Geog. Acct of Pa., 5, 37; 1,200 houses in 1708: Oldmixon, British Empire, I, 151; 10,000 souls in 1722: Gov. Keith to BT, Proprieties R: 42, Vol. XI, in HSPT; 2,400 houses and 12,000 souls in 1731: Holmes, Annals, I, 551; 1,621 taxables, 1,097 voters, and 8,000 souls in 1735: Mellick, Story of an Old Farm, 51; 1,700 houses and 10,000 inhabitants according to Gov. Thomas in 1740-41: Chalmers Coll., R.I., 33, NYPL; 1,500 houses and 13,000 people according to Sec'y Peters in 1744: Watson, Annals of Phila., II, 404;

10,000 people in *1746*: Kalm, *Travels*, I, 57; 2,076 houses and 16,000 population in *1749*; 2,300 houses and 18,000 population in *1753*: Pownall, *Memorial*, 61; 14,563 inhabitants in *1753*: Watson, *Annals of Phila.*, III, 237; 20,000 inhabitants in *1755*: Pownall, "Desc. of Streets and Main Roads about Phila.," in *Pa. Mag. Hist.*, XVIII, 212.

c Bristol had 50 houses in *1708*: Oldmixon, *British Empire*, I, 175.

d Chester (town) had 200 families in *1708*; Newton had 20 or 30 houses; Radnor had 50 families: Oldmixon, *British Empire*, I, 154, 177. Chester County had 2,157 taxables in *1732*; 2,532 in *1737*: *Pa. Votes and Proc.*, IV, 226.

e The county had 41 English and 87 German taxables in *1718*; 176 taxables in *1719*; 237 taxables in *1721*; 350 in *1724*; 384 in *1725*: Eshleman, "Assessment List," in *Lancaster Co. Hist. Soc. Papers*, XX, 160-94. Lancaster (town) had 311 taxables in *1751*: *Pa. Votes and Proc.*, IV, 226.

f York (town) had 63 houses in *1749*; and 210 in *1754*: Stevenson and Peters, in *Pa. Archs.*, 2d Series, VII, 247.

g In this and the following tables for Pa., totals of columns are given as found in the source cited. When no total is given in the source, it has been computed and placed in brackets, as here. When the total given is incorrect, the true sum has been presented in brackets beside that found in the source used, as in table B.

h *1760*: *Pa. Votes and Proc.*, V, 120; *1770*: *Pa.* CR, XIV, 336; *1779*: Hazard, *Reg. of Pa.*, IV, 12; *1785*: *Ibid.*, IV, 12. Cf. Miss Stella Sutherland's list, C below.

i Philadelphia city in *1760* was estimated at 18,000 or 20,000 inhabitants: Burnaby, *Travels*, 59; 2,969 houses and about 31,318 population: Pownall, *Memorial*, 61; 2,960 houses and 18,756 inhabitants: Mease, *Picture of Phila.*, 31. In *1769* it had 4,474 houses; and Pownall estimated 35,000 population; *Memorial*, 61; but Mease gives 28,042: *Picture of Phila.*, 31. Germantown had 350 houses in *1758* according to Acrelius, "Desc. of Cond. of Swedish Churches," in *Pa. HS Mem.*, XI, 143; 300 houses in *1760* according to Rev. Mr. Mill, in Perry, *Hist. Colls. Re. Am. Col. Church*, II, 287; or 500 houses in *1760*: Burnaby, *Travels*, 62.

j Bristol in *1758* had 90 houses: Acrelius, "Desc. of Cond. of Swedish Churches," in *Pa. HS Mem.*, XI, 143.

k Chester (town) had 120 houses in *1758*: Acrelius, "Desc. of Cond. of Swedish Churches," in *Pa. HS Mem.*, XI, 143; 30 odd families in *1760*: Mr. Craig to S.P.G., in Perry, *Hist. Colls. Re. Am. Col. Church*, II, 290.

l Lancaster (town) had about 500 houses from *1755* to *1760*: Pownall, "Desc. of Streets and Main Roads about Phila.," in *Pa. Mag. Hist.*, XVIII, 212; Acrelius, "Desc. of Cond. of Swedish Churches," in *Pa. HS Mem.*, XI, 143; Burnaby, *Travels*, 62; 600 houses in *1764*: Mr. Barton to S.P.G., in Perry, *Hist. Colls. Re. Am. Col. Church*, II, 315, 369.

m York (town) had 190 houses in *1758*: Acrelius, "Desc. of Cond. of Swedish Churches," in *Pa. HS Mem.*, XI, 143.

n Maxatawney Township contained 119 taxables in *1757*: Levan, "Maxatawney Prior to 1800," in *Pa. German Soc. Proc.*, IV, 79. Reading in *1752* had 130 dwelling houses, 106 families consisting of 378 persons: *Pa. Votes and Proc.*, IV, 204; 210 families in *1763*, or about 1,300 persons: Mr. Murray to S.P.G., in Perry, *Hist. Colls. Re. Am. Col. Church*, II, 346.

o Bethlehem had 898 white inhabitants and 82 Indians in *1756*: in *Pa. Archs.*, III, 52-53, 70-76.

p Philadelphia city had 5,470 houses and 21,767 inhabitants, exclusive of army and strangers, in *1777* by census taken for Gen. Cornwallis: Watson, *Annals of Phila.*, II, 407. Capt. Montresor noted 35,000 total inhabitants, 23,000 being in the city, 2,000 in the suburbs, and 10,000 in the Liberties: "Journal," in *Pa. Mag. Hist.*, V, 414. In *1783* the city had 6,000 houses: Watson, *Annals of Phila.*, III, 238. Rossiter estimates 37,800 population: *Cent. Pop. Growth*. In *1786* there were 4,500 houses: Webster, *N.Y. Directory for 1786*, 22.

q Buckingham had 173 dwellings in *1787*, 1,173 whites and 13 black inhabitants, according to enumeration: Watson, "Acct of Buckingham and Solebury," in *Pa. HS Mem.*, I, 288. Solebury in *1787* had 166 dwellings, 928 white and no black inhabitants: *Ibid.*

I. LISTS OF TAXABLES — *Continued*

C. TAXABLES FOR 1772-83 [v]

Counties	Date		
Bedford	1779 1555 taxables;	102 single freemen; 28 Negroes [w]	
Berks	1779 4415 taxables;	661 freemen; 164 Negroes [x]	
Bucks	1779 3467 taxables;	634 single men; 479 servants [y]	
Chester	1779 3609 taxables; 1215 freemen; 1433 inmates; 303 servants [z]		
Cumberland	1779 4539 taxables;	935 freemen; 649 Negroes [aa]	
Lancaster	1779 6710 taxables; 1107 freemen; 387 inmates; 439 Negroes [ab]		
Northampton	1772 2432 taxables;	234 freemen [ac]	
Philadelphia			
Without the city	1779 7437 taxables [ad]		
Philadelphia city	1779 4102 taxables [ad]		
Northumberland	1778-80 1397 taxables [ae]		
Washington	1781 2722 taxables;	570 single men; 448 Negroes [af]	
Westmoreland	1783 2596 taxables;	183 single men [ag]	
York	1779 5946 taxables;	570 single men; 448 Negroes [ah]	

r The county contained 807 Negro slaves in *1780*: Clark, "Lancaster's Relation to Slavery," in *Lancaster Co. Hist. Soc. Hist. Papers*, XV, 53. Lancaster (town) in *1786* had 678 houses and 4,000 inhabitants: Landis, "Lancaster Houses," *ibid.*, XXVI, 136. Harrisburg in *1788* had 100 houses: "Journals of Rev. Mr. Cutler," in N.J. HSP, 2d Series, III, 78.

s York (town) was estimated at 2,000 to 3,000 inhabitants in *1777* by Anburey, *Travels*, II, 274; and in *1783* by Smyth, *Tour in U.S.*, II, 279.

t Reading had 400 houses in *1777*: Watson, *Memoirs*, 39.

u Bethlehem had 600 souls in *1777*: "Wm. Whipple's Journey to N.H.," in *Pa. Mag. Hist.*, X, 368; 36 dwelling houses and about 61 families in *1780*: John Ettwein to Lewis Weiss, in *Pa. Mag. Hist.*, II, 155. Easton contained 60 or 70 dwelling houses in *1777*: "Acct of Wm. Whipple's Journey to N.H.," in *Pa. Mag. Hist.*, X, 369.

v Volumes XII-XXII of the *Pennsylvania Archives*, 3d Series, contain tax lists for varying dates. The table given above represents an attempt to count the taxables for the year 1779 (the lists for that year are most complete) or as near that date as possible. This calculation was supplied by Miss Stella Sutherland.

w *Penn. Archives*, III, Vol. XXII, pp. 157-201.

x *Ibid.*, Vol. XVIII, pp. 175-301.

y *Ibid.*, Vol. XIII, pp. 3-111.

z *Ibid.*, Vol. XII, pp. 127-225.

aa *Ibid.*, Vol. XX, pp. 117-248.

ab *Ibid.*, Vol. XVII, pp. 489-685.

ac *Ibid.*, Vol. XIX, pp. 5-78.

ad *Ibid.*, Vol. XIV, pp. 471-743.

ae *Ibid.*, Vol. XIX, pp. 405-38.

af *Ibid.*, Vol. XXII, pp. 699-782.

ag *Ibid.*, Vol. XXII, pp. 369-453.

ah *Ibid.*, Vol. XXI, pp. 3-164.

120 DELAWARE

II. Census of 1790 [a]

| COUNTIES | FREE WHITES | | | OTHER FREE | SLAVES | TOTAL |
| | Males | | Females | | | |
	Over 16	Under 16				
Alleghany	2,636	2,743	4,772	12	159	10,322
Bedford	2,887	3,841	6,316	34	46	13,124
Berks	7,714	7,551	14,648	201	65	30,179
Bucks	6,575	5,947	12,037	581	261	25,401
Chester	7,489	6,596	13,166	543	145	27,939
Cumberland	4,821	4,537	8,456	206	223	18,243
Dauphin	4,908	4,622	9,179	57	238	19,004
Delaware	2,532	2,112	4,489	289	50	9,472
Fayette	3,425	3,416	6,154	48	282	13,325
Franklin	4,022	3,860	7,170	273	330	15,655
Huntingdon	1,872	2,089	3,537	24	43	7,565
Lancaster	9,713	8,070	17,471	545	348	36,147
Luzerne	1,236	1,331	2,313	13	11	4,904
Mifflin	1,954	1,949	3,558	42	59	7,562
Montgomery	6,001	5,385	10,985	441	113	22,925
Northampton	6,013	6,405	11,646	133	23	24,220
Northumberland	4,191	4,726	8,046	109	89	17,161
Philadelphia	14,486	10,845	26,520	2,101	384	54,336
Washington	5,327	7,291	11,006	12	265	23,901
Westmoreland	4,013	4,355	7,483	39	128	16,018
York	9,213	9,527	17,671	837	499	37,747
Total	110,788	106,948	206,363	6,537	3,737	434,373
	[111,028]	[107,198]	[206,623]	[6,540]	[3,761]	[435,150]

DELAWARE
GENERAL

Delaware Settlements to 1682

1644 105 male inhabitants in New Sweden. From list of Gov. Printz, in Johnson, *Swedish Settlements*, II, 70-710.
1648 83 male inhabitants. *Ibid.*, 710-15.
1653 200 souls, including women and children. Quoted from a letter of Gov. Printz, by Keen, "New Sweden, or Swedes on the Del.," in Winsor, *Narr. and Crit. Hist.*, IV, 469.
1655 220 male inhabitants, including officers, soldiers, servants, and freemen. From Rising's Journal, Doc. XII, and Pvt. Letters, in Johnson, *Swedish Settlements*, II, 716-22.
1671 130 persons on the quit-rent list. NYCD, XII, 490-92.

a U.S. Bureau of Census, *Heads of Families, Pa.*, 8-11.

1677   443 total tithables: 136 tithables, list in Upland Court Recds., in
       Pa. HS Mem., VII, 77-80; 307 tithables, list of tithables living in
       the jurisdiction of the Court of New Castle on the West Shore of
       the Delaware, Recds. of the Court of New Castle, in *Pa. Mag.
       Hist.*, III, 352-54.

1680   201 families, according to detailed local census of persons residing
       on the Delaware River. List in NYCD, XXII, 646-49.

Delaware Counties

1687   314 taxables. List, in Scharf, *Hist. of Del.*, I, 154.

1688   12,000 inhabitants in Pa. and Del. *See* Thirteen Colonies: General,
       1688.

1693   942 persons; 188 Swedish families. Acrelius, "Desc. of Cond. of
       Swedish Churches," in *Pa. HS Mem.*, XI, 190-93.

       931 individuals, and 139 families. Watson, *Annals of Phila.*, II, 230-
       32.[1]

1734   70,000 inhabitants in the three Lower Counties. Petition of R.
       Penn, in *Acts of Privy Council*, Unbound Papers, 234, 439.

1775   30,000 total population. *See* Thirteen Colonies: General, 1775.

       For taxables for Kent and Sussex counties in 1774, and 1784, and
       inhabitants by the census of 1782, see page below.

1783   35,000 population. *See* Thirteen Colonies: General, 1783.

1785   37,000 inhabitants. Webster, in *N.Y. Directory for 1786*, 21.

1786   50,000 population. *See* Thirteen Colonies: General, 1786.

1787   37,000 population. *See* Thirteen Colonies: General, 1787.

1790   59,096 total inhabitants: free white males over 16, 11,783; free
       white males under 16, 12,143; free white females, 22,384; other
       free persons, 3,899; slaves, 8,887. U. S. Bureau of Census, *Heads
       of Families, Pa.*, 8.

LOCAL

Counties	1774 [a] Taxables	1784 [a] Taxables	1782 [a] Census
Kent	1,642	1,827	9,782
Sussex	2,636	2,926	12,660

Christina Bridge

1758   70 or 80 houses. Acrelius, "Desc. of Cond. of Swedish Churches," in
       Pa. HS Mem., XI, 144.

[a] The *1774* taxables, the census for *1782*, and the *1784* taxables are taken from unpublished manuscripts in the State House in Dover, Delaware. No lists are available for
Newcastle. These lists were supplied by Miss Stella Sutherland.

[1] Watson cities no authority for his list, but states that the census was taken for
William Penn.

Dover

1722   40 families. Humphreys, S.P.G., 166.

1733   15 or 16 families. Mr. Frazer to S.P.G., in Perry, *Hist. Colls. Re.
           Am. Col. Church,* V, 70.

1758   100 houses. Acrelius, "Desc. of Cond. of Swedish Churches," in *Pa.
           HS Mem.,* XI, 144.

1776   50 families. *North Am. and W. Ind. Gazetteer,* under "Dover."

Horekill

1671   47 souls. List, in NYCD, XII, 522.

1675   8 males. (Probably only freeholders included.) List in *ibid.,* XII,
           589.

Kent County

1751   1,320 taxables. Mr. Neill to S.P.G., *ibid.,* V, 97.

1759   7,000 population. Hawkins, *Missions of the Church of England,* 324,
           citing *Journal of S.P.G.,* Vol. XV, 279.

1760   1,500 taxables, which "are not more than one-third of the souls."
           Mr. Inglis' Acct. in Perry, *Hist. Colls. Re. Am. Col. Church,* II,
           313.

1785   2,022 taxables: St. Jones' Hundred and East Dover, lying east of
           St. Jones' River, 114; Duck Creek Hundred, 309; Little Creek
           Hundred, 180; Kenton Hundred, 129; North and South Murder-
           kill, West Dover, and East Dover lying west of St. Jones' Creek,
           769; Mispillion Hundred, 521. Lists in Scharf, *Hist. of Del.,*
           II, 1086, 1095-96, 1118-19, 1124-25, 1145-47, 1175-77.

Lewis-Town

1758   100 houses, inhabitants mostly pilots. Acrelius, "Desc. of Cond. of
           Swedish Churches," in *Pa. HS Mem.,* XI, 144.

New Amstel (New Castle)

1657   60 men capable of bearing arms. Vice-Director Alrichs to Com-
           missioners of the Colonies on the Delaware, in NYCD, II, 16.
           20 families, mostly Swedes, not more than 5 or 6 families belong
           to our nation (Dutch). Letter from Evert Pieterson, in *N.Y. Eccl.
           Recds.,* I, 401.

1659   30 families. Letter from Stuyvesant, Sept. 17, 1659, in NYCD, XII,
           254.

1675   17 males. (Probably only freeholders included.) List in *ibid.,* XII,
           589.

Newcastle

1705   2,500 population. Hawkins, *Hist. Notices,* 118; also Humphreys,
           S.P.G., 163.

1728   2,500 souls. Holmes, *Annals*, I, 543.
1758   240 houses. Acrelius, "Desc. of Cond. of Swedish Churches," in
       Pa. HS Mem., XI, 144.
1760   100 houses. Burnaby, *Travels*, 57.
1785   5,000 to 6,000 houses. Mandrillon, *Le Spectateur américain*, 264.

Newcastle County

1787   1,997 taxables: Christiana Hundred, 875; Brandywine Hundred,
       330; Red Lion Hundred, 126; Appoquinimunk Hundred, 477;
       New Castle Hundred, 189. Lists, in Scharf, *Hist. of Del.*, II, 639,
       851-52, 902, 966, 1018-20.

Newport

1758   70 or 80 houses. Acrelius, "Desc. of Cond. of Swedish Churches," in
       Pa. HS Mem., XI, 144.

Sussex County

1785   2,787 taxables: Lewis and Rehoboth Hundred, 176; Cedar Creek
       Hundred, 392; Broadkiln Hundred, 429; Indian River Hundred,
       253; North West Fork Hundred, 334; Broad Creek Hundred,
       222; Nantichoke Hundred, 209; Little Creek Hundred, 299;
       Dagsborough Hundred, 204; Baltimore Hundred, 269. Lists, in
       Scharf, *Hist. of Del.*, II, 1216-17, 1250-51, 1258-59, 1271-72,
       1279-80, 1287, 1296-97, 1317-18, 1336-37, 1341.

Wilmington

1739   610 inhabitants. Scharf, *Hist. of Del.*, II, 639.
1758   260 houses. Acrelius, "Desc. of Cond. of Swedish Churches," in
       Pa. HS Mem., XI, 144.
1775   1,172 white; 57 colored inhabitants. Scharf, *Hist. of Del.*, II, 639.
1785   400 houses. Webster, in *N.Y. Directory for 1786*, 22.

MARYLAND

GENERAL

1633   200 English. Humphreys, S.P.G., 28.
1642   207 tithables: St. Mary's Hundred, 28; Kent County, 70; St.
       George's Hundred, 30; St. Clement's Hundred, 20; St. Michael's
       Hundred, 45; Mattapanian, 14. Assembly Proc., *Md. Archs.*, I,
       142-46.
1660   8,000 English. Fuller, *Worthies of Eng.*, III, 418; Bancroft, I, 176.
1665   16,000 inhabitants. Oldmixon, *British Empire*, I, 191.[1]
1675   6,610 tithables: St. Mary's County, 924; Kent County, 300; Ann
       Arundel County, 816; Calvert County, 1,091; Charles County,

---

[1] Dexter thinks this figure too high.

124   MARYLAND

785; Talbott County, 1,018; Baltimore County, 319; Dorchester County, 355; Somersett County, 603; Cecil County, 399. Council Proc., *Md. Archs.*, XV, 50-54.

1676 20,000 souls. Letter from Rev. Mr. Yeo, 1676, from MSS. in State Paper Office, in Anderson, *Hist. of Church of Eng. in Am.*, II, 395.[2]

1688 25,000 inhabitants. *See* Thirteen Colonies: General, 1688.

1690 10,400 taxables. Gov. Seymour, Ans. Quer., June 23, 1708, in CSPC, 1706-8, 758, No. 1570.

1693 4,000 men able to bear arms. *See* Thirteen Colonies: General, 1693.

1694 9,847 taxables. CSPC, 1696-97, 425, No. 864.

9,747 taxables. See page 127. List in Council Proc., *Md. Archs.*, XXV, 255.

1695 10,390 taxables. See page 127. List in Council Proc., *Md. Archs.*, XXV, 255; also total in CSPC, 1696-97, 425, No. 864.

1696 10,381 taxables. See page 127. List in Council Proc., *Md. Archs.*, XXV, 255: total also in CSPC, 1696-97, 425, No. 864.

1697 10,516 taxables. See page 127. CSPC, 1696-97, 424, No. 864.

11,030 taxables, including Prince George's Co., 514 taxables. Council Proc., *Md. Archs.*, XXIII, 92.

1699 3,000 freemen. *See* Thirteen Colonies: General, 1699.

1701 32,258 total inhabitants: 12,214 taxables, 20,044 untaxables. CSPC, 1701, 152, No. 314 ii; also in Council Proc., *Md. Archs.*, XXV, 255; see page 128.

25,000 population. *See* Thirteen Colonies: General, 1701.

1704 34,912 total population. Gov. Seymour to BT, in CSPC, 1704-5, 553, No. 1210, iii; also in Council Proc., *Md. Archs.*, XXV, 256. For list by counties, see page 128. Also in Repr. BT, Sept. 8, 1721, *Kings MS.*, 205, fol. 18, pp. 31-32, in LCT; and NYCD, V, 605.

1707 33,833 [33,883] souls, white and black, viz.: Christian men, 7,090; Christian women, 6,325; children, 12,808; white servants, 3,003; slaves, 4,657. Gov. Seymour, Ans. Quer., June 23, 1708, in CSPC, 1706-8, 758, No. 1570; also in Council Proc., *Md. Archs.*, XXV, 258.

1710 42,741 total inhabitants: 34,796 whites; 7,945 Negroes. CSPC, 1710-11, 252, No. 474 i; see page 128; Council Proc., *Md. Archs.*, XXV, 258-59; Repr. BT to King, Sept. 8, 1721, *Kings MS.*, 205, fol. 18, pp. 31-32, in LCT. Cf. NYCD, V, 604.

1712 46,151 total inhabitants according to census. See page 129. Council

[2] Dexter quotes this but thinks it too high. However, it accords well with the preceding figure of 6,610 tithables.

Proc., *Md. Archs.*, XXV, 259. Also in *Chalmers Coll.*, Md., I. NYPL, and in CSPC, 1712-14, 8, No. 11.

1715 50,270 inhabitants: 40,740 whites, 9,530 slaves. Board's Ans. Quer., Sept., 1721, *Chalmers Coll.*, Md., I, NYPL. 50,200 total population: 40,700 whites; 9,500 blacks. *See* Thirteen Colonies: General, 1715.

1719 80,000 inhabitants: 55,000 whites; 25,000 blacks. Repr. BT to King, Sept. 8, 1721, *Kings MS.*, 205, fol. 18, pp. 31-32, in LCT; and in NYCD, V, 605. Also in *Chalmers Coll.*, Md., I. NYPL.

1721 8,000 militia. Repr. BT to King, Sept. 8, 1721, *Kings MS.*, 205, fol. 18, pp. 31-32, in LCT; also in NYCD, V, 605.

1724 4,642 families, plus 1,400 taxables. (3 parishes omitted.) See page 129. Ans. Quer. by parishes, in Perry, *Hist. Colls. Re. Am. Col. Church*, IV, 190-231.

1728- 80,000 souls, whites and Negroes, exclusive of Indians. Benedict
1729 Leonard Calvert to Hearne, March 18, 1728-29, in *Md. Hist. Mag.*, XI, 283.

1729 12,159 taxables, excluding Prince George's parish, unknown. Ans. Three Quer. proposed by the Gov., in *Md. Archs.*, XXVIII, 449-52. See page 129.

1732 96,000 total inhabitants, whereof 21,000 are blacks. Sec'y Janssen to BT, Feb. 23, 1732, in Ass'bly Proc., *Md. Archs.*, XXXVII, 588. Cf. Anon., *State of British and French Colonies in North Am., 1755*, 137.

1733 31,440 tithables. See page 129. List in Council Proc., *Md. Archs.*, XXXVIII, 52-53.

1740 10,000 militia. *See* Thirteen Colonies: General, 1740.

1741 36,000 taxables. Jones to Bishop of London, in Perry, *Hist. Colls. Re. Am. Col. Church*, IV, 323.

1743 50,000 taxables. Ass'bly Proc., *Md. Archs.*, XLII, 660.

1748 130,000 inhabitants: 94,000 whites, 36,000 blacks; 12,000 militia. Gov. Ogle, Ans. Quer., Dec. 21, 1748, in Council Proc., *Md. Archs.*, XXVIII, 469.

1749 Same estimate as for 1748. Gov. Ogle, Ans. Quer., Dec. 19, 1749, *Proprieties V*: 65, (Vol. XVIII), in HSPT. 100,000 white inhabitants with 12,500 militia. Repr. BT, in NYCD, VI, 993. 85,000 inhabitants. *See* Thirteen Colonies: General, 1749.

1754 104,000 white inhabitants; 44,000 blacks. Bancroft, II, 389-91.

1755 153,564, total inhabitants, according to census as follows:

Census	Free	Servants	Convicts	Total
Men	24,058	3,576	1,507	29,141
Women	23,521	1,824	386	25,731

Census	Free	Servants	Convicts	Total
Boys	26,637	1,049	67	27,752 [27,753]
Girls	24,141	422	21	24,584
Whites	98,357	6,870 [6,871] a	1,981	107,208 [107,209]

	Mulattoes	Negroes
Men	739	10,947
Boys, slaves	577	11,054
Boys, free	419	
Women	639	9,007
Girls	1,030	11,103
Useless	188	653
Total	3,592	42,764

Md. Recds., Miscel., 1755-75, 11, in Force, *Transcripts,* (copied from Dr. Ezra Stiles' MSS.) in LCT.

100,000 whites; or 140,000 inhabitants (40,000 Negroes). *See* Thirteen Colonies: General, 1755.

1756　107,963 white inhabitants; 46,225 blacks and mulattoes; 16,500 militia. Gov. Sharpe, Ans. Quer., Aug. 23, 1756, from Correspondence, I, 353, in *Md. Archs.*, VI, 353-54; also in *Md. Archs.*, XXXI, 145-46.

1760　90,000 inhabitants, exclusive of slaves. Burnaby, *Travels*, 53.

1761　114,332 white inhabitants; 49,675 blacks; 18,000 militia. Gov. Sharpe, Ans. Quer., Dec. 21, 1761,[3] in Council Proc., *Md. Archs.*, XXXII, 25.

　　　40,000 whites; and 60,000 blacks. Burke, *European Settlements*, II, 233. Cf. Wynne, *Hist. Brit. Empire in Am.*, I, 241.

1765　720,000 inhabitants in Va. and Md., 180,000 men. *See* Thirteen Colonies: General, 1765.

1770　300,000 people D'Auberteuil, *Essais historiques et politiques*, 28.

1774[4]　320,000 total inhabitants; or 220,000; or 114,332. *See* Thirteen Colonies: General, 1774.

1775　74,350 taxables. See page 131. Perry, *Hist. Colls. Re. Am. Col. Church*, IV, 343-45.

a In this and the following tables for Md., totals of columns are given as found in the source cited. When the total given was incorrect, the true sum has been presented in brackets beside that found in the source, as here. When no total was given in the source, it was computed and placed in brackets; see page 131.

[3] Sharpe gave the same figures in his Ans. Quer., Jan. 14, 1762 (see *Kings MS.*, 205, fol. 251, in LCT; and *Proprieties X*: 8, Vol. XXI, in HSPT); and in a letter to Calvert, June, 1763 (Sharpe Correspondence, III, 92, in *Md. Archs.*, XIV, 92).

[4] See also table on page 131 giving taxables for counties at various dates between 1766 and 1774.

250,000 total population. *See* Thirteen Colonies: General, 1775.
1782 254,050 total inhabitants: 170,688 whites; 83,362 Negro slaves. Morse, *American Geography*, 350. Cf. Smyth, *Tour of the U.S.*, II, 187; Robin, *New Travels*, 53; Mandrillon, *Le Spectateur américain*, 279; Webster, in *N.Y. Directory for 1786*, 21. See page 132.
1783 220,700 population. *See* Thirteen Colonies: General, 1783.
1786 320,000 total inhabitants. *See* Thirteen Colonies: General, 1786.
1787 218,000 population, including 80,000 Negroes: or 174,000 whites, and 80,000 blacks. *See* Thirteen Colonies: General, 1787.
1790 319,728 total inhabitants, as follows: free white men over 16, 55,915; free white men under 16, 51,339; free white females, 101,395; other free persons, 8,043; slaves, 103,036. U.S. Bureau of Census, *Heads of Families, Md.*, 9. See page 133.

LOCAL

I. LISTS OF TAXABLES

A. TAXABLES FOR 1694 TO 1697 a

Counties	1694	1695	1696	1697 d
Ann Arundell b	1,539	1,525	1,564	1,564
Baltimore	468	871	495	483
Calvert	1,787	1,791	1,045	1,822
Cecil	....	496	669	671
Charles	895	....	991	731
Dorchester	661	1,509	628	628
Kent	447	618	515	680
Prince George	....	1,450	658	[514] e
St. Mary's c	1,006	1,014	1,049	1,005
Somerset	1,439	649	1,388	1,388
Talbot	1,505	467	1,379	1,544
	9,747	10,390	10,381	10,516 [11,030]

a Figures for *1694, 1695, 1696*, from *Md. Archs.*, XXV, 255; and for *1697*, from CSPC, 1696-97, 424, No. 864.

b St. Ann's parish in *1696* had 374 taxables: "Vestry Proc., St. Ann's Parish," in *Md. Hist. Mag.*, VI, 325.

c St. Mary's (town) had 30 houses in *1678*: Lord Baltimore, Ans. Quer., in *Md. Archs.*, V, 266.

d The original list is by parishes in counties, but they have been added together for purposes of tabulation.

e Prince George County figures are not given in this list. This figure is taken from Council Proc., in *Md. Archs.*, XXIII, 92. With Prince George County the total number of taxables is 11,030.

I. LIST OF TAXABLES — *Continued*

B. TAXABLES FOR 1701 f

Counties	Taxables	Untaxables	Total
Ann Arundel	1,809	2,312	4,121
Baltimore g			
Calvert	1,248	1,569	2,817
Cecil	870	1,134	2,004
Charles	946	1,686	2,632
Dorchester	868	1,749	2,617
Kent	707	1,223	1,930
Prince George	963	1,395	2,358
St. Mary's	1,277	2,236	3,513
Somerset	1,680	3,724	5,404
Talbot	1,846	3,016	4,862
	12,214	20,044	32,258

C. TAXABLES FOR 1704 h

Counties	Masters	Freewomen and Serv.	Free Children	Freemen and Serv.	Servants Boys and Girls	Slaves	Fit to Bear Arms
Ann Arundel i	765	1,058	1,418	503	145	672	1,272
Baltimore	364	418	632	235	74	204	803
Calvert	309	560	942	619	243	938	928
Cecil	407	489	716	430	95	198	837
Charles	408	485	931	390	197	578	868
Dorchester	305	512	814	418	64	199	723
Kent	264	413	608	393	54	159	639
Prince George	416	530	1,166	464	92	436	880
St. Mary's	418	617	1,065	938	151	326	1,356
Somerset	804	1,167	1,436	642	83	305	1,546
Talbot	712	914	1,207	822	115	460	1,534
	5,172	7,163	10,935	5,854	1,313	4,475	11,386

Total Inhabs. [34,912]

D. TAXABLES FOR 1710 j

Counties	Masters and Taxable Men	White Women	White Children	Negroes
Ann Arundel k	1,014	793	1,443	1,529
Baltimore	733	558	1,098	438
Calvert	708	560	1,014	934

f Md. Archs., XXV, 255.

g Baltimore County in *1699* had 647 taxables: List in *Md. Hist. Mag.*, XII, 1-10.

h Md. Archs., XXV, 256.

i St. Ann's Parish had 363 taxables in *1705*; 414 in *1706*; 440 in *1707*; 421 in *1708*; and 436 in *1709*: "Vestry Proc., St. Ann's Parish," in *Md. Hist. Mag.*, VII, 64.

j Md. Archs., XXV, 258-59.

k St. Ann's Parish had 430 taxables in *1710* and 426 in *1711*: "Vestry Proc., St. Ann's Parish," in *Md. Hist. Mag.*, VII, 64.

I. LIST OF TAXABLES — *Continued*

Counties	Masters and Taxable Men	White Women	White Children	Negroes
Cecil	497	406	856	197
Charles	951	641	1,199	638
Dorchester	499	430	909	343
Kent	974	753	547	479
Prince George	845	637	1,215	1,297
Queen Anne	808	644	1,241	374
St. Mary's	1,088	827	1,538	668
Somerset	1,871	1,194	2,670	579
Talbot	1,103	851	1,681	470
	11,091	8,294	15,411	7,945

Total [42,741]

E. TAXABLES FOR 1712 [1]

Counties	Masters and Taxable Men	White Women	White Children	Negroes
Ann Arundel [m]	985	885	1,574	1,559
Baltimore	785	572	1,114	452
Calvert	644	597	1,080	1,179
Cecil	504	435	873	285
Charles	993	783	1,507	724
Dorchester	759	747	1,582	387
Kent	830	575	996	485
Prince George	790	600	1,198	1,202
Queen Anne	1,011	843	1,446	550
St. Mary's	998	812	1,768	513
Somerset	1,616	1,368	2,787	581
Talbot	1,114	864	1,708	492
	11,025	9,077	17,641	8,408
	[11,029]	[9,081]	[17,633]	

Total [46,151]

F. TAXABLES FOR 1724 TO 1733 [n]

Counties	1724	Taxables 1729	Taxables 1733
Ann Arundel	......	....	3,551
St. Ann's Parish [o]	130 fam.		
St. James' Parish	150 fam.		
Baltimore	......	....	2,924

[1] *Md. Archs.*, XXV, 259.

[m] St. Ann's Parish had 430 taxables in *1712*; 430 in *1714*; 443 in *1715*; 497 in *1716*; 504 in *1717*; 514 in *1718*: "Vestry Proc., St. Ann's Parish," in *Md. Hist. Mag.*, VII, 64, 65, 66.

[n] Figures for *1724* in Perry, *Hist. Colls. Re. Amer. Col. Church*, IV, 190-231; for *1729*, *Md. Archs.*, XXVIII, 449-52; for *1733*, *ibid.*, XXXVIII, 52-53.

I. List of Taxables — *Continued*

Counties	*1724*	*Taxables 1729*	*Taxables 1733*
St. Paul's Parish	363 fam.		
Calvert	......	....	1,968
Christ Church Parish	230 fam.		
All Saints Church Parish	208 fam.		
Cecil	......	....	1,787
St. Stephen's Parish [p]	......	1,011	
St. Mary Ann's Parish	......	569	
Charles [q]	......	....	2,624
Dorchester	......	....	1,950
Gt. Choptank Parish	1,000 tax.		
Dorchester Parish	400 tax.		
Kent	......	....	2,096
Christ Church Parish	100 fam.		
	260 tax.		
St. Paul's Parish	100 com.[r]		
Shrewsbury Parish	3-400 pers.		
	100 com.		
Prince George	......	....	3,924
St. Paul's Parish	120 fam.	916	
King George's Parish	1,200 tax.	1,025	
St. Barnaby's Parish	300 fam.	1,148	
Prince George's Parish			
Queen Anne's	......	....	2,391
St. Paul's Parish	542 fam.	1,147	
Christ Church Parish	....	324	
St. Luke's Parish	......	822	
St. Mary's and Charles	......	....	2,395
King and Queen Parish	200 fam.		
All Faith Parish	204 fam.		
Wm. and Mary Parish			
Port Tobacco and Durham Parish	300 fam.		
Somerset	......	....	3,492
Stepney Parish	400 fam.	925	
Coventry Parish	300 fam.	795	
Somerset Parish	......	586	
Allhallows Parish	......	826	

o St. Ann's Parish in *1723* had 663 taxables; 744 in *1725*; and 809 in *1729*: "Vestry Proc. St. Ann's Parish," in *Md. Hist. Mag.*, VII, 177, 281; VIII, 275.

p St. Stephen's Parish had 520 taxables in *1714*; 726 in *1721*; 1,011 in *1723*; and 1,443 in *1743*: Johnston, *Hist. of Cecil Co., Md.*, 212, 215. A third parish, North Elk, had 569 taxables in *1723*: *Ibid.*, 212.

q For Charles County *1724* see St. Mary's and Charles.

r Communicants. The estimates for *1724* are sometimes given in families, sometimes in taxables. Those for *1729* and *1733* are given always in taxables.

I. LIST OF TAXABLES — *Continued*

Counties	1724	Taxables 1729	Taxables 1733
Talbot	......	....	2,338
St. Peter's Parish	344 fam.	954	
St. Michael's Parish	300 fam.	969	
St. Paul's Parish		243	

Total [31,440]

G. TAXABLES FOR 1766 TO 1774 s

Counties	Year	Taxables
Anne Arundel	1774	877
Baltimore	1771	1,397
Calvert	1774	402
Cecil	1766	403
Charles	1774	742
Dorchester	1770	1,021
Somerset	1774	980
Frederick	1773	665
Harford	1773	665
Kent	1769	773
Prince George	1772	754
Queen Ann's	1775	258
St. Mary's	1774	588
Talbot	1772	454
Worcester	1774	1,031

H. TAXABLES FOR 1775 t

Baltimore County		St. Mary's County	
St. George's Parish	1800	King and Queen Parish	1600
St. John's Parish	3100	All Faiths Parish	1400
St. Thomas Parish	2100	St. Andrew Parish	1200
St. Paul's Parish	2150	William and Mary Parish	1450
Ann Arundel County		Charles County	
Queen Caroline Parish	1700	Durham Parish	1100
St. Margaret and Westminster Parish	900	William and Mary Parish	1450
St. Anne's Parish	1450	Port Tobacco Parish	2300
All Hallows Parish	1200	Trinity Parish	1500
St. James' Parish	1400	Frederic County	
Calvert County		Prince George's Parish	3500
All Saints Parish	1350	All Saints' Parish	5000
Christ Church Parish	1400	Prince George County	
		Queen Ann's Parish	1800

s From bound unpublished manuscripts, "Index to the Debt-Books," in the Land Office at Annapolis. It should be noticed that they include no Negroes, and that the numbers are manifestly too low. This calculation was supplied by Miss Stella Sutherland.
t "Estimated Number of Taxables in 1775." Perry, *Historical Collections, IV*, 343-44.

I. List of Taxables — *Continued*

St. Paul's Parish	1650	St. Peter's Parish	1450
King George's Parish	2400	St. Michael's Parish	1500
Cecil County		Dorchester County	
St. Mary Anne Parish	1400	Dorchester Parish	1200
St. Stephen's Parish	1500	Great Choptank Parish	1800
St. Augustine's Parish	750	St. Mary, Whitechapel	2000
Kent County		Somerset County	
St. Paul's Parish	1200	Somerset Parish	1600
Chester Parish	1250	Stepney Parish	3000
Shrewsbury Parish	1600	Coventry Parish	1550
Queen Ann's County		Worcester County	
Christ Church Parish	800	All Hallow's Parish	1500
St. John's Parish	1200	Worcester Parish	1400
St. Paul's Parish	1450		
St. Luke's Parish	1300	Total Taxables	[74,350]
Talbot County			

II. Censuses

A. Census of 1782 [a]

Counties	Whites
Anne Arundel	9,370
Baltimore	17,878
Calvert	4,012
Caroline	6,230
Cecil	7,749
Charles	9,804
Dorchester	8,927
Frederick	20,495
Harford	9,377
Kent	6,165
Montgomery	10,011
Prince George	9,864
Queen Ann's	7,767
St. Mary's	8,459
Somerset	7,787
Talbot	6,744
Washington	11,488
Worcester	8,561
	[170,688]

[a] Morse, Jedidiah, *American Geography*, 350. *See also* note a page 46.

II. CENSUSES — *Continued*

B. CENSUS OF 1790 b

COUNTY	FREE WHITES Males Over 16	Under 16	Females	OTHER FREE PERSONS	SLAVES	TOTAL
Alleghany	1,068	1,283	2,188	12	258	4,809
Ann Arundel c	3,142	2,850	5,672	804	10,130	22,598
Baltimore Co.d	5,184	4,668	9,101	604	5,877	25,434
Baltimore Town e	3,866	2,556	5,503	323	1,255	13,503
Calvert	1,091	1,109	2,011	136	4,305	8,652
Charles f	2,565	2,399	5,160	404	10,085	20,613
Frederick g	7,010	7,016	12,911	213	3,641	30,791
Harford	2,872	2,812	5,100	775	3,417	14,976
Montgomery h	3,284	2,746	5,649	294	6,030	18,003
Prince George i	2,653	2,503	4,848	164	11,176	21,344
St. Mary's	2,100	1,943	4,173	343	6,985	15,544
Washington j	3,738	3,863	6,871	64	1,286	15,822
Total Western Shore	38,573	35,748	69,187	4,136	64,445	212,089
Caroline	1,812	1,727	3,489	421	2,057	9,506
Cecil k	2,847	2,377	4,831	163	3,407	13,625

b U.S. Bureau of Census, *Heads of Families, Md.*, 9.

c The county in *1776* had 3,192 whites and 3,853 blacks according to census: Brumbaugh, *Md. Recds.*, 407-31. Annapolis had 150 houses in *1760*: Burnaby, *Travels*, 51; and 260 houses in *1785*: Webster, in *N. Y. Directory for 1786*, 22.

d The county in *1773* had 10,498 taxables: Griffith, *Annals of Baltimore*, 51.

e Baltimore in *1752* had about 25 houses or about 100 inhabitants: Scharf, *Hist. of Md.*, I, 420; 5,934 inhabitants in *1775* according to census: Griffith, *Annals of Baltimore*, 62; 8,000 inhabitants in *1782*: McSherry, *Hist. of Md.*, 316; 12,000 to 15,000 inhabitants in *1783*: Smyth, *Tour in U.S.*, II, 186; 1,950 houses in *1786*: Webster in *N.Y. Directory for 1786*, 22.

f The county in *1776* had 1,800 males over 18: Brumbaugh, *Md. Recds.*, 297-312.

g The county in *1776* had 1,457 whites and 79 blacks according to census: Brumbaugh, *Md. Recds.*, 177-257. Fredericktown had 2,000 inhabitants in *1776*: Smyth, *Tour in U.S.*, II, 257; 400 houses in *1786*: Webster, in *N.Y. Directory for 1786*, 22. All Saints Parish in *1753* had 2,215 taxables: Gov. Sharpe to Calvert, from Sharpe Correspondence, II, 343, in *Md. Archs.*, IX, 343.

h Georgetown in *1776* had about 60 houses. Towns in Maryland, in "An Estimate of Produce," in *Chalmers Coll.*, Md., II. NYPL.

i St. John's and Prince George Parishes had 8,441 inhabitants in *1776* according to census: Brumbaugh, *Md. Recd.*, 1-89.

j Hagerstown in *1773* was estimated at 150 houses. "Journal of James Whitelaw," in *Vt.* HSP, 1906, 139.

k Charlestown had 89 taxables in *1768*, of which 12 were Negro slaves; 102 taxables in *1771*, including 17 Negro slaves; 92 taxables in *1774*, including 11 Negro slaves: Johnston, *Hist. Cecil Co., Md.*, 273; 60 houses in *1776*: Towns in Maryland, in "An Estimate of Produce," *Chalmers Coll.*, Md., II, NYPL.

II. Censuses — *Continued*

County	Free Whites			Other Free Persons	Slaves	Total
	Males		Females			
	Over 16	*Under 16*				
Dorchester [l]	2,541	2,430	5,039	528	5,337	15,875
Kent [m]	1,876	1,547	3,325	655	5,433	12,836
Queen Anne	2,158	1,974	4,039	618	6,674	15,463
Somersett [n]	2,185	1,908	4,179	268	7,070	15,610
Talbot	1,938	1,712	3,581	1,076	4,777	13,084
Worcester [o]	1,985	1,916	3,725	178	3,836	11,640
Total Eastern Shore	17,342	15,591	32,208	3,907	38,591	107,639
Grand Total	55,915	51,339	101,395	8,043	103,036	319,728

VIRGINIA

General

1607   82 to 100 planters and others; 2,565 fighting men in Indian tribes.
Smith, *Tour*, I, 116-18, 153.

104 persons [left by Capt. Newport, June 15, 1607]. "Percy's Observations," in Purchas, *Pilgrimes*, IV, 1689. Cf. Brown, *Genesis*, I, 166.

1608   200 persons [with those brought by Capt. Newport in 1608]. Proc. of English Colonie in Va., Purchas, *Pilgrimes*, IV, 1719.

1609   200 persons [in two years increased but to 200]. Smith, *Va.*, I, 242.

490 persons [upon Smith's departure in 1609]. Smith, *Works*, 486.

60 men [left of 500 six months after Capt. Smith's departure]. Smith, *Va.*, II, 2.

80 persons. "Spelman's Relation" [Aug., 1609], in Brown, *Genesis*, I, 483-88.

240 persons [when Sir Thomas Gates arrived in 1609]. Crashaw, "Epistle Dedicatorie," *ibid.*, II, 611-20.

1610   350 people. "About 200 souls were found by Lord De la Ware . . . He brought 150, so the population must have been about 350." Brown, *First Republic*, 129.

1611   200 men.[1] Lord De la Ware, "A Short Relation, June 25, 1611," in Brown, *Genesis*, I, 478.

l Cambridge had 50 houses in *1776: Ibid.*
m Chester Town had about 200 houses in *1776: Ibid.*
n Vienna had 30 houses in *1776: Ibid.*
o Snow Hill and Princess Ann were estimated at 50 houses each in *1776: Ibid.*
[1] Brown, *First Republic*, 138, quotes this figure, but thinks it too high; that Delaware must have left less than 150 persons, the decrease due to Indian massacres and sickness.

1612 700 people. Letter of De Molina, May 28, 1613, *ibid.*, II, 646-52.

700 men. "New Life of Va.," in Force, *Tracts*, Vol. I, Tract VII, 13.

1613 350 remaining. Letter of De Molina, May 28, 1613, in Brown, *Genesis*, II, 646-52.

300 remaining. Gondomar to Philip II, Oct. 5, 1613, *ibid.*, II, 659-62.

1614 400, not full 400 men. Quoted from Howes' Chronicle, *ibid.*, I, 689.

250 persons, men, women, and children. Molina to Gondomar, June 14, 1614, *ibid.*, II, 743-46.

1616 351 persons: officers and laborers, 205; farmers, 81; with women and children making a total of 351. Rolfe, "Relation of State of Va.," in *Va. Hist. Reg.*, I, 108-10.

1617 400 people. Beverley, *Va.*, 33.

1618 400 men, women, and children. Rept. of Treasurer, Abst. of Proc. of Va. Co., in *Va.* HSC, VII, 64.

400 people. "A Briefe Decl. of the Plantation of Va.," in *Va.* CR, 80.

1619 2,400 souls. Note of Shipping, July 30, 1619, in CSPC, 1574-1660, 22, No. 46.

1,000 persons at Easter, 1619. Brown, *First Republic*, 308-9, quoting Sir Edwin Sandys.[2]

400 people, April 29, 1619. Answer of Gen'l Ass'bly in Va. to a Decl. of the State of the Colonie in Va., *Journal, House of Burgesses*, 1619-58/9, 22.

1620 887 persons, by census. Brown, *First Republic*, 328-29.[2]

2,200 persons. 1,200 persons have come this year, and 1,000 remain of those who had come before. "A Decl. of the State of the Colony in Va.," by the Va. Council, in Force, *Tracts*, Vol. III, Tract V, 5; also in Purchas, *Pilgrimes*, IV, 1775.

1621 4,000 inhabitants, Petition of Va. Co. to Lords of Council, in *Va.* HSC, VII, 144.

843 English people by census of 1621. Brown, *First Republic*, 415.

1622 1,240 English people by census of March, 1622. *Ibid.*, 464.

1623 2,500 people. Abst. of Proc. of Va. Co., Ans. to Capt. Butler, May 7, 1623, in *Va.* HSC, VII, 193.

1,277 inhabitants, Feb. 16, 1623-24. "List of the Living," in *Va.* CR, 37-54. Cf. CSPC, 1675-76, III, 57, No. 2.

1,700 persons. Quoted from John Wroth writing in 1623, in Brown, *Genesis*, II, 1064.

[2] Brown, *First Republic*, 328-29, thinks Sandys' figures about correct, as the census of March, 1620, fixed the population at 887, and less than 134 had arrived since Nov., 1619. He continues by citing the census of Dec., 1618, 600; arrival between Dec., 1618, and Nov., 1619, 840 immigrants, making a total with those in Va. of 1,440; but there had died *en route* and in Va. about 500, leaving about 900 alive.

136 VIRGINIA

1,800 persons survived the massacre and pestilence. Purchas, *Pilgrimes*, IV, 1792, based on Va. Co.'s repts.

1624 1,275 persons, including 22 Negroes. See page 143. "List of the Living in Va., Feb. 16, 1623-24," supposedly sent by Davison to Ferrar, in CSPC, 1574-1660, III, 57, No. 2. Cf. *ibid.*, III, No. 28.

1624- 1,232 persons according to census. See page 144. Hotten, *Original*
1625 *Lists*, 201-65; also *Va. Mag. Hist.*, VII, 364-67.

1,227 inhabitants, including 2 Indians and 23 Negroes. See page 144. Brown, *First Republic*, 617-27.

1,200 people, "whereof able men about 700." "A Brief Decl. of the State of Va. in Feb., 1624-25," by Capt. John Harvey, in *Chalmers Coll.*, Va., I, 27. NYPL.

1628 3,000 persons. Letter from Gov., Council, and Burgesses to King, March 26, 1628, in CSPC, 1574-1660, IV, 89, No. 45.

1629? 4-5,000 English in the colony. "Relation of the Present State of Va.," by Capt. Will. Perse [Peirce?], *ibid.*, 1574-1660, V, 100, No. 24.

1630 2,500 inhabitants. Gov. Harvey to the Privy Council, May 29, 1630, in CSPC, 1574-1660, V, 117, No. 95; also in *Chalmers Coll.*, Va., I, NYPL.

1634 4,914 men, women, and children. See table, page 145. Number of inhabitants taken, 1634, in *Va.* CR, 91.

1635 5,119 inhabitants. 205 arrived from Bermuda since list made. In CSPC, VII, 201, No. 55; also in *Chalmers Coll.*, Va., I, 18.

1648 15,000 English; 300 Negro servants. "A Perfect Desc. of Va.," in MHSC, 2d Series, IX, 105.

1653 3,435 tothables. See page 145. *Journal, House of Burgesses*, 1619-58/59, 88-89.

1660 30,000 population. Bancroft, I, 151-52.

1663 40,000 people. Berkeley, *Discourse of Va.*, 6.[3]

1665 15,000 men can be mustered in Va., whereof 2/3 are servants and 1/3 masters. Notes on New Eng., evidently submitted by the Commission of 1665, in *Egerton MS.*, 2395, fol. 415, in LCT.

40,000 population. Yonge, *Site of old Jamestowne*, 30, citing *Winder Papers*, I, 187.

80,000 population. *See* Thirteen Colonies: General, 1665.

1671 40,000 persons, men, women, and children, of which 2,000 are black slaves, 6,000 Christian servants for a short time. Gov. Berkeley, Ans. Quer.,[4] in Hening, *Statutes of Va.*, II, 515.

1675 50,000 inhabitants. Repr. of Agents to King, in Chalmers, *Annals*, I, 338.

[3] Berkeley makes this estimate in a discussion of Va.'s commerce.
[4] These Ans. Quer. are mentioned in CSPC, 1669-74, 232, No. 565, but not abstracted.

1677 15,000 (men?). Petition of Sir John Berry and Col. Moryson to
Mr. Watkins [simply mentions figure], in CSPC, 1677-80, 19,
No. 55.

1681 80-100,000 souls, Capt. Morris . . . believes, *Va. Mag. Hist.*, XXV,
373, citing *Col. Entry Bk.*, No. 106, pp. 297-98.
15,000 fighting men. Rept. of Lord Culpepper, Dec. 12, 1681, in
CSPC, 1681-85, 155, No. 319.
70,000 or 80,000 population, of which 15,000 servants, 3,000 blacks.
Lord Culpepper to Lds. of Trade, in CSPC, 1681-85, 157, No.
320.

1682 15,162 tithables. See table IV, page 145. *Journal, House of Burgesses,* 1659/60-93, 176-83.

1688 50,000 inhabitants. *See* Thirteen Colonies: General, 1688.

1689 4,300 militia: "3,000 foot and 1,300 horse." Col. Effingham's Acct.
of Govt. of Va., in *Chalmers Coll.* Va., II, NYPL. Also in
CSPC, 1689-92, 44, No. 148.

1690 6,570 militia. Repr. of BT, in NYCD, V, 607.

1693 6,000 men able to bear arms. *See* Thirteen Colonies: General, 1693.

1696 19,566 tithables; 8,299 [8,298] militia; 2,020 horse and 6,278 foot.
Gov. Andros, Ans. Quer., April 22, 1697, CO 5: 1309, No. 16,
fol. 73, in LCT; and in CSPC, 1696-97, 455, No. 956.

1697 70,000 inhabitants. (Estimated on basis of tithables.) Gov. Andros
to BT, July 1, 1697, CO 5: 1309, No. 24, fol. 161, in LCT; also
in CSPC, 1696-97, 530, No. 1131.
362 Indian bowmen in the province. Andros to BT, in CSPC, 1696-
97, 456, No. 956.
20,000 tithables. ("The country of Va. is very ill peopled.") Col.
Hartwell, Ans. Quer., Sept. 13, 1697, CO 5: 1309, No. 30, fol.
143, in LCT.

1698 20,523 tithables. See page 145. Gov. Nicholson to BT, July 1, 1699,
CO 5: 1310, No. 39, fol. 319; and same to same, Dec. 2, 1701, A,
CO 5: 1312, No. 19, XI; also Repr. BT to King, Sept. 8, 1721,
Kings MS., 205, fol. 21, p. 37, in LCT; also in CSPC, 1701, 635,
No. 1040, XI.

1699 21,606 tithables; 36,434 untaxables; 58,040 total. See page 145.
CO 5: 1312, No. 19, XI, in LCT; CSPC, 1701, 635, No. 1040, XI.
5,000 freemen. *See* Thirteen Colonies: General, 1699.
4,625 militia: 1,014 horse, 3,236 foot, 375 officers. See Table V,
page 146. Gov. Nicholson to BT, Dec. 2, 1701, A, CO 5: 1312,
No. 19, V, in LCT.
58,000 inhabitants. *Brit. Mus. Add. MSS.*, 30372; Dexter, *Hist.
Papers*, 171.

1700 24,291 tithables. See page 147. Gov. Nicholson to BT., Dec. 2, 1701,

CO 5: 1312, No. 2, III, in LCT; CSPC, 1701, 640, No. 1041 [total only].

80,000 population in Va. and Carolinas. *See* Thirteen Colonies: General, 1700.

1701   54,934 inhabitants: 20,634 tithables; 34,700 untithables. See page 147. Gov. Nicholson to BT, Dec. 2, 1701, A, CO 5: 1312, No. 19, X, in LCT; CSPC, 1701, 556, No. 913 [total only].

       8,915 militia: 2,117 horse, 6,435 foot, 363 officers; also 2,123 horse, 6,016 foot. See page 146. Gov. Nicholson to BT, Dec. 2, 1701, A, CO 5: 1312, No. 19, VII and IV, in LCT.

       10,417 militia: 2,143 horse, 1,985 dragoons, 4,971 foot, 1,318 officers. (Taken Oct., 1701.) Gov. Nicholson to BT, Dec. 2, 1701, B, CO 5: 1312, No. 20, XLI, in LCT.

       8,000 militia.[5] Col. Rob't Quary on State of Defence of Va., CO 5: 1312, Pt. II, fol. 29, in LCT.

       40,000 total population. *See* Thirteen Colonies: General, 1701.

1702   25,099 tithables. See page 147. Sec. E. Jennings to BT, July 18, 1702, CO 5: 1312, No. 38 (iii), in LCT; CSPC, 1702, 474, No. 767, III.

       26,245 tithables. See Table VI, page 147. Gov. Nicholson to BT, March 13, 1702-3, CO 5: 1313, No. 16 (ix), Enc. No. 20, in LCT.

       60,606 souls: 25,023 tithables; 35,583 women and children. Census of Va., 1702, in Beverly, *Va.*, App.

       10,000 and some odd hundred of miltia. Governor's Message, in CVSP, I, 78.

1703   26,771 tithables. See page 149. Gov. Nicholson to BT, Oct. 22, 1703, CO 5: 1313, No. 33 (xii), in LCT; CSPC, 1702-3, 762, No. 1176, XII.

       10,556 militia: 1,403 officers; 2,161 horse; 1,794 dragoons; 5,198 foot. See page 148. Abstract of militia of Va. taken in 1703. Gov. Nicholson to BT, Oct. 22, 1703, CO 5: 1313, No. 33 (xi), in LCT.

1704   26,928 tithables. See page 149. Gov. Nicholson to BT, May 31, 1704, CO 5: 1314, No. 21 (ii), in LCT; CSPC, 1704-5, 154, No. 361 (ii).

1705   27,053 tithables.[6] See page 149. Acct. of Tithables taken . . . Apr. 1705. Gov. Nicholson to BT, July 25, 1705, CO 5: 1314, No. 63, (v), in LCT; CSPC, 1704-5, 596, No. 1277 (v); Repr. BT to King, Sept. 8, 1721, *Kings MS.*, 205, fol. 21, p. 37, in LCT.

---

[5] Not above that figure. Complaining of "the weak and defenceless condition."

[6] According to Hening, *Statutes of Va.*, III, 258, (1705) all male persons 16 and over, all Negro, mulatto and Indian women 16 and up, not free, are tithable.

1708 30,000 tithables, of whom 12,000 were negroes. "Increase in three years about 3,000, mostly imported Negroes." Col. Jennings, Ans. Quer., Nov. 27, 1708, CO 5: 1316, No. 16, in LCT; CSPC, 1708-9, 158, No. 216; *Va. Trans.*, 306.

10,632 militia: 1,060 officers, 2,211 horse, 1,221 dragoons, 6,140 foot. Col. Jennings to BT, Nov. 27, 1708, CO 5: 1316, No. 16 (iv), in LCT.

1710 444 men, total of abstract of muster rolls. Gov. Nicholson to BT, May 16, 1710, CO 5: 9, fol. 104, in LCT.

1712 12,051 freemen fit to bear arms, and an equal number of Negroes and other servants; 700 Indians. Gov. Spotswood, Ans. Quer., July 25, 1712, in *Spotswood Letters*, I, 166-67; also in CSPC, 1712-14, 15, No. 25.

1714 31,540 tithables. See page 149. Gov. Spotswood to BT, Jan. 27, 1714-15, CO 5: 1317, fol. 265, in LCT; Repr. BT, to King, Sept. 8, 1721, *Kings MS.*, 205, fol. 21, p. 37, in LCT.

1715 31,658 tithables. Gov. Spotswood, Ans. Quer., Feb. 7, 1715, in *Spotswood Letters*, II, 140.

15,000 militia: 11,000 foot and 4,000 horse. *Ibid.*, 211.

72,500 white and 23,000 Negro population. Intro. by R. A. Brock, *Spotswood Letters*, I, xi.

95,000 population: 72,000 white, 23,000 negro. *See* Thirteen Colonies: General, 1715.

100,000 whites in all . . . militia . . . about 10,000 men. Mr. Byrd of Va. before Parliament, July 15, *Journal of BT*, 1714/5-18, 54.

1721 84,000 souls. (Computed on the basis of 14,000 militia in 1715, supposed to be 1/6 of whole.) Repr. BT to King, Sept. 8, 1721, *Kings MS.*, 205, fol. 20, p. 35, in LCT; also in NYCD, V, 607.

1722 37,750 tithables. Table in *Va. Hist. Reg.*, IV, 19. See page 150.

1723 39,761 tithables. *Ibid.*, 67. See page 150.

1724 43,877 tithables. See page 150. Acct. of Tobacco Plants tended in Va., 1724, in Maj. Drysdale's letter, Jan. 29, 1724-25, in CO 5: 1319, fol. 439, Q:86, in LCT.

8,056 families, with 1,400 tithables from parishes where no family estimate is given. Ans. Quer. by Ministers, in Perry, *Hist. Colls. Re. Am. Col. Church*, I, 261-318.

1726 45,857 tithables. See page 150. Present State of Va. for year 1726, Maj. Drysdale, Ans. Quer., June 29, 1727, CO 5: 1320, fol. 107-12, in LCT.

45,266 tithables. According to Table in *Va. Hist. Reg.*, IV, 74.

30,000 inhabitants. *See* Thirteen Colonies: General, 1726.

1729 48,196 tithables. (Without Brunswick, Caroline, and Goochland.)

Present State of Va., 1729, Maj. Gooch to BT, Sept. 7, 1729, CO 5: 1322, fol. 237-40, in LCT. See page 150.

1730   114,000 souls. On basis of 51,000 tithables. See note a, page 145. Maj. Gooch, Ans. Quer., July 23, 1730, CO 5: 1322, fol. 125, in LCT.

12,230 militia: 4,550 horse, and 7,680 foot. CO 5: 1322, fol. 126.

1740   12,000 militia. See Thirteen Colonies: General, 1740.

1742   134,000 inhabitants, whites and blacks. Increased in past 10 years 20,000, mostly white people. 16,000 militia. Gov. Gooch, Ans. Quer., Aug. 11, 1742, CO 5: 1325, V:32, in LCT.

1743   130,000 inhabitants: 42,000 blacks, 88,000 whites. Gov. Gooch, Ans. Quer., Aug. 22, 1743, CO 5: 1326, V:40, fol. 32, in LCT.

1744   140,000 inhabitants, white and black. 15,660 militia: 176 companies on foot, and 102 troops of horse, reckoning the companies at 60 men each, and the troops at 50.[7] Gov. Gooch, Ans. Quer., Dec. 21, 1744, CO 5: 1326, V:55, fol. 214, p. 8, in LCT.

1749   135,000 souls: 85,000 tithables, 40,000 being blacks. See page 150 and note b, page 145. Gov. Gooch, Ans. Quer., 1749, CO 5: 1327, fol. 174, W:30/9, in LCT; also in Va. Mag. Hist., III, 118-19.

13,800 militia: 176 companies of foot; 100 troops horse. Gov. Gooch, Ans. Quer., 1749, CO 5: 1327, fol. 174, W:3/9, in LCT.

85,000 inhabitants. See Thirteen Colonies: General, 1749.

1750   13,800 militia. [See above, 1749.] Col. Thos. Lee, Pres. of Council, Ans. Quer., Sept. 29, 1750, CO 5: 1327, fol. 242, p. 12; W:42/2/2, in LCT.

1754   168,000 white, 116,000 black inhabitants. Bancroft, II, 389-91.

1755   103,407 tithables: 45,329 whites, 60,078 blacks. See page 150. Va. List of Tithables, Gov. Dinwiddie to BT, Feb. 23, 1756, CO 5: 1328, fol. 443, 444, W:209, in LCT.

230,000 inhabitants; 28,000 militia. Gov. Dinwiddie, Ans. Quer., Feb. 10, 1755, CO 5: 1328, fol. 329, W:185, in LCT; also in Dinwiddie Papers, I, 387.

300,000 inhabitants, of which 1/2 Negroes. Rev. S. Daires to member of S.P.G., March, 1755, in Foote, Sketches of Va., I, 285.

125,000 white inhabitants with 28,000 militia. Rept. of BT, in NYCD, VI, 993.

125,000 whites; or 230,000 total. See Thirteen Colonies: General, 1755.

1756   293,472 inhabitants, white and black, computed as follows: 43,329 white tithables times four equals 173,316; 60,078 Negro tithables times two equals 120,156. 36,000 militia. Gov. Dinwiddie to BT, Feb. 23, 1756, in CO 5: 1328, fol. 437, in LCT; also in Din-

[7] This same militia estimate is given for June 10, 1747, in CO 5: 1326, V: 99, fol. 477.

widdie Papers, II, 344-45; and *Va.* HSC, IV. Cf. Pownall, *Memorial*, 60.

1759 104,815 tithables. Gov. Fauquier, Ans. Quer., Jan. 30, 1763, CO 5: 1330, fol. 546, in LCT.[8]

1761 113,287 tithables. *Ibid.*

1762 121,022 tithables. *Ibid.*

1763 340,000 souls, with whites and blacks nearly equal. 28,826 militia. Gov. Fauquier, Ans. Quer., Jan. 30, 1763, CO 5: 1330, fol. 545-46, in LCT; also *Kings MS.*, 205, fol. 264, pp. 540-41, in LCT.

1764 200,000 population. Pownall, *Memorial*, 60.

1765 720,000 inhabitants in Va. and Md., 180,000 men. *See* Thirteen Colonies: General, 1765.

1766⎱ 120,000 tithables for 1766 and for 1769. *Va. Journal, House of*
1769⎰ *Burgesses*, 1761-65, 178. (In Treasury statement.)

1770 447,008 inhabitants, white and black, according to computation as follows: 131,000 tithables, 55,958 white, the rest black men and women. Allowing 3 children to each pair of Negro tithables, the whole number of Negroes is 187,606. Allowing 50,863 women to the white men tithables, the ratio being commonly stated as 11 to 10, and 3 children to every woman, there will be 152,589 children.[9] Quoted from "Concise Account" at bottom of map by Col. John Henry, in *Wm. and Mary Coll. Quar.*, XIV, 85; also in *Hist. Mag.*, Sept., 1863, VII, 286-88.

1772 153,000 tithables. Jefferson, "Notes on Va.," *Writings*, III, 187.

1773 155,278 tithables. From Amelia Co. Order Book, in *Va. Mag. Hist.*, XXVIII, 81-82.

1774 300,000 whites and 200,000 blacks. ("A very rough guess.") 60,000 militia. 120 or 130 tributary Indians. Lord Dunmore to Earl of Dartmouth, Ans. Quer., March 18, 1774, CO 5: 1352, fol. 21-22, in LCT. Cf. Smyth, *Tour in U.S.*, I, 72.

640,000 population; or 560,000, or 300,000. *See* Thirteen Colonies: General, 1774.

300,000 in population. Pownall, *Memorial*, 60.

1775 300,000 in population. De Witt, *Abstract of Census of Mass., 1855*, 195.

400,000 total population. *See* Thirteen Colonies: General, 1775.

1776 41,115 men available for military duty. List, in *Va. Mag. Hist.*, XVIII, 34-35.

1782 567,614 population estimate obtained as follows: 53,289 free males above 21 years. 211,698 slaves of all ages and sexes. 23,766 not

[8]Burnaby, *Travels*, 17, and Jefferson, "Notes on Va.," *Writings*, III, 187, estimate 200,000 to 300,000 inhabitants on the basis of 105,000 tithables.

[9] On the basis of the figures given, the total number of inhabitants should be 447,016.

distinguished, but said to be tithable slaves. Numbers above 16 and below equal. Therefore multiply tithables by 2, which is 47,532, added to 211,698 gives 259,230 slaves. 53,289 being all free males above 21, estimate the number between 16 and 21 as 17,763, males under 16 as 17,052, and a total of 284,208 free inhabitants of all ages, which added to slaves, gives 543,438 inhabitants exclusive of 8 counties for which were no returns.[10] Estimate for these counties 12,644 free inhabitants and by proportion 11,532 slaves. Added to above estimates, we have 296,852 free inhabitants, and 270,762 slaves; 567,614 total inhabitants of every age, sex, and condition. Jefferson, "Notes on Va.," *Writings*, III, 187-92.

For partial census of Va. in 1782, see page 152.

1783　For partial census of Va. in 1783, see page 152.

400,000 population. *See* Thirteen Colonies: General, 1783.

1784　For partial census of Va. in 1784, see page 152.

1785　448,008 inhabitants, white and black; 73,000 tithables, 55,985 [white?], the residue Negroes. Letter of John Joyce, in *Va. Mag. Hist.*, XXIII, 410.

For partial census in 1785, see page 152.

1786　650,000 inhabitants. *See* Thirteen Colonies: General, 1786.

1787　420,000 inhabitants, including 280,000 Negroes; or 300,000 whites and 300,000 blacks. *See* Thirteen Colonies: General, 1787. For partial census, see page 152.

1788　352,000 whites; 236,000 Negroes in Va. Randolph's figures in speech in Convention of 1788. Brock thinks them too low. Grigsby, "Hist. of Va. Fed. Convention," in Va. HSC, IX, 124 and note.

800,000 and over in population: 503,248 whites; 12,880 free colored; and 305,257 slaves. Grigsby, "Hist. of Va. Fed. Convention," in Va. HSC, IX, 8.

1790　823,599 total inhabitants according to census: white, 499,341; black 311,280; all others, 12,978. 897,276 is the total, including Ky. Tatham, "A Topographical Analysis of the Commonwealth of Va. Compiled for the years 1790-1791," in Appendix to Jefferson, *Notes on Va.* (1853 ed.).

738,308 inhabitants, including Ky.: whites, 442,115; blacks, 293-427; "including all other persons, 738,308." Grigsby, "Hist. of Va. Fed. Convention," in Va. HSC, IX, 8n, 124n.

70,825 families appear upon my census returns of the district of Va. Gen. Edw. Carrington to Alex. Hamilton,[11] Oct. 4, 1791, in *Wm. and Mary Coll. Quar.*, 2d Series, II, 142.

---

[10] Jefferson's method of obtaining his summary figures is confusing and apparently not accurate, but the estimates have been given as found in the source cited.

[11] Gen. Carrington was marshal of the U.S. District Court of Va., and had charge of the 1790 Census. *Wm. and Mary Coll. Quar.*, 2d Series, II, 139 (ed. note).

747,610 total population according to census: free white males over 16, 110,936; free white males under 16, 116,135; free white females, 215,046; other free persons, 12,866; 292,627. See page 154. Edw. Carrington, Dist. Marshal, U.S. Bureau of Census, *Heads of Families, Va.*, 8.

LOCAL

I. LIST OF THE LIVING IN VIRGINIA, FEB. 16, 1623-24 [a]

College Land	29	
Neck of Land	41	
West and Sherlow Hundred	45	
Jordon's Journey	42	
Flourdieu Hundred	63	(incl. 11 Negroes)
W. and Sherlow Hundred	24	
Chaplain's Choice	24	
James City	182	(incl. 3 Negroes)
In the Main	88	
James Island	39	(incl. 1 Negro)
Neck of Land	25	
Over the River	33	
At the Plantation over against James City	77	(incl. 1 Negro)
At the Glass House	5	
Archer's Hoop	14	
Hogg Island	31	
Martin's Hundred	24	
Warwick Squeak	33	(incl. 4 Negroes)
Indian Thicket	11	
Elizabeth City	319	(incl. 2 Negroes)
Buckrow	30	
Bass Choice	20	
Eastern Shore	76	
	1,275	(incl. 22 Negroes)

a CSPC, 1574-1660, III, 57, No. 2.

II. Census of 1624-25 [a]

SETTLEMENT	WHITE			NEGRO			SUM TOTAL
	Male	Female	Total	Male	Female	Total	
Colledge Land	20	2	22				
Neck of Land [b]	25	19	44				
W. and Sherley Hund	44	16	60				
Jordan's Journey	36	19	55				
Chaplain Choice and							
Truelove's Co.	13	4	17				
Piersey's Hund.	40	9	49	4	3	7	
Pasheayghs	35	8	43				
The Maine	30	6	36				
James City	122	53	175	3	6	9	
Neck of Land [c]	126	19	145	1	0	1	
Hog Island	40	13	53				
Martin's Hund.	20	7	27				
Mulbury Island	25	5	30				
Wariscoyack	8	..	8	1	1	2	
Basses Choyse	16	3	19				
Newportes Newes	20	..	20				
Elizabeth City	198	59	257	2	1	3	
Elizabeth City be-							
yond Hampton Rd.	78	20	98	1	0	1	
Eastern Shore	44	7	51				
	940	269	1,209	12	11	23	1,232

Summary of Inhabitants, 1624-25

Place	Free	Servants	Children	Negroes	Total
Henrico	18	3	1		22
Charles City	119	84	26	7	236
James City	204	226	35	10	475
Elizabeth City	235	157	43 + 2 Inds.	6	443
Eastern Shore	32	17	2		51
	[608] [d]	[487]	[109]	[23]	[1,227]

Total: 432 males, 176 females — free   ⎱   1,095   ⎱

441 males, 46 females — servants ⎰ emigrants ⎰   1,202 English

107 children

                                            2 Indians

11 males, 10 females, 2 children — Negroes   23 Negroes

                                            1,227

a *Va. Mag. Hist.*, VII, 364-67; Brown, *First Republic*, 617-27.
b In Charles City.   c In James City.
d In this and the following tables for Va., totals of columns are given as found in the source cited. When no total was given, it was computed and placed in brackets, as here. When the total given was incorrect, the true sum has been presented in brackets beside that found in the source used, as on page 145.

III. List of the Number of Men, Women, and Children in the Several Counties of Va., 1634 [a]

Henrico	419
Charles City	511
James City	886
Warrick	811
Warrowerguyoake	522
Elizabeth City Co.	854
Charles River Co.	510
Accomacke Co.	396
	4,914
	[4,909]

IV. Lists of Tithables from 1653 to 1699 [b]

Counties [c]	1653	1682	1698	1699 Tithables	Untithables
Accomack	...	583	866	854	1,814
Charles City	532	714	1,052	1,260	2,639
Elizabeth City	395	287	427	453	735
Essex	...	...	871	1,018	1,584
Gloucester	367	2,005	2,326	2,514	3,216
Henrico	...	471	699	724	1,498
Isle of Wight	673	735	732	781	1,985
James City [d]	...	982	1,084	1,059	1,701
King and Queen	...	...	1,483	1,664	2,642
Lancaster [e]	...	421	636	869	1,224
Middlesex	...	546	764	658	883
Nansemond	...	755	775	781	1,790

a Va. CR, 91. "After this list was brought in there arrived a Ship of Holland with 145 persons from Bermudas; and since that 60 more in an English ship from Bermudas also." Chalmers *Coll.*, Va., I, 18. NYPL.

b "The rule for computing the number of inhabitants is by the List of Tithables on which the Publick Tobacco Taxes are laid. These are all white male persons above 16 years of age, and all blacks, male and female, above the same age . . . The white women, married and unmarried, and the white and black children under 16 years of age [are accounted] to be treble the number of white tithables." Gov. Gooch, Ans. Quer., July 23, 1730, in CO 5: 1322, fol. 125. Gov. Dinwiddie multiplied white tithables by 4 for the total number of whites (*Dinwiddie Papers*, II, 353-352). But according to other computations, the ratio of women to men was considered as 10 to 11 (Col. John Henry, "Concise Acct.," in *Wm. and Mary Coll. Quar.*, XIV, 85); and the number of persons under 16 was held to be equal to the number of those over. Therefore 3 would seem to be more nearly correct. Compare also these groups in the census of 1790.

c The lists differ from the originals in that the counties have been arranged in alphabetical order for the sake of convenience and consistency throughout the tables. Sources for *1653*, *Journal, House of Burgesses*, 1619-58/9, 88-89; for *1682*, ibid., 1659/60-93, 176-83; for *1698*, CO 5: 1310, No. 39, fol. 319; for *1699 ibid.*

d Jamestown (James City) in *1697* had 20 or 30 houses: Dr. Blair's Statement to BT, Aug. 25, 1697, in CSPC, 1696-97, 585, No. 1262.

e Lancaster County in *1654* had 502 tithables: List, in *Va. Mag. Hist.*, V, 158-60.

IV. LISTS OF TITHABLES FROM 1653 TO 1699 — *Continued*

Counties	1653	1682	1698	1699 Tithables	Untithables
New Kent	...	1,802	1,056	1,116	2,056
Norfolk	...	694	674	684	1,572
Northampton f	500	555	615	681	1,369
Northumberland	450	624	997	1,088	931
Princess Anne	...	...	646	620	1,351
Rappahanock g	...	1,053			
Richmond	...	...	1,036	1,262	1,278
Stafford h	...	407	679	708	1,152
Surry i	518	486	662	664	1,350
Warwick	...	306	463	474	888
Westmoreland	...	695	887	936	1,605
York j	...	1,041	1,093	738	1,171
Total	[3,435]	15,162	20,523	21,606	36,434

V. MILITIA IN 1699 AND 1701 k

Counties	1699 Horse	Foot	1701 (A) Horse	Foot	1701 (B) Horse	Foot
Accomack	...	...	98	339		
Charles City m	...	...	203	422	164 l	390
Elizabeth City n	54	145	54	142	...	142
Essex o	...	...	128	272		
Gloucester	...	...	121	473	121	473
Henrico p	111	210	98	247		

f Northampton County in *1666* had 424 tithables: 372 white, 52 Negroes. Compiled by T. B. Robertson from County Recds., in *Va. Mag. Hist.*, X, 194-96, 258-63.

g This county must have been renamed, as it never appears in later lists. never appears in later lists.

h Stafford County in *1699* had 474 persons cultivating tobacco: From County Recds., in CVSP, I, 68.

i Surry County in *1668* had 434 tithables. List, in *Wm. and Mary Coll. Quar.*, VIII, 160-64.

j York County in *1662* had 1,140 tithables: Extracts from County Recds., *ibid.*, XXVI, 33; in *1693*, 1,040 tithables: *Ibid.*, XXVI, 37.

k *1699*, given in CO 5: 1312, No. 19, V: *1701*, given in *ibid.*, 1312, No. 19, VII and IV.

l Accomack is bracketed with Northampton.

m Charles City County in *1700* had 178 horse, 431 foot in militia: Nicholson to BT, Dec. 2, 1701, CO 5: 1312, Pt. I, F 6, Encl. No. 19, in LCT. In *1702* it had 7 officers and 54 dragoons in militia: Nicholson to BT, July 29, 1702, *ibid.*, 1312, Pt. II, fol. 40 (xlv), Encl. No. 32.

n Elizabeth City County in *1700* had 169 horse and 488 foot in the militia: Nicholson to BT, Dec. 2, 1701, *ibid.*, Pt. I, F 6, Encl. No. 19.

o Essex County in *1700* had 72 horse and 113 foot in the militia: Nicholson to BT, Dec. 2, 1701, *ibid.*

p Henrico also had 21 dragoons. The original lists included a column for dragoons, but as Henrico was the only county with a troop and as the dragoons are apparently not included in the total, this column was omitted for purpose of tabulation. In *1700*, it had a militia of 88 horse and 218 foot: Nicholson to BT, Dec. 2, 1701. *Ibid.*

V. MILITIA IN 1699 AND 1701 — *Continued*

	1699		1701 (A)		1701 (B)	
Counties	*Horse*	*Foot*	*Horse*	*Foot*	*Horse*	*Foot*
James City	...	415	123	278	113	318
Isle of Wight	129	321	140	374	140	374
King and Queen q	...	...	...	...	189	459 r
Lancaster	46	224	48	229	42	229
Middlesex s	...	...	45	137	56	143
Nansemond	133	403	142	449	142	449
New Kent t	...	...	120	89	120	89
Norfolk	...	307	48	332	48	334
Northampton	...	...	70	227	70	277
Northumberland	109	317	109	359	130	164
Princess Anne	50	201	69	215	69	215
Richmond	105	272	122	382	122	382
Stafford	...	...	84	261	84	261
Surry	...	...	62	288	60	284
Warwick u	51	...	49	152	49	152
Westmoreland	167	190	130	228	133	318
York	...	...	68	322	68	322
	1,014	3,236	2,117	6,435	2,123	6,016
	[955]	[3,005]	[2,131]	[6,217]	[1,920]	[5,775]

Summary	*1699*		*1701*		*1701*	
Horse	1,014	[955]	2,117	[2,131]	2,123	[1,920]
Foot	3,236	[3,005]	6,435	[6,217]	6,016	[5,775]
Officers	375		363			
Total	4,625	[4,335]	8,915	[8,711]		

VI. LISTS OF TITHABLES FOR 1700 TO 1702 a

	1700	1701		1702 (A)	1702 (B)
Counties		*Tithables*	*Untithables*		
Accomack	1,041	867	1,763	1,041	1,041
Charles City	1,327	1,260	2,639	1,493	1,327

q King and Queen County in *1700* had 169 horse and 488 foot in the militia: Nicholson to BT, Dec. 2, 1701, *ibid.*

r King and Queen County is given twice.

s Middlesex County in *1700* had 49 horse and 179 foot in the militia: Nicholson to BT, Dec. 2, 1701, *ibid.*

t New Kent County in *1702* had 15 officers and 239 foot in the militia: Nicholson to BT, July 29, 1702, in CO 5: 1312, Pt. II, fol. 40 (xlv), Encl. No. 32.

u Surry County in *1700* had 60 horse and 285 foot in militia: Nicholson to BT, Dec. 2, 1701, CO 5: 1312, Pt. I, fol. 6, Encl. No. 19; in *1702* it had 17 officers, 72 horse, 45 dragoons, and 233 foot in militia: Nicholson to BT, July 29, 1702, CO 5: 1312, Pt. II, fol. 40 (xlv), Encl. No. 32.

a Sources for *1700*, CO 5: 1312, No. 20, III; for *1701*, CO 5: 1312, No. 19, X; for *1702* (A), Gov. Nicholson's List of Tithables, March 13, 1702-3, CO 5: 1313, No. 16

VI. LISTS OF TITHABLES FOR 1700 TO 1702 — *Continued*

Counties	1700	1701		1702 (A)	1702 (B)
		Tithables	*Unthithables*		
Elizabeth City	478	448	719	429	478
Essex	1,034	1,078	1,584b	1,221	1,034
Gloucester	2,626	2,514	3,206	2,959	2,626
Henrico	863	724	1,498	963	863
James City c	1,193	1,055	1,693	1,365	1,193
Isle of Wight	876	750	1,873	922	876
King William	....	....	....	806	803
King and Queen	1,848	1,667	2,629	1,539	1,848
Lancaster	926	869	1,214	876	926
Middlesex	814	658	883	821	814
Nansemond	1,030	767	1,512	1,040	1,030
New Kent	1,245	1,117	2,049	1,432	1,245
Norfolk	693	684	1,572	700	693
Northampton	693	681	1,369	728	693
Northumberland	1,189	1,088	931	1,163	1,189
Princess Ann	727	620	1,351	698	727
Richmond	1,358	1,307	1,230	1,337	1,358
Stafford d	828	715	1,170	901	828
Surry	737	664	1,350	834	739
Warwick	505	474	895	506	505
Westmoreland	1,080	936	1,605	1,207	1,083
York	1,180	769	1,149	1,244	1,180
Total	24,291	20,634	34,700	26,245	25,099
		[21,712]	[35,884]	[26,225]	

VII. MILITIA IN 1703 a

Counties	Com. and Noncom. Officers	Horse	Dragoons	Foot
Henrico	53	79	171	124
Charles City	37	43	34	97
Prince George	46	58	81	144
Isle of Wight	71	150	40	305
Nansemond	58	123	105	200
Norfolk	28	60	37	193
Princess Ann	43	50	28	186
Elizabeth City	27	33	35	4 [*sic*]

(ix), Encl. No. 20; for *1702* (B), Sec. Jennings' List of Tithables, July 18, 1702, CO 5: 1312, No. 38 (iii).

b In transcript (erased) in pencil.

c Jamestown had about 20 houses according to Gov. Bellomont, in CSPC, 1700, 92, No. 167.

d Another report of Nicholson for *1702* gives 61 officers, 90 horse, 45 dragoons, and 150 foot, in CO 5: 1312, Pt. II, fol. 40 (xiv), Encl. No. 32, in LCT.

a CO 5: 1313, No. 33 (xi).

VII. MILITIA IN 1703 — *Continued*

Counties	Com. and Noncom. Officers	Horse	Dragoons	Foot
Accomack	72	135	242	123
Northampton	37	60	90	118
Warwick	30	37	39	140
James City	81	83	50	286
New Kent	28	111	...	215
King William	50	62	80	172
King and Queen	79	104	120	225
Gloucester	116	146	...	625
Essex	68	105	40	204
Lancaster	56	66	91	137
Stafford	46	73	56	182
Richmond	59	171	46	349
Westmoreland	64	80	101	250
Northumberland	90	98	205	172
York	61	96	30	269
Middlesex	26	32	73	106
Surry	17	79	...	248
	1,403	2,161	1,794	5,198
	[1,343]	[2,134]		[5,074]

VIII. LISTS OF TITHABLES FOR 1703 TO 1714 [a]

Counties	1703	1704	1705	1714
Accomack	1,061	1,061	1,061	1,055
Charles City	551	550	571	553
Elizabeth City	478	478	478	610
Essex	1,261	1,262	1,307	1,653
Gloucester	294	2,945	2,880	2,804
Henrico	1,018	1,020	1,020	1,335
James City [b]	1,435	1,435	1,423	1,535
Isle of Wight	734	923	923	1,223
King William	884	884	936	1,226
King and Queen	1,545	1,546	1,574	1,814
Lancaster [c]	909	909	909	1,019
Middlesex	807	807	824	926
Nansemond	1,117	1,017	1,017	1,250
New Kent	1,482	1,482	1,453	1,852
Norfolk	693	693	714	891
Northampton	716	728	728	831
Northumberland	1,188	1,180	1,180	1,272

a Sources for *1703*, CO 5: 1313, No. 33 (xii) ; for *1704*, *ibid.*, 1314, No. 21 (ii) ; for *1705*, *ibid.*, 1314, No. 63 (v) ; for *1714*, *ibid.*, 1317, fol. 265.

b Jamestown had 60 or 70 houses in *1708*: Oldmixon, *British Empire*, I, 273.

c Lancaster in *1716* had 1,065 tithables: *Wm. and Mary Coll. Quar.*, XXI, 106-12.

VIII. List of Tithables for 1703 to 1714 — *Continued*

Counties	1703	1704	1705	1714
Prince George	1,016	1,024	1,024	1,040
Princess Anne	728	728	728	921
Richmond	1,483	1,483	1,489	1,799
Stafford	892	892	892	1,069
Surry	844	855	895	1,320
Warwick	577	518	536	604
Westmoreland	1,229	1,229	1,229	1,543
York	1,279	1,279	1,262	1,395
Total	26,771	26,928	27,053	31,540
	[24,221]			

IX. List of Tithables for 1722 to 1755 [a]

Counties	1722	1723	1724	1726	1729	1749	1755 Whites	1755 Blacks
Accomack	1,055	1,263	1,290	1,300	1,474	2,353	1,506	1,135
Albemarle	....	....	....	....	....	1,725	1,344	1,747
Amelia [b]	....	....	....	....	....	2,383	1,251	1,652
Augusta [c]	....	....	....	....	....	1,423	2,273	40
Brunswick	....	....	....	160	....	1,765	1,299	976
Bedford	....	....	....	....	....	....	357	143
Caroline	....	....	....	....	....	3,551	1,208	2,674
Charles City	918	922	1,088	1,082	1,081	1,506	537	1,058
Chesterfield	....	....	....	....	....	....	841	1,198
Culpepper	....	....	....	....	....	....	1,221	1,217
Cumberland	....	....	....	....	....	....	704	1,394
Dinwiddie [d]	....	....	....	....	....	....	784	1,175
Elizabeth City	654	753	823	813	778	1,070	316	812
Essex [e]	2,158	2,171	2,413	2,472	2,694	2,610	889	1,711
Fairfax	....	....	....	....	....	1,586	1,312	921
Frederick	....	....	....	....	....	1,581	2,173	340
Gloucester	3,109	3,260	3,451	3,421	3,473	4,307	1,137	3,284
Goochland	....	....	....	....	....	2,773	569	935
Halifax	....	....	....	....	....	....	629	141
Hampshire	....	....	....	....	....	....	558	12
Hanover	1,324	1,465	1,750	1,941	2,134	3,108	1,169	2,621

a Figures for *1722* in *Va. Hist. Reg.*, IV, 19; *1723, ibid.*, 67; *1724*, CO 5: 1319, fol. 439, Q:86; *1726, ibid.*, 1320, fol. 107-12; *1729, ibid.*, 1322, fol. 237-40; *1749, ibid.*, 1327, fol. 174, W:30/9; *1755, ibid.*, 1328, fol. 443, 444, W:209.

b Amelia County in *1769* had 4,903 tithables: From Amelia Co. Order Book, *Va. Mag. Hist.*, XXVIII, 82.

c Augusta County, in *1747* had 1,670 tithables, according to parish levy, Sept. 21, 1747: Peyton, *Hist. of Augusta Co.*, 98.

d Dinwiddie County in *1767* had 2,864 tithables: From Amelia Co. Order Book, *Va. Mag. Hist.*, XXVIII, 82.

e Essex County in *1753* had 559 men in militia: CVSP, I, 247.

IX. LIST OF TITHABLES FOR 1722 TO 1755 — *Continued*

Counties	1722	1723	1724	1726	1729	1749	1755 Whites	1755 Blacks
Henrico	1,842	1,922	2,227	2,453	2,767	2,979	529	898
Isle of Wight f	1,715	1,686	1,849	1,844	2,075	3,244	810	966
James City	1,286	1,265	1,327	1,347	1,242	1,543	394	1,254
King George	915	1,016	1,130	1,300	1,275	1,744	720	1,068
King and Queen	2,337	2,482	2,670	2,685	2,850	2,899	944	2,103
King William	1,918	2,045	2,294	2,389	2,518	2,392	702	1,834
Lancaster	1,147	1,065	1,233	1,249	1,390	1,538	486	1,124
Louisa	....	....	....	....	....	1,519	655	1,452
Lunenburg	....	....	....	....	....	1,519	1,209	903
Middlesex	1,055	1,120	1,192	1,150	1,139	1,400	371	1,056
Nansemond g	1,437	1,466	1,567	1,692	1,847	2,153	989	1,264
New Kent	1,190	1,216	1,296	1,348	1,364	1,610	465	1,209
Norfolk	1,094	1,127	906	1,188	1,245	2,190	1,132	1,408
Northampton	809	871	986	1,044	1,033	1,529	609	902
Northumberland	1,521	1,563	1,715	1,723	1,572	2,176	980	1,434
Orange h	....	....	....	....	....	2,679	627	1,016
Princess Anne	954	1,000	1,185	1,046	1,147	1,559	840	880
Prince George	1,315	1,387	1,562	1,624	1,795	3,190	650	1,138
Prince William	....	....	....	....	....	2,222	1,384	1,414
Prince Edward	....	....	....	....	....	....	416	410
Richmond	1,020	1,394	1,551	1,450	1,839	1,837	761	1,236
Southampton	....	....	....	....	....	....	973	1,036
Spotsylvania i	....	....	800	950	919	1,782	665	1,468
Stafford j	1,503	1,554	1,747	1,800	2,060	1,811	889	1,126
Surry	1,701	1,712	1,924	2,049	2,190	3,367	587	1,006
Sussex	....	....	....	....	....	....	778	1,388
Warwick	581	631	692	701	675	818	181	665
Westmoreland	1,763	1,880	2,007	2,011	1,998	2,471	944	1,588
York	1,439	1,525	1,202	1,625	1,622	2,054	562	1,567
Total	37,750 [37,760]	39,761	43,877	45,857	[48,196]	85,919 [85,966]	43,329	60,078 [59,999]

f Isle of Wight County in *1724* had 700 assessed persons: Discussion of Isle of Wight Co. Recds., in *Wm. and Mary Coll. Quar.*, VII, 210.

g Suffolk in Nansemond County in *1745* had 60 or 70 houses: "Wm. Logan's Journal," in *Pa. Mag. Hist.*, XXXVI, 5.

h Orange County in *1735* had 1,111 tithables: From Orange Order Book, 1735-45, in Morton, *Hist. of Rockbridge Co., Va.*, 54.

i St. George's Parish in Spotsylvania County in *1735* had 1,500 tithables: Transcribed from the Vestry Book, in Slaughter, *Hist. of St. George's Parish*, 18.

j Falmouth in Stafford County in *1759* had 18 or 20 houses: Burnaby, *Travels*, 34.

X. CENSUS AND TITHABLES FOR 1782 TO 1789

Counties	Whites	Blacks	Total	Date	Reference a
Accomac	812	2,749	3,561	1787	Tithables
Albemarle	908	4,409	5,317	1782	Tithables
Amelia	5,549	8,749	14,298	1782	H. F.
Amherst	5,964	3,852	9,816	1783	H. F.
Augusta	1,311	1,182	2,493	1782	Tithables
Bedford	5,497	1,653	7,150	1783	CVSP, III, 551
Berkeley	1,315	1,921	3,236	1782	Tithables
Botetourt	922	823	1,745	1785	Tithables
Brunswick b	...	...	6,449	1782	Tithables
Buckingham	759	3,160	3,919	1782	Tithables
Campbell	1,307	1,059	2,366	1785	Tithables
Caroline	965	3,712	4,677	1783	Tithables
Charles City	472	2,729	3,201	1787	Tithables
Charlotte	3,790	3,442	7,232	1783	H. F.
Chesterfield	4,885	5,961	10,846	1783	H. F.
Culpepper	1,863	6,352	8,215	1782	Tithables
Cumberland	2,670	3,882	6,552	1782	H. F.
Dinwiddie c	840	5,746	6,586	1782	Tithables
Elizabeth City	904	648	1,552	1782	Tithables
Essex	2,489	2,817	5,306	1785	H. F.
Fairfax	5,154	3,609	8,763	1782	H. F.
Fauquier	1,747	5,168	6,915	1782	Tithables
Fluvanna	1,985	1,330	3,315	1782	H. F.
Frederick	4,786	767	5,553	1782	H. F.
Gloucester	3,151	2,764	5,915	1783	H. F.
Goochland	614	3,852	4,466	1782	Tithables
Greenbriar d	515	167	682	1783	Tithables
Greensville	1,845	2,691	4,536	1783	H. F.
Halifax	5,335	3,290	8,625	1782	H. F.
Hampshire	7,469	513	7,982	1782	CVSP, III, 371
Hanover	3,707	5,184	8,891	1782	H. F.
Henrico	1,339	6,961	8,300	1787	Tithables
Henry	1,168	1,723	2,891	1782	Tithables
Isle of Wight	3,760	2,948	6,708	1782	H. F.
James City	493	1,832	2,325	1782	Tithables

a As the records of the Virginia Census of 1782-83, to be found in the Virginia volume of *Heads of Families* in Census of 1790 here referred to as H. F., are incomplete,
the tithables from unpublished manuscripts in the Archives Division of the State Library
at Richmond, Virginia, have been used to fill in the gaps; these were kindly supplied
by Miss Sutherland.

b The inscription on the outside of the 1782 Brunswick list reads "6449 Persons
white and black."

c *Wm. and Mary Coll. Quar.*, XXVI, 97-106, 196-201, 250-58, gives Dinwiddie 849
white tithables and 5,746 blacks.

d Morton, O. F.: *Hist. of Monroe Co., W. Va.*, 71 (Extracts from Col. Records), gives
811 as the number of white tithables; no blacks mentioned.

X. Census and Tithables for 1782 to 1789 — *Continued*

Counties	Whites	Blacks	Total	Date	Reference
King and Queen e	549	2,827	3,376	1782	Tithables
King George	450	2,040	2,490	1782	Tithables
King William	877	3,443	4,320	1782	Tithables
Lancaster	1,541	2,567	4,108	1783	H. F.
Loudon	947	8,704	9,651	1783	Tithables
Louisa	No figures available				
Lunenburg	750	3,406	4,156	1782	Tithables
Mecklenburg	6,397	4,927	11,324	1782	H. F.
Middlesex	1,167	2,282	3,449	1783	CVSP, III, 373
Monongalia	2,302	81	2,383	1782	H. F.
Montgomery	1,560	319	1,879	1787	Tithables
Nansemond	2,842	2,567	5,409	1783	H. F.
New Kent	1,617	2,957	4,574	1782	H. F.
Norfolk	5,365	3,096	8,461	1782	CVSP, III, 386
Northumberland	3,809	3,925	7,734	1782	CVSP, III, 412
Orange	3,410	2,848	6,258	1782	H. F.
Pittsylvania	5,304	1,835	7,139	1782	H. F.
Powhatan	1,468	2,669	4,137	1783	H. F.
Prince Edward	1,552	1,468	3,020	1783	H. F.
Prince George	476	3,303	3,779	1782	Tithables
Prince William	877	3,443	4,320	1782	Tithables
Princess Anne	3,999	2,656	6,655	1783	CVSP, III, 552
Richmond	2,947	3,885	6,832	1783	CVSP, III, 552
Rockbridge f	755	471	1,226	1782	Tithables
Rockingham g	2,947	3,885	6,832	1783	Tithables
Shenandoah	7,908	347	8,255	1783	H. F.
Southampton	5,286	4,953	10,239	1784	CVSP, III, 553
Spotsylvania	696	4,714	5,410	1782	Tithables
Stafford	2,483	428	2,911	1785	H. F.
Surry	2,389	2,729	5,118	1782	H. F.
Sussex	2,923	3,696	6,619	1782	H. F.
Warwick	569	776	1,345	1782	H. F.
Westmoreland h	410	4,536	4,946	1782	Va. Mag. Hist., Vol. X, 229
Washington	1,062	383	1,445	1782	Tithables
Williamsburg, city of	722	702	1,424	1782	H. F.
York	2,063	699	2,762	1782	Tithables

e In addition to the blacks and whites for which exact numbers are given, the tax lists include "635 freemen and slaves."

f Morton, O. F.: *Hist. of Monroe Co., W. Va.*, 369-77 gives 771 white tithables and 503 blacks.

g The lists of tithables give a total of 2,947 white persons; see, too, CVSP, III, 634, in which Rockingham has 3,657 white persons in 1784.

h Westmoreland had 410 slave owners in 1782.

XI. Census of 1790 [a]

COUNTIES	FREE WHITES			OTHER FREE PERSONS	SLAVES	TOTAL
	Males		Females			
	Over 16	Under 16				
Augusta east of North Mt.	2,048	1,665	3,438	40	1,222 }	
Augusta west of North Mt.	551	572	986	19	345 }	10,886
Albemarle	1,703	1,790	3,342	171	5,579	12,585
Accomack	2,297	2,177	4,502	721	4,262	13,959
Amherst	2,056	2,235	3,995	121	5,296	13,703
Amelia	1,709	1,697	3,278	106	11,307	18,097
Botetourt	2,247	2,562	4,432	24	1,259	10,524
Buckingham	1,274	1,537	2,685	115	4,168	9,779
Berkley	4,253	4,547	7,850	131	2,932	19,713
Brunswick	1,472	1,529	2,918	132	6,776	12,827
Bedford	1,785	2,266	3,674	52	2,754	10,531
Cumberland	885	914	1,778	142	4,434	8,153
Chesterfield	1,652	1,557	3,149	369	7,487	14,214
Charlotte	1,285	1,379	2,535	63	4,816	10,078
Culpeper	3,372	3,755	6,682	70	8,226	22,105
Charles City	532	509	1,043	363	3,141	5,588
Caroline	1,799	1,731	3,464	203	10,292	17,489
Campbell	1,236	1,347	2,363	251	2,488	7,685
Dinwiddie	1,790	1,396	2,853	561	7,334	13,934
Essex	908	869	1,766	139	5,440	9,122
Elizabeth City	390	388	778	18	1,876	3,450
Fauquier	2,674	2,983	5,500	93	6,642	17,892
Fairfax	2,138	1,872	3,601	135	4,574	12,320
Franklin	1,266	1,629	2,840	34	1,073	6,842
Fluvanna	589	654	1,187	25	1,466	3,921
Frederick Division	1,757	1,653	3,041	49	1,319 }	
Ditto	2,078	2,517	4,269	67	2,931 }	19,681
Gloucester	1,597	1,523	3,105	210	7,063	13,498
Goochland	1,028	1,059	2,053	257	4,656	9,053
Greensville	669	627	1,234	212	3,620	6,362
Greenbrier	1,463	1,574	2,639	20	319	6,015
Henrico	1,823	1,170	2,607	581	5,819	12,000
Hanover	1,637	1,412	3,242	240	8,223	14,754
Hampshire	1,662	1,956	3,261	13	454	7,346
Harrison	487	579	947	...	67	2,080
Hardy	1,108	2,256	3,192	411	369	7,336
Halifax	2,214	2,320	4,397	226	5,565	14,722
Henry	1,523	1,963	3,277	165	1,551	8,479
Isle of Wight	1,208	1,163	2,415	375	3,867	9,028

a U.S. Bureau of Census, *Heads of Families, Va.*, 9-10.

XI. CENSUS OF 1790 — *Continued*

COUNTIES	FREE WHITES			OTHER FREE PERSONS	SLAVES	TOTAL
	Males		Females			
	Over 16	Under 16				
James City	395	359	765	146	2,495	4,070 [4,160]
King William	723	732	1,438	84	5,151	8,128
King and Queen	995	1,026	2,138	75	5,143	9,377
King George	757	781	1,585	86	4,157	7,366
Lunenburg	1,110	1,185	2,252	80	4,332	8,959
Loudon	3,677	3,992	7,080	183	4,030	18,962
Lancaster	535	542	1,182	143	3,236	5,638
Louisa	957	1,024	1,899	14	4,573	8,467
Mecklenburg	1,857	2,015	3,683	416	6,762	14,733
Middlesex	407	370	754	51	2,558	4,140
Monongalia	1,089	1,345	2,168	12	154	4,768
Montgomery	2,846	3,744	5,804	6	828	13,228
Norfolk	2,650	1,987	4,291	251	5,345	14,524
Northampton	857	743	1,581	464	3,244	6,889
New Kent	605	587	1,199	148	3,700	6,239
Northumberland	1,046	1,137	2,323	197	4,460	9,103 [9,163]
Nansemond	1,215	1,167	2,331	480	3,817	9,010
Orange	1,317	1,426	2,693	64	4,421	9,921
Ohio	1,222	1,377	2,308	24	281	5,212
Prince Edward	1,044	1,077	1,961	32	3,986	8,100
Prince William	1,644	1,797	3,303	167	4,704	11,615
Prince George	965	822	1,600	267	4,519	8,173
Powhatan	623	548	1,115	211	4,325	6,822
Pendleton	568	686	1,124	1	73	2,452
Pittsylvania	2,008	2,447	4,083	62	2,979	11,579
Princess Anne	1,169	1,151	2,207	64	3,202	7,793
Richmond	704	697	1,517	83	3,984	6,985
Randolph	221	270	441	...	19	951
Rockingham	1,816	1,652	3,209	...	772	7,449
Russell	734	969	1,440	5	190	3,338
Rockbridge	1,517	1,532	2,756	41	682	6,548 [6,528]
Spotsylvania	1,361	1,278	2,532	148	5,933	11,252
Stafford	1,341	1,355	2,769	87	4,036	9,588
Southampton	1,632	1,546	3,134	559	5,993	12,864
Surry	732	651	1,379	368	3,097	6,227
Shenandoah	2,409	2,779	4,791	19	512	10,510
Sussex	1,215	1,174	2,382	391	5,387	10,554 [10,549]
Warwick	176	158	333	33	990	1,690
Washington	1,287	1,440	2,440	8	450	5,625
Westmoreland	815	754	1,614	114	4,425	7,722
York	530	461	1,124	358	2,760	5,233
Total	110,936	116,135 [116,115]	215,046	12,866	292,627 [292,717]	747,610 [747,680]

NORTH CAROLINA

GENERAL

1663   300 families.[1] Oldmixon, British Empire, I, 369.

1664   800 persons in Cape Feare.[2] "A Brief Desc. of Prov. of Carolina," in Hawks, *Hist. of N.C.*, II, 38.

1677   1,400 tithables, "a third part whereof at least being Indians, Negroes and women."[3] Rept. to Proprietors, in N.C. CR, I, 260.

       4,000 inhabitants. Bancroft, I, 425.

1688   8,000 population in the Carolinas. *See* Thirteen Colonies: General, 1688. [This included territory later the colony of Georgia.]

1694   787 tithables. General Court Recds., in N.C. CR, I, 428.

       4,000 inhabitants. Ashe, *Hist. of N.C.*, I, 145. [Based on a rent-roll among MS. recds. at Edenton, N.C.].

1696   60 or 70 scattered families. Memorial of Edw. Randolph, Nov. 10, 1696, in N.C. CR, I, 467.

1700   80,000 in Va. and Carolinas. *See* Thirteen Colonies: General, 1700.

1701   5,000 inhabitants, besides Negroes and Indians. Quoted in Humphreys, S.P.G., 25.

       5,000 population. *See* Thirteen Colonies: General, 1701.

1715   11,200 total population: 7,500 whites and 3,700 blacks. *See* Thirteen Colonies: General, 1715.

1717   2,000 tithables, according to Col. Thomas Pollock. N.C. CR, II, 296.

1720   1,600 tithables, mostly whites; not 500 blacks in the government. Memorial from Messrs. Boone and Barnwell, in N.C., CR, II, 396.

1721   1,600 tithables, about one-third blacks. Rept. BT to King, Sept. 8, 1721, *Kings MS.*, 205, fol. 22, p. 40, in LCT; NYCD, V, 609; also in N.C. CR, II, 419.

       2,500 white souls. Gov. Eden to S.P.G., in N.C. CR, II, 430.

1725   10,000 souls. Humphreys, S.P.G., 142.

1726   5,000 inhabitants. *See* Thirteen Colonies: General, 1726.

1732   30,000 whites, and 6,000 Negroes. 5,000 militia and at least another thousand not enrolled. Gov. Burrington, Ans. Quer., Jan. 1, 1732-33, in N.C. CR, III, 433.[4]

[1] Rivers gives this estimate in Winsor, *Narr. and Crit. Hist.*, V, 305 n., and says he obtains these figures also from the sec. of state.

[2] Same for 1666 in reprint of "Brief Description" in N.C. CR, I, 156, (Swain Coll.).

[3] Tithables [1715] included all white males above 16 years and all Negroes, male and female, over the age of 12. N.C. CR, II, 889. In 1723 free Negroes, mulattoes, and other persons of mixed blood were specifically included. *Ibid.*, XXIII, 106.

[4] Saunders, "Prefatory Notes," N.C. CR, II, xvii, makes this comment: "From the testimony of Pollock, Burrington, and McCulloh, therefore, [see 1717, 1732, and 1735] it would seem that the estimate of population in N.C. in 1729 usually accepted by historians is much too low. Counting both black and white, the population would seem to have been three times greater. According to historians the population was between 10,000 and 12,000. According to contemporary statements, it must have been nearer to 30,000 or 35,000." Dexter quotes the Humphreys figure for 1725, but thinks it too low.

1735 40,000 whites. Petition of Henry McCulloh, in N.C. CR, IV, 156.

1740 2,000 militia. *See* Thirteen Colonies: General, 1740.

1742 7,000 inhabitants male and female, from 16 to 60, plus 3,000 population in Hanover County. Moir to S.P.G., in N.C. CR, IV, 608.

1744 1,400 tithables. House to the Council, in N.C. CR, IV, 748.

1748 5,596 taxables. See page 160. Broadside *"Table of taxables in the province of N.C. from 1748 . . . to 1770,"* in MHS.

1749 8,290 taxables. See page 160. *Ibid.*
      45,000 inhabitants. *See* Thirteen Colonies: General, 1749.

1750 9,214 taxables. See page 160. Broadside *"Table of taxables in the province of N.C. from 1748 . . . to 1770,"* in MHS.

1751 9,437 taxables. See page 160. *Ibid.*

1752 9,943 taxables. See page 160. *Ibid.*
      20,000 whites, about 10,000 Negro slaves. Rowan's Dispatches, in Moore, *Hist. of N.C.*, 63.
      15,000 to 20,000 inhabitants. J. MacSparren to Col. Cary, in Updike, *Hist. of Church in Narragansett*, I, 489.

1753 22,605 taxables. See page 160. Broadside *"Table of taxables in the province of N.C. from 1748 . . . to 1770,"* in MHS.

1754 24,460 taxables. See page 161. *Ibid.*
      15,400 militia, horse and foot, and about 1,500 in the out parts that do not list themselves; about 1,000 exempt from mustering. 10,000 slaves of 12 years and upwards. Pres. Rowan to BT,[5] in N.C. CR, V, 124. For incomplete returns from counties, see page 162.
      24,861 total taxables: 12,393 white men, 7,186 Negro men and women. 2,774 Indian warriors. See page 162. N.C. CR, V, 320-32.
      90,000 total inhabitants: 70,000 whites, 20,000 blacks. Bancroft, II, 389-91.

1755 25,965 taxables. See page 161. Broadside *"Table of taxables in the province of N.C. from 1748 . . . to 1770,"* in MHS.
      24,607 total taxables; 12,823 militia. See page 163. N.C. CR, V, 575.
      50,000 white inhabitants, with 13,000 men capable of bearing arms. Rept. of BT, in NYCD, VI, 993.
      45,000 inhabitants. Anon., *State of British and French Colonies in North Am., 1755*, 138.
      50,000 whites; or 80,000 total. *See* Thirteeen Colonies: General, 1755.

1756 26,908 taxables. See page 161. Broadside *"Table of taxables in the province of N.C. from 1748 . . . to 1770,"* in MHS.

[5] On the basis of these and previously cited figures, Saunders would estimate the population at 90,000 in 1752, (N. C. CR, IV. xx), and 100,000 in 1754 (*Ibid.*, V, xxxix).

25,737 total taxables: 12,069 white taxables; 13,668 black taxables; 12,931 militia. See page 163. N.C. CR, V, 603.

72,000 whites. Gov. Dobbs to Earl of Loudoun,[6] in N.C. CR, V, 600-601.

1757 27,094 taxables. See page 161. Broadside *"Table of taxables in the province of N.C. from 1748 . . . to 1770,"* in MHS.

1758 27,336 taxables. See page 161. *Ibid.*

1759 30,385 taxables. See page 161. *Ibid.*

1760 25,226 taxables.[7] See page 164. *Ibid.*

80,000 whites. Gov. Dobbs to S.P.G., in N.C. CR, VI, 223.

1761 36,219 taxables. See page 164. Broadside *"Table of taxables in the province of N.C. from 1748 . . . to 1770,"* in MHS.

34,000 taxables, of which 22,000 are white men of 16 and 12,000 Negroes, male and female. The whole number of souls must be near 88,000. The militia is about 16,000. Returns for the 14 southern counties are: 7,473 white taxables, 16-60; and 6,535 black taxables, male and female, 13 years and over; 2,208 Indian warriors. Gov. Dobbs' Ans. Quer., in N.C. CR, VI, 613-14.

1762 36,433 taxables. See page 164. Broadside *"Table of taxables in the province of N.C. from 1748 . . . to 1770,"* in MHS.

1763 36,469 taxables. See page 164. *Ibid.*

1764 40,576 taxables. See page 164. *Ibid.*

24,000 white taxables, and consequently near 100,000 souls; and above 100,000 [*Sic.* 10,000?] male and female taxable Negroes.[8] Gov. Dobbs to BT, in N.C. CR, VI, 1027.

1765 41,065 taxables. See page 164. Broadside *"Table of taxables in the province of N.C. from 1748 . . . to 1770,"* in MHS.

45,912 total taxables: 28,542 white taxables, 17,370 black and mulatto taxables.[9] See page 165. N.C. CR, VII, 145-46.

120,000 inhabitants; 30,000 men. *See* Thirteen Colonies: General, 1765.

1766 43,664 taxables. See page 167. Broadside *"Table of taxables in the province of N.C. from 1748 . . . to 1770,"* in MHS.

48,610 total taxables: 16,183 white male taxables, and 12,923 black

---

[6] Gov. Dobbs also observes: "You will see also the list of taxables is not compleat . . . if they had been properly returned I believe the whites who are males above 16 would be about 18,000."

[7] This total is incomplete. The broadside is so badly worn away on the folds that the returns for seven counties are partially or completely undecipherable. See page 164.

[8] On p. 1041, N.C. CR, VI, Gov. Dobbs in a letter to the S.P.G. gives the above figures for the white inhabitants, but only 10,000 for the Negroes. Comparison with the total given in the broadside indicates that the estimate of 100,000 is probably an error for 10,000.

[9] The return for Rowan Co. is for 1766. See page 166.

and mulatto taxables, male and female. See page 165. N.C. CR, VII, 288-89.[10]

29,706 white men above 18 capable of bearing arms; "which at 4 to a family (deducting the Heads of Taxables) are 119,164 souls." See page 165. Mr. Woodmason's Acct. of N.C., in N.C. CR, VII, 283-84.

1767 46,627 taxables. See page 167. Broadside *"Table of taxables in the province of N.C. from 1748 . . . 1770,"* in MHS.

51,044 total taxables; 17,700 white taxables, 12,382 black taxables. See page 166. N.C. CR, VII, 559. (Enclosed in Gov. Tryon's letter, April 25, 1769.)

1768 46,701 taxables. See page 167. Broadside *"Table of taxables in the province of N.C. from 1748 . . . to 1770,"* in MHS.

1769 51,456 taxables. See page 167. *Ibid.*

1770 25,681 taxables. See page 167.[11] *Ibid.*

58,000 taxables. *North Am. and West Ind. Gazetteer,* under "N.C."

1771 60,000 solvent taxables, according to revenue act of 1771, which implies a population of some 250,000 souls. Saunders, "Prefatory Notes," in N.C. CR, IX, xv. For taxables in the counties of the "Northern District," see page 168.

1774 270,000 inhabitants, the estimate of Congress of 300,000 being exaggerated by 30,000 at least. Smyth, *Tour of the U.S.,* I, 235.[12]

64,000 taxables, and 10,000 Negroes and mulattoes. *North Am. and West Ind. Gazetteer,* under "N.C."

300,000 total population; or 260,000. *See* Thirteen Colonies: General, 1774.

1775 30,000 fighting men; 10,000 Negroes. Gov. Martin to Lord Dartmouth, in N.C. CR, X, 46.

200,000 total population. *See* Thirteeen Colonies: General, 1775.

1783 200,000 population. *See* Thirteeen Colonies: General, 1783.

1784 25,000 militia. "Our Delegates . . . stated the number of our militia at 40,000 . . . The number of inhabitants in some of the States have been taken from the militia rolls by counting five inhabitants for every Man on the roll . . . I have some reason to believe our fencible militia were much nearer 25 than 40 thousand. Hugh Williamson to Gov. Martin, Sept. 30, 1784, *N.C. State Recds.,* XVII, 95-96.

[10] A note states that this list was enclosed in Gov. Tryon's letter, but there is nothing to indicate the identity of the letter.

[11] These returns are evidently incomplete, since there are none for fourteen counties: Bertie, Bladen, Chowan, Cumberland, Currituck, Duplin, Hyde, Mecklenburg, Northampton, Onslow, Orange, Pitt, Rowan, and Tryon.

[12] Dexter uses the figure 300,000 from John Adams' account of the Congressional estimates, but thinks 260,000 a closer estimate. Rossiter gives 260,000.

1786 123,785 total inhabitants: 74,374 whites, 37,324 blacks. According to incomplete census. See page 169. *N.C. State Recds.*, XVIII, 433-34.

224,000 total inhabitants: 164,000 whites; 60,000 blacks. Webster, in *N.Y. Directory for 1786*, 21.

300,000 total inhabitants. *See* Thirteen Colonies: General, 1786.

1787 200,000 including 60,000 Negroes; or 181,000 whites. *See* Thirteen Colonies: General, 1787.

1790 393,751 total population: free white males over 16, 69,988; free white males under 16, 77,506; free white females, 140,710; other free persons, 4,975; slaves, 100,572. U.S. Bureau of Census, *Heads of Families, N.C.*, 8. See page 170.

LOCAL

I. LISTS OF TAXABLES AND MILITIA

A. TAXABLES FROM 1748 TO 1753 a

Counties	1748	1749	1750	1751	1752	1753
Anson	....	....	516	588	965	702
Beaufort	832	1,000	1,009	866	866	1,200
Bertie	....	....	....	....	....	1,706
Bladen	800	705	903	988	949	899
Carteret	320	375	387	399	435	442
Chowan	....	....	....	....	....	1,400
Craven	1,278	1,374	1,214	1,435	1,543	1,629
Currituck	....	....	....	....	....	70–b
Duplin	....	....	377	477	553	554
Edgecomb	....	....	....	....	....	2,103
Granville	870	922	1,0–8 b	991	969	1,004
Hyde	396	429	414	412	400	409
Johnston	908	1,009	1,048	1,190	1,160	1,340
New Hanover	192	1,890	1,688	1,438	1,487	2,037
Northampton	....	....	....	....	....	1,753
Onslow	....	586	650	653	616	711
Orange	....	....	....	....	....	1,108
Pasquotank	....	....	....	....	....	1,180
Perquimans	....	....	....	....	....	1,028
Tyrrell	....	....	....	....	....	700
	[5,596] c	[8,290]	[9,214]	[9,437]	[9,943]	[22,605]

a From a broadside entitled "A Table of taxables in the province of North Carolina from 1748 . . . to 1770," belonging to the Massachusetts Historical Society.

b One digit is undecipherable, because the paper is worn away on the folds. This digit has been added in the total as zero.

c In this and the following tables for North Carolina, totals of columns are given as found in the source cited. When the total given is incorrect, as in Table C, (White

I. Lists of Taxables and Militia — *Continued*

B. Taxables from 1754 to 1759 d

Counties	1754	1755	1756	1757	1758	1759
Anson e	600	854	450	364	178	350
Beaufort f	1,241	1,311	1,302	1,211	1,285	1,252
Bertie	1,789	1,876	1,871	1,941	1,892	1,892
Bladen g	684	661	664	933	1,064	1,010
Carteret	447	422	449	508	479	527
Chowan h	1,456	1,536	1,592	1,287	1,413	1,420
Craven	1,644	1,836	1,836	1,967	2,049	2,090
Currituck	707	717	721	705	706	811
Cumberland	323	377	371	612	348	394
Dobbs	....	....	....	....	....	1,054
Duplin	629	626	678	766	795	896
Edgecomb	2,190	2,410	2,414	2,222	2,050	1,331
Granville	1,200	1,318	1,304	1,655	1,852	2,097
Halifax	....	....	....	....	....	2,029
Hyde	415	424	425	485	488	520
Johnston	1,298	1,541	1,871	1,673	1,653	1,756
New Hanover	2,008	2,210	2,228	2,159	2,371	2,250
Northampton	1,805	1,875	1,933	1,963	1,955	2,210
Onslow	716	778	753	721	761	799
Orange e	1,281	1,124	1,415	1,595	1,860	1,856
Pasquotank	1,200	1,223	1,250	1,332	1,229	1,247
Perquimans	1,117	1,136	1,023	1,173	1,240	1,198
Rowan e	1,000	1,000	1,531	1,034	1,034	747
Tyrrell	710	710	827	788	634	649
	[24,460]	[25,965]	[26,908]	[27,094]	[27,336]	[30,385]

taxables for 1754), the true sum has been presented in brackets beside that found in the source. When no total was given in the original, as in these tables, it has been computed and placed in brackets at the foot of the column.

d From a broadside entitled "A Table of taxables in the province of North Carolina from 1748 . . . to 1770," belonging to the Massachusetts Historical Society.

e Anson County in *1748* had 200 to 300 white tithables on the Peedee River: Petition to Governor, in N.C. CR, IV, 888. Anson, Orange, and Rowan Counties in *1746* had 100 fighting men: *Ibid.*, IV, Pref. Notes, xxi; also Pres. Rowan to BT, in *ibid.*, V, 24; in *1753* had 3,000 fighting men, "for the most part Irish Protestants and Germans, and dayley increasing": Pres. Rowan to BT, *ibid.*, V, 24.

f Bath in Beaufort District in *1709* had 12 houses: Mr. Gordon to S.P.G., *ibid.*, I, 715; in *1745* had 30 houses: "Journal of Wm. Logan," in *Pa. Mag. Hist.*, XXXVI, 10.

g Bladen Precinct in *1732* had 30 families, including the Freeholders: Petition to the Gov. and Council, N.C. CR, III, 450.

h Chowan Precinct in *1702* had 285 tithables: Vestry Book of St. Paul's Parish, in *ibid.*, I, 559; in *1743* had 1,126 tithables: "Acct. for erecting a magazine," in *N.C. Hist. Gen. Reg.*, II, 198; in *1745* had 1,200 tithables: Letter from Clement Hall to S.P.G., in N.C. CR, IV, 753. Edenton in Chowan County in *1729* had 40 or 50 houses: Byrd, *Hist. of Div. Line*, I, 59.

I. LISTS OF TAXABLES AND MILITIA — *Continued*

C. TAXABLES AND MILITIA IN 1754 [1]

COUNTIES	TAXABLES			TOTAL	MILITIA
	White	Black			
	Male	*Male*	*Female*		
Anson	810	40	20	870	
Beaufort	637	267	218	1,306 n	587
	120	40	24		
Bertie	1,220	289	200	1,709 o	720
Bladen	338	226	120	684	477 r
Carteret	...	...	...	400 p	209
Chowan	...	...	...	1,481 o	652
Craven	870	468	308	1,646	
Cumberland	...	...	...	850 p	
Currituck j	470	80	70	629 p	345
Duplin	560 n	105	63	628	39
Edgecombe	1,611	508	416	2,535	1,317
Granville	779	261	165	1,205	734
Hyde	237	100	83	420	252
Johnston	...	...	...	1,425	893
New Hanover k	362	799	575	1,736	508
Northampton l	902	510	324	1,736	739
Onslow	448	151	96	695	352
Orange f	950	35	15	1,000 q	
Pasquotank m	563	266	100	929	590
Perquimans	...	...	...	1,117	379
Rowan f	1,116	30	24	1,170	
Tyrrel	500	100	90	690	337
	12,393 [12,493]	4,275	2,911	24,861	[9,130]

i N.C. CR, V, 320, 161-63.

j Currituck in *1707* had 1,300 souls: Martin, *Hist. of N.C.*, I, 251; in *1754* had 839 souls: Humphreys, S.P.G., 134; in *1710* had 539 inhabitants in the parish of whom 97 are Negroes, 1 Quaker, 5 or 6 of no professed religion, the rest of the Established Church: Letter of J. Adams to S.P.G., in N.C. CR, I, 722.

k Hanover County in *1742* had 3,000 inhabitants, two-thirds whereof were Negroes: Letter from James Moir to S.P.G., in *ibid.*, V, 605. Wilmington in *1754* had 70 families; Gov. Dobbs to Earl of Halifax, *ibid.*, V, 158. Brunswick in *1754* had 20 families: Gov. Dobbs to the Earl of Halifax, *ibid.*, V, 158.

l Northampton County in *1748* had 676 total militia: *N.C. State Recds.*, XXII, 273.

m Pasquotank in *1709* had 1,332 inhabitants, including 211 Negroes: Letter of James Adams to S.P.G. in N.C. CR, I, 720.

n Including "184 not distinguished in total." This figure should evidently be 460. Compare total for Duplin and total white male taxables.

o "Not distinguished in the return."   p "Computed."

q "Not returned."

r "50 families . . . a lawless people."

I. LISTS OF TAXABLES AND MILITIA — *Continued*

D. TAXABLES AND MILITIA FOR 1755 [t]

COUNTIES	MILITIA	TAXABLES		
		White	*Black*	*Total*
Anson	790	810	60	870
Beaufort	680	771	567	1,383 [v]
Bertie	794	...	...	1,876
Bladen	441	338	346	684
Carteret	230	...	...	400
Chowan	830	...	...	1,481
Craven	631	989	934	1,923
Cumberland				
Currituck	393	474	150	620
Duplin	340	460	168	628
Edgecomb	1,317	1,611	924	2,538
Granville	734	779	426	1,205
Hyde	248	237	183	420
Johnston	894	...	...	1,425
New Hanover [u]	508	362	1,374	1,736
Northampton	676	902	834	1,736
Onslow	308	448	247	695
Orange	490	950	50	1,000
Pasquotank	581	563	366	929
Perquimans	357	...	...	1,176
Rowan	996	1,116	54	1,160
Tyrell [w]	438	477	335	722
Troops of horse	149			
Total	12,823 [12,825]	[11,287]	[7,018]	24,607

E. TAXABLES AND MILITIA FOR 1756 [x]

COUNTIES	MILITIA	TAXABLES		
		White	*Black*	*Total*
Anson	790	810	60	870
Beaufort	680	771	567	1,383 [y]
Bertie	902	...	...	1,876

t N.C. CR, V, 575-76.

u Wilmington had 106 taxables: Town Recds. in *Jas. Sprunt Hist. Mono. and Publ.*, IV, 71.

v The totals for this county, Currituck, Edgecomb, Rowan, and Tyrell are not accurate on the basis of the figures given for whites and blacks.

w Tyrell County in *1758* had 505 total militia: *N.C. State Recds.*, XXII, 390.

x N.C. CR, V, 603.

y The totals for this county, Rowan, and Tyrell are not accurate on the basis of the figures given for whites and blacks.

I. Lists of Taxables and Militia — *Continued*

Counties	Militia	Taxables			Horse	
		White	*Black*	*Total*		
Bladen	441	338	346	684	Bladen	33
Carteret	230	...	...	400	Bertie	44
Chowan	830	...	...	1,481	Duplin	39
Craven	631	989	934	1,923	New Hanover	33
Cumberland	...	302	74	376		—
Currituck	390	470	150	620		149
Duplin	340	460	168	628		
Edgecomb	1,317	1,674	1,091	2,765		
Granville	734	835	470	1,305		
Hyde	249	276	148	424		
Johnson	894	1,242	397	1,639		
New Hanover	508	396	1,420	1,816		
Northampton	676	902	834	1,736		
Onslow	308	448	247	695		
Orange	490	...	...	1,113		
Pasquotank	581	563	366	929		
Perquimans	357	...	...	1,176		
Rowan	996	1,116	54	1,176		
Tyrell	438	477	335	722		
Horse	149					
Total	12,931	12,069	[7,661]	25,737		

F. Taxables from 1760 to 1765.[z]

Counties	1760	1761	1762	1763	1764	1765
Anson	600	776	776	776	745	644
Beaufort	1,2–2 aa	712	716	742	751	740
Bertie	665	840	1,631	1,–66 aa	1,641	1,426
Bladen	1,112	1,207	1,200	1,244	1,244	1,114
Brunswick	....	....	....	....	1,318	1,184
Bute	....	....	....	....	1,757	1,798
Carteret	503	528	541	541	594	657
Chowan	1,480	1,500	1,500	1,400	1,400	1,510
Craven	? aa	2,239	2,120	2,120	2,266	2,344
Currituck	6— aa	857	807	737	800	717
Cumberland	? aa	611	693	873	1,005	1,109
Dobbs	? aa	1,273	1,339	1,400	1,485	1,607
Duplin	? aa	1,029	1,055	1,085	1,085	881
Edgecomb	1,3— aa	1,663	1,666	1,566	1,480	1,557
Granville	2,009	2,877	2,828	3,128	1,362	1,479

z From a broadside entitled "A Table of taxables in the province of North Carolina from 1748 . . . to 1770," belonging to the Massachusetts Historical Society.

aa These figures are undecipherable, because the paper is worn away on the folds. Missing digits have been added in the total as zero.

I. LISTS OF TAXABLES AND MILITIA — *Continued*

Counties	1760	1761	1762	1763	1764	1765
Halifax	2,291	2,706	2,425	1,985	2,286	2,476
Hertford	1,324	1,488	1,392	1,384	1,496	1,552
Hyde	525	569	568	588	689	588
Johnston	817	973	982	1,282	1,282	1,298
Mecklenburg	....	....	....	791	1,071	1,217
New Hanover	2,003	2,670	2,790	2,356	1,747	1,805
Northampton	2,210	2,270	2,280	2,131	2,109	2,300
Onslow	780	873	877	890	1,050	1,017
Orange	1,928	2,627	2,427	2,669	3,028	3,064
Pasquotank	1,410	1,411	1,292	1,215	1,225	1,098
Perquimans	1,174	1,320	1,299	1,303	1,470	1,485
Pitt	....	987	995	1,093	1,061	1,062
Rowan	669	1,373	1,486	1,486	2,295	2,520
Tyrrell	624	840	748	618	834	816
	[25,226]	[36,219]	[36,433]	[36,469]	[40,576]	[41,065]

G. TITHABLES AND MILITIA FOR 1765 AND 1766 ab

COUNTIES	1765			1766			
	White	Black	Total	White	Black	Total	Militia
Anson	584	131	715	...	...	786	800
Beaufort ac	411	470	881	432	476	908	742
Bertie	636	877	1,513	...	...	1,745	1,634
Bladen	604	633	1,237	...	...	1,262	1,244
Brunswick ad	209	1,106	1,315	229	1,177	1,406	186
Bute	...	...	2,078	1,172	967	2,139	200
Carteret	411	931	1,342	460	269	729	541
Chowan	610	1,017	1,627	616	1,082	1,698	745
Craven	1,284	1,320	2,604	1,391	1,298	2,689	1,175
Cumberland	866	366	1,232	900	387	1,287	652
Currituck	...	...	796	...	...	875	709
Dobbs	1,176	609	1,785	1,211	643	1,854	954
Duplin	848	130	978	883	359	,1,242	1,085
Edgecombe	...	...	1,739	...	...	2,066	1,207
Granville	974	701	1,675	926	809	1,735	2,882
Halifax	...	...	2,628	...	...	2,894	2,029

ab List of taxables, N.C., CR, VII, 145-46, 288-89; militia, *ibid.*, VII, 283-84.

ac Bath had 2,000 inhabitants in *1762*, of whom 1,700 were members of the Anglican Church: Hawkins, *Hist. Notices*, 86. St. Thomas' Parish was estimated to have about 2,100 inhabitants in *1760*; 1,000 whites and 400 taxable negroes in *1761*; 800 taxables in all in *1764*; and 1,100 white inhabitants in *1765*: Stewart to S.P.G., in N.C. CR, VI, 315-16, 562, 1056; VII, 126.

ad St. Philip's Parish, which included Brunswick Co. and part of Bladen Co., had 800 taxables and 200 families in *1762*: Macdowell to S.P.G., in *ibid.*, VI, 729-30.

I. Lists of Taxables and Militia — *Continued*

COUNTIES	1765			1766			
	White	*Black*	*Total*	*White*	*Black*	*Total*	*Militia*
Hertford	...	...	1,567	...	...	1,667	1,393
Hyde	402	251	653	430	286	716	604
Johnston	984	458	1,442	1,003	511	1,514	899
Mecklenberg	...	...	1,352	...	...	1,461	791
New Hanover ae	529	1,476	2,005	507	1,531	2,038	446
Northampton	...	...	2,434	...	...	2,497	1,169
Onslow	678	451	1,129	...	...	1,192	978
Orange	2,825	579	3,404	3,324	649	3,973	2,699
Pasquotank	...	...	1,106	740	606	1,346	850
Perquimans	...	...	1,531	527	1,017	1,544	
Pitt	750	429	1,179	798	470	1,268	741
Rowan	...	...	3,059	...	...	3,059	1,486
Tyrell	538	368	906	634	386	1,020	996
	28,542	17,370	45,912	16,183	12,923	48,610	29,706
	[15,319]	[12,303]					[29,837]

H. Taxables for 1767 af

Counties	*White*	*Black*	*Total*
Anson ag	696	173	869
Beaufort	410	481	891
Bertie	...	...	1,829
Bladen	791	716	1,507
Brunswick ah	224	1,085	1,309
Bute	1,299	941	2,240
Carteret ai	470	290	760
Chowan	...	...	1,653
Craven aj	1,378	1,520	2,898
Currituck ak	...	...	889
Cumberland	899	362	1,261
Dobbs	1,268	706	1,974

ae New Hanover in *1763* had 2,670 taxables, of whom only 509 were white persons, the rest Negroes: *Ibid.*, VI, 986.

af N.C. CR, VII, 539.

ag Anson County in *1769* had 896 taxables: Acct. of Sheriff of County, in N.C. CR, VIII, 256.

ah The town of Brunswick in *1773* had 50 or 60 houses: Smyth, *Tour in the U.S.*, II, 88. Waccamaw in *1774* had 30 families: Rev. Mr. Christian to S.P.G., N.C. CR, IX, 1022.

ai The town of Beaufort in Carteret County in *1773* had 60 families and upwards: Petition to Gov. Martin, in *ibid.*, IX, 641.

aj Newbern in Craven County in *1775* had 600 population: Vass, *Hist. of Presby. Church in New Bern*, 76; in *1787* had 500 or 600 houses: Attmore, "Journal of a Tour to N.C.," in *Jas. Sprunt Hist. Mono. and Publ.*, XVII, No. 245.

ak Currituck in *1771* had 572 total number of militia: Returns, in N.C. CR, IX, 58-59.

I. LISTS OF TAXABLES AND MILITIA — *Continued*

Counties	White	Black	Total	
Duplin	1,071	437	1,508	
Edgecomb	...	...	2,260	
Granville al	1,022	906	1,928	
Halifax	...	...	2,806	
Hertford am	...	...	1,690	
Hyde an	441	282	723	
Johnson ao	1,129	567	1,696	
Mecklenburg	...	...	2,163	
New Hanover ap	511	1,492	2,003	
Northampton	...	...	2,557	
Onslow	716	500	1,216	
Orange	3,573	729	4,300	[4,302]
Pasquotank	433	359	792 as	
Perquimans	...	...	1,472	
Pitt aq	775	448	1,223	
Rowan ar	...	...	3,643	
Tyrrell	594	390	984	
	17,700	12,382	51,044	
		[12,384]	[51,046]	

I. TAXABLES FROM 1766 TO 1770 at

Counties	1766	1767	1768	1769	1770 av
Anson	708	783	800	807	963
Beaufort	779	803	783	74—au	177
Bertie	1,629	1,647	1,154	1,914	
Bladen	1,136	1,357	1,435	1,274	
Brunswick	1,266	1,179	1,341	1,351	1,496
Bute	1,871	1,974	2,398	2,473	2,629

al Granville in *1771* had 487 total militia: *N.C. State Recds.*, XXII, 160-67.

am Hertford County in *1772* had 621 total militia: Returns, in N.C. CR, IX, 296-97.

an Hyde County in *1774* had 376 total militia: Returns, in *ibid.*, IX, 1050.

ao Johnston County in *1774* had 390 total militia: Returns, in *ibid.*, IX, 1075-77.

ap Wilmington in New Hanover County in *1773* had 200 houses: Smyth, *Tour in the U.S.*, II, 87.

aq Pitt County in *1773* had 566 total militia: Returns, in *ibid.*, IX, 696.

ar Rowan County in *1771* had 2,000 taxables in the upper settlement of the Catawba River, on the Yadkin River, and at Three Creeks: Petition to Gov. Martin, in *ibid.*, IX, 91; in *1775* had 2,817 taxables given in by militia captains: *Ibid.*, X, 252-53, 280, 319; Salisbury in *1786* had 50 dwelling houses: Watson, *Memoirs*, 294.

as The taxables for this county are less than in *1766*. Gov. Tryon attributes this fact, not to any decrease in inhabitants, but to the failure of some justices to make returns from their districts. Gov. Tryon to Lord Hillsborough, in N.C. CR, VIII, 32.

at From a broadside entitled "A Table of taxables in the province of North Carolina from 1748 . . . to 1770," belonging to the Massachusetts Historical Society.

au These figures are undecipherable, because the paper is worn away on the folds. The missing digits have been added in the total as zero.

av These returns are evidently incomplete.

I. LISTS OF TAXABLES AND MILITIA — *Continued*

Counties	1766	1767	1768	1769	1770
Carteret	657	684	713	736	483
Chowan	1,577	1,663	1,519	1,589	
Craven	2,421	2,609	2,654	2,506	
Currituck	808	849	863	913	938
Cumberland	1,159	1,135	1,179	1,186	
Dobbs	1,669	1,777	1,812	1,858	2,038
Duplin	1,118	1,358	1,365	1,387	
Edgecomb	1,988	2,155	2,153	2,346	2,237
Granville	1,394	1,791	1,849	1,925	2,040
Halifax	2,445	2,559	2,594	2,759	2,760
Hertford	1,501	1,521	1,564	1,606	1,620
Hyde	645	651	665	671	
Johnston	1,363	1,527	1,681	1,709	1,950
Mecklenburg	1,315	1,917	1,208	1,136	
New Hanover	1,835	1,803	1,991	2,056	2,048
Northampton	2,325	2,412	2,235	2,263	
Onslow	1,073	1,095	1,140	1,138	
Orange	3,576	3,870	3,281	3,467	
Pasquotank	1,202	790	1,392	2,922	2,010
Perquimans	1,390	1,452	1,487	1,660	1,527
Pitt	1,142	1,101	1,121	1,162	
Rowan	2,754	3,279	3,636	3,852	
Tyrrell	918	886	688	951	765
Tryon	....	....	....	1,099	
	[43,664]	[46,627]	[46,701]	[51,456]	[25,681]

J. TAXABLES FOR 1770 TO 1772 [NORTHERN DISTRICT ONLY]

Counties	Taxables aw	Date
Bertie	2105	1771
Bute	2629	1771
Chatham	1282	1772
Chowan	1669	1771
Currituck	1042	1770
Edgecombe	2489	1770
Grenville	2474	1771
Halifax	3070	1771
Hertford	1813	1771
Northampton	2647	1771
Orange	2906	1771

aw This list of taxables is taken from an unpublished bound manuscript in the archives of the North Carolina Historical Commission at Raleigh, North Carolina. The volume is entitled "The Tax Book of the Northern District." No tax book corresponding to it for the Southern District has been found. This table was kindly supplied by Miss Stella Sutherland.

I. Lists of Taxables and Militia — *Continued*

Counties	Taxables	Date
Pasquotank	2203	1771
Perquimans	1793	1772
Tyrell	959	1771

[29,081]

II. Censuses

A. Census of 1786 [a] [*Incomplete*]

COUNTIES [b]	WHITES			BLACKS		TOTAL
	Males 21-60	Other Males	Females	From 12 to 60	Other Blacks	
Franklin	740	1,069	1,814	931	913	5,475
Tyrrell	552	966	1,488	374	379	3,859
Pasquotank	615	1,023	1,551	789	815	4,793
Northampton	763	1,329	1,966	1,721	1,564	7,043
New Hanover [c]	579	722	1,397	1,332	1,012	5,042
Duplin	734	1,356	1,997	605	548	5,248
Warren	735	1,399	2,499	1,792	1,870	8,295
Addition to above						701
Richmond	380	757	1,126	168	154	2,585
Caswell	1,273	2,748	3,611	1,110	1,097	9,839
Chowan [d]	463	641	970	992	716	3,782
Nash	650	1,269	1,850	799	709	5,277
Edgecomb	1,045	1,977	2,985	1,271	1,202	8,480
Halifax [e]	1,088	814	3,145	2,638	2,552	10,327
Gates	543	901	1,361	927	1,183	4,917
Granville	733	1,486	2,149	925	954	6,247
Addition to above						4,055
Sampson	565	1,197	1,786	384	338	4,268
Hyde	496	584	1,282	430	376	3,421
Surry [f]	340	837	436	105	94	1,559
	[12,294]	[21,075]	[33,413]	[17,293]	[16,476]	105,213 [g]

Total whites	66,782	Total blacks	33,769
	Total whites and blacks	105,213	

To this total should be added 25 counties, whose names are undecipherable, having a total of 18,572, of which 7,592 were whites and 3,555 blacks.

a *N.C. State Recds.*, XVIII, 433-34.

b Davidson County in *1785* had 700 militia: Blount to Ind. Commsrs., *N.C. State Recds.*, XVII, 580: Morgan District, which included Burke, Lincoln, Rutherford, and Wilkes, in *1786* had 3,071 total militia: Returns, *ibid.*, XVII, 786.

c Wilmington District, in New Hanover County, in *1780* had 112 taxables (in some cases apparently heads of families): *Ibid.*, XV, 190-92.

d Edenton in Chowan County in *1777* had 135 dwellings: Watson, *Memoirs*, 44.

e Halifax, the town, in *1778* had 45 dwellings: *Ibid.*, 70; and in *1782* had 25 dwelling houses: Letter Book of Lt. Enos Reeves, from Extracts in *Pa. Mag. Hist.*, XXI, 378.

f Salem in Surry County in *1786* had 40 dwellings: Watson, *Memoirs*, 293.

g Totals for counties of Franklin, Tyrrell, Northampton, Duplin, Halifax, Gates, and

II. Censuses — *Continued*

B. Census of 1790 h

DISTRICTS	FREE WHITES			OTHER FREE	SLAVES	TOTAL
	Males		Females			
	Over 16	Under 16				
Edenton						
Bertie	1,762	1,841	3,514	348	5,141	12,606
Camden	727	759	1,477	30	1,040	4,033
Chowan	460	446	876	7	1,647	3,436
Edentontown	181	113	306	34	941	1,575
Currituck	1,017	1,024	1,960	115	1,103	5,219
Gates	790	775	1,515	93	2,219	5,392
Hertford	814	823	1,533	216	2,442	5,828
Pasquotank	951	1,034	1,810	79	1,623	5,497
Perquimans	885	923	1,717	37	1,878	5,440
Tyrell	807	959	1,777	35	1,166	4,744
	8,394	8,697	16,485	994	19,200	53,770
Fayette						
Anson	1,034	1,183	2,047	41	828	5,133
Cumberland	1,397	1,362	2,661	49	1,666	7,135
Fayetteville i	394	195	398	34	515	1,536
Moore	849	968	1,570	12	371	3,770
Richmond	1,096	1,205	2,116	55	583	5,055
Robeson	1,131	1,141	2,244	277	533	5,326
Sampson	1,145	1,281	2,316	140	1,183	6,065
	7,046	7,335	13,352	608	5,679	34,020
Halifax						
Edgecombe	1,659	1,879	3,495	70	3,152	10,255
Franklin	1,089	1,400	2,316	37	2,717	7,559
Halifax	1,835	1,778	3,403	443	6,506	13,965
Martin	1,064	1,009	2,022	96	1,889	6,080
Nash	1,143	1,426	2,627	188	2,009	7,393
Northampton	1,334	1,273	2,503	462	4,409	9,981
Warren	1,070	1,319	2,220	68	4,720	9,397
	9,194	10,084	18,586	1,364	25,402	64,630
Hillsborough						
Caswell	1,801	2,110	3,377	72	2,736	10,096
Chatham	1,756	2,160	3,664	9	1,632	9,221
Granville	1,581	1,873	3,050	315	4,163	10,982
Orange	2,433	2,709	4,913	101	2,060	12,216

Sampson are not accurate on basis of figures given ; the grand total would then be 105,307.

h U.S. Bureau of Census, *Heads of Families, N.C.*, 8, 9-10.

i Fayetteville town not included in Cumberland.

II. Censuses — *Continued*

Districts	Free Whites			Other Free	Slaves	Total
	Males		Females			
	Over 16	Under 16				
Randolph	1,582	1,952	3,266	24	452	7,276
Wake ʲ	1,772	2,089	3,688	180	2,463	10,192
	10,925	12,893	21,958	701	13,506	59,983
Morgan						
Burke	1,706	2,115	3,683	11	595	8,110
Lincoln	2,053	2,294	4,037	...	935	9,319
Rutherford	1,577	2,121	3,502	2	609	7,811
Wilkes	1,615	2,251	3,739	2	549	8,156
	13,902 ˡ	17,562	29,922	30	5,376	66,792
	[6,951]	[8,781]	[14,961]	[15]	[2,688]	[33,396]
Newbern						
Beaufort	951	926	1,824	129	1,632	5,462
Carteret	718	707	1,502	92	713	3,732
Craven	1,709	1,538	3,227	337	3,658	10,469
Dobbs	1,162	1,293	2,478	45	1,915	6,893
Hyde	795	718	1,522	37	1,048	4,120
Johnston	1,039	1,119	2,083	64	1,329	5,634
Jones	736	794	1,541	70	1,681	4,822
Pitt	1,461	1,507	2,915	25	2,367	8,275
Wayne	1,064	1,219	2,256	37	1,557	6,133
	9,635	9,821	19,348	836	15,900	55,540
Salisbury						
Guilford	1,607	1,799	3,242	27	516	7,191
Iredell	1,118	1,217	2,239	3	858	5,435
Mecklenburg	2,378	2,573	4,771	70	1,603	11,395
Montgomery	967	1,121	1,798	5	834	4,725
Rockingham ᵏ	1,173	1,413	2,491	10	1,100	6,187
Rowan	3,288	3,837	6,864	97	1,742	15,828
Stokes	1,846	2,104	3,778	13	787	8,528
Surry	1,531	1,762	3,183	17	698	7,191
	13,908	15,826	28,366	242	8,138	66,480
Wilmington						
Bladen	837	830	1,683	58	1,676	5,084
Brunswick	380	398	779	3	1,511	3,071
Duplin	1,035	1,187	2,054	3	1,383	5,662

ʲ The only other return for Wake Co. is one for 577 militia in *1772*: N.C. CR, IX, 344.

ᵏ Including Salisbury town.

ˡ The totals for Morgan County should be just half those given, as in each column sub-figures used to make up the totals for Burke, Lincoln, Rutherford, and Wilkes were added again to give the entire total for Morgan.

II. Censuses — *Continued*

DISTRICTS	FREE WHITES			OTHER FREE	SLAVES	TOTAL
	Males		Females			
	Over 16	Under 16				
New Hanover	834	695	1,497	67	3,738	6,831
Onslow	828	939	1,788	84	1,748	3,639 [5,387]
	3,914	4,049	7,801	215	10,056	26,035
Grand Total	69,988	77,506	140,710	4,975	100,572	393,751
	[69,967]	[77,486]	[140,857]		[100,569]	[393,854]

SOUTH CAROLINA

GENERAL

1671   Not 150 men fit to bear arms. Gov. West to Ashley, Carteret, and Colleton, March 21, 1671, in CSPC, 1669-74, 183, No. 472.

       200 and odd souls. Wm. Owen, letter from Ashley River, March 21, 1671, *ibid.*, 185, No. 473.

1672   406 people: 268 men able to bear arms,[1] 69 women, 59 children or persons under 16. Dalton to Lord Ashley, Jan. 20, 1672, *ibid.*, 1669-74, 321, No. 736.

1680   1,000 or 1,200 souls. Ash "A Compleat Discovery of S.C.," in Carroll, *Hist. Colls.*, II, 82.

1682   2,500 population. Increase due to vast number of arrivals. *Ibid.*, 82.[2]

1688   8,000 in the Carolinas. *See* Thirteen Colonies: General, 1688. [This included territory later the colony of Georgia.]

1699   1,500 militia, white men, and not above 1,100 families, English and French[3]; 50,000 slaves, and 4 Negroes to one white man. Edw. Randolph to BT, March 16, 1698-99, in CSPC, 1699, 104-6, No. 183; also *Proprieties*, III, C: 22, fol. 170, in HSPT.

1700   5,000 to 6,000 inhabitants, besides Indians and Negroes. Hewitt, "Hist. Acct. of S.C.," in Carroll, *Hist. Colls.*, I, 132.

1701   7,000 persons, besides Negroes and Indians. Humphreys, S.P.G., 25.

       7,000 population. *See* Thirteen Colonies: General, 1701.

1703   7,150 total inhabitants, as follows:[4]

[1] Ed. note: A mistake for 278 men.

[2] Dexter quotes this. Rossiter says 2,200.

[3] McCrady, *S.C. Under Proprietary Gov't.*, 315, estimates about 5,500 inhabitants from this figure if each family averaged 5 persons.

[4] The Gov. and Council give increases and decreases from the data for 1708, q.v. These figures result from the appropriate addition and subtraction.

	Slaves		
Freemen	1,460	Negro men	1,500
Free women	940	Negro women	900
White men servants	110	Indian men	100
White women servants	90	Indian women	150
White children	1,200	Negro children	600
		Indian children	100

Gov. and Council to Lds. Proprietors, May 17, 1708, in *Chalmers Colls.*, Carolina, I, 11. NYPL.

1705 590 families, 980 slaves, as follows:

Parish	Families	Slaves
Goose Creek	120	200
W. Branch Cooper R. (St. John's)	70	180
E. Branch Cooper R.	100	200
Wandoe River	100	100
Ashley River	100	150
Stone River	100	150

Rev. Samuel Thomas to S.P.G., in *S.C. Hist. and Gen. Mag.*, V, 31, 32, 34, 37.

1708 9,580 souls, as follows:[5]

Whites		Slaves	
Freemen	1,360	Negro men	1,800
Free women	900	Negro women	1,100
Servants men	60	Negro children	1,200
Servants women	60	Indian men	500
Children	1,700	Indian women	600
		Indian children	300

Gov. and Council to Lds. Proprietors, May 17, 1708, *Chalmers Coll.*, Carolina, I, 11. NYPL.

12,000 souls in all.[6] Oldmixon, in Carroll, *Hist. Colls.*, II, 460.

1715 2,000 men able to bear arms; 16,000 Negroes. Petition to BT, in N.C. CR, II, 197.

1,500 fighting men. *Spotswood Letters*, II, 120.

1,400 men. Mr. Beresford of Carolina before Parl., July 28, 1715, in BT, *Journals*, 1714-15 to 1718, 64.

1,500 white men. Gov. Craven to Lord Townshend, in N.C. CR, II, 178.

16,750 total population: 6,250 whites, 10,500 Negroes. *See* Thirteen Colonies: General, 1715.

1719 1,000 housekeepers, 2,000 white men, and about 7,000 slaves. Ex-

[5] Same figures given for 1708, in S.C. HSC, II, 217, and for Sept. 17, 1709, in CSPC, 1708-9, 466, No. 759.

[6] Dexter quotes this figure, but Rossiter gives 9,500.

tract of a letter dated Charlestown in S.C., Nov. 18, 1719. Rec'd with Mr. Sec'y Cragg's letter. *Proprieties*: Vol. X, Q: 195, in HSPT.

1,600 fighting men, or 6,400 white inhabitants. Gov. Johnson, Ans. Quer., Jan. 12, 1719-20, *Proprieties*: Vol. X, Part ii, Q: 204-5, in HSPT; also in S.C. HSC, II, 239.

1720 9,000 white inhabitants; 12,000 blacks; 2,000 militia of men between 16 and 60. Gov. Boone, Ans. Quer., Aug. 23, 1720, in CO 5: 358, A: 7; also in Ans. Quer. by Committee of Assembly, Jan. 29, 1719-20, *Proprieties*: Vol. X, Part ii, Q: 204-5, in HSPT. Cf. Repr. BT, to King, Sept. 8, 1721, *Kings MS.*, 205, fol. 23, p. 42, in LCT; and NYCD, V, 610; N.C. CR, II, 421; and Barnwell to BT, in *Brit. Hist. MSS. Comm. Rep.*, XI, Part iv, 254.

17,048 inhabitants: 1,305 taxables, white men, or 5,220 total white population; 11,828 slaves. By exact lists as delivered by inquisitors. Transcript of recds. in State Paper Office (probably by "titular Gov. Moore"), *Chalmers Coll.*, Carolina, I, 97. NYPL.

1724 14,000 white inhabitants. Glen, "Desc. of S.C.," and Hewitt, "Hist. Acct. of S.C.," in Carroll, *Hist. Colls.*, II, 261; I, 266.

1726 16,000 inhabitants. *See* Thirteen Colonies: General, 1726.

1732 10,000 or 12,000 inhabitants. Holmes, *Annals*, I, 554.

1734 3,500 men in S.C. and Ga. available for militia. Memorial of S.C. Council to King, Hewitt, "Hist. Acct. of S.C.," in Carroll, *Hist. Colls.*, I, 304.

1737 5,000 white fighting men, and 22,000 Negroes. Abstract of rept. of Mr. Crockett, S.C. merchant, "Journal of the Earl of Egmont," in *Brit. Hist. MSS. Comm. Rept.* LXIII (5), 201.

1740 4,000 militia. *See* Thirteen Colonies: General, 1740.

1741 5,000 whites, and 40,000 blacks. "Impartial Inquiry into the State and Utility of the Province of Ga.," Ga. HSC, I, 167. Cf. Rept. of Comm. in 1743, in CO 5: 388, fol. 174, p. 309.

1742 4,000 effective men in the province. Papers in the State Paper Office, S.C. HSC, III, 289.

5,500 provincial militia, and 49,000 slaves. Anon., *State of British and French Colonies in North Am., 1755*, 138.

1745 10,000 white inhabitants, men, women, and children, and 40,000 Negroes. "Reasons humbly offered for granting Liberty to Export Rice directly from S.C.," John Fenwick and Peregrine Furye, in CO 5: 371, H: 79.

1747 25,000 whites and 40,000 Negroes. Gov. Glen to BT, April 28, 1747, *ibid.*, 371, H: 100.

1749 25,000 white inhabitants, and 39,000 Negroes at least; 5,000 militia men between 16 and 60; 300 fighting men among the Catawbas.

Gov. Glen to BT, July 19, 1749, *ibid.*, 372, I : 47; and *Kings MS.*, 205, fol. 296-98, p. 607, in LCT.[7]

30,000 inhabitants. *See* Thirteen Colonies: General, 1749.

1750   64,000 population. Pownall, *Memorial*, 60.

1751   25,000 white people and 40,000 Negroes. Gov. Glen to BT, June 24, 1751, in CO 5: 372, K: 29.

1752   25,000 white population, with 5,000 militia. Rept. of BT, in NYCD, VI, 993.

1753   30,000 white inhabitants. (Refers to provincial census.) Mills, *Statistics of S.C.*, 177.

1754   40,000 white, 40,000 black inhabitants. Bancroft, II, 389-91.

1755   30,000 souls, on basis of 5,000 militia. Anon., *State of British and French Colonies in North Am., 1755*, 138.[8]

25,000 white inhabitants; or 110,000 total (50,000 Negroes). *See* Thirteen Colonies: General, 1755.

1756   5,500 militia. Rivers, "The Carolinas" (quoting letter by Gov. Lyttleton in *Chalmers Coll.*), in Winsor, *Narr. Crit. Hist.*, V, 335n.

5,000 to 6,000 men in the militia, and 16,000 to 18,000 male Negro slaves 16 and upward. "Strength of the Province of S.C.," by Charles Pinckney, Dec. 2, 1756, in CO 5: 375, K: 147.

1757   6,594 militia. See page 176. "Return of Muster Rolls from Colonels . . . of militia, May 4, 1757." With Gov. Lyttleton's letter of Sept. 15, 1757, in *ibid.*, 376, L: 5.

1763   30,000 to 40,000 whites; 70,000 slaves, Negroes. Milligan, "Desc. of S.C.," in Carroll, *Hist. Colls.*, S.C., II, 478-79.

1765   40,000 white inhabitants, on basis of 7,000 to 8,000 militia; 80,000 to 90,000 Negroes. Hewitt, "Hist. Acct. of S.C.," in Carroll, *Hist. Coll.*, S.C., I, 503.

180,000 inhabitants; 45,000 men. *See* Thirteen Colonies: General, 1765.

1766   10,000 militia and 117 regulars. Return of Regular Troops and Militia . . . in 1766. Encl. in Gov. Montagu's letter of Dec. 8, 1766, in CO 5: 378, N: 51.

1769   45,000 whites; 80,000 Negroes; 125,000 total population. Lt. Gov. Bull to BT, Dec. 5, 1769, *ibid.*, 379, O: 34. Also *ibid.*, 393, p. 9.

1770   10,000 militia, and 75,178 Negroes. "The State of S.C.," by Lt. Gov. Bull, Nov. 30, 1770, *ibid.*, 394, pp. 14, 26; also in *Chalmers Coll.*, Carolina, II, 15. NYPL.

[7] Also called "Glen's Desc. of S.C." under date of 1750 in Carroll, *Hist. Coll.*, II, 218-19.

[8] Cf. N.C. "Our number of whites are near double the number of what are in your Province." Gov. Dobbs of N.C. to Gov. Glen of S.C. in N.C. CR, V, 389-90.

115,000 population. Pownall, *Memorial*, 60.[9]

5,480 [6,136] men on the northwest frontier: 756 men in Congaree, Amelia, and Orangeburgh Townships; 2,005 men between Broad and Congaree Rivers; 2,110 men between Broad and Black Rivers; 1,265 men above Congaree River. Lt. Gov. Bull to BT, June 7, 1770, in CO 5: 379, fol. 237.

1773   65,000 whites; 110,000 Negroes; 175,000 total population. McCrady, *S.C. under Royal Gov't*, 807. (Quotes Rept. of Historical Commission of Charlestown Library Society, 1835). Also in *North Am. and W. Ind. Gazetteer*, under "S.C."

1774   225,000 total population; 180,000 population; and 60,000 are various estimates. *See* Thirteen Colonies: General, 1774.

200,000 total population, the Congressional estimate of 225,116, of which one-fifth are whites, being exaggerated by about 25,116. Smyth, *Tour in the U.S.*, I, 207.

1775   60,000 whites, and 80,000 to 100,000 Negroes. Henry Laurens to M. Marbois in 1780, *Corr. of Henry Laurens*, 181.

70,000 white inhabitants, and 104,000 Negroes; 14,000 militia. MS. Notes of Dr. George Milligan, in *Chalmers Coll.*, Carolina, II, 75. NYPL.

200,000 total population. *See* Thirteen Colonies: General, 1775.

1783   170,000 population. *See* Thirteen Colonies: General, 1783.

1785   188,000 total population; 108,000 whites, 80,000 blacks. Webster, in *N.Y. Directory for 1786*, 21.

1786   225,000 total inhabitants. *See* Thirteen Colonies: General, 1786.

1787   150,000 inhabitants including 80,000 Negroes; or 93,000 white inhabitants. *See* Thirteen Colonies: General, 1787.

1790   249,073 total population, according to census, as follows: free white males over 16, 35,576; free white males under 16, 37,722; free white females, 66,880; other free persons, 1,801; slaves, 107,094. U.S. Bureau of Census, *Heads of Families, S.C.*, 8. See page 177.

Local

I. Return of Muster Rolls from Colonels . . . of Militia, May 5, 1757[a]

	Men
Three troops horse	115
Charlestown reg. foot	912
Reg. foot, Col. Izard	829
Granville regiment	449

a With Gov. Lyttleton's letter of Sept. 15, 1757, in CO 5: 376, L: 5.

[9] Pownall, *Memorial*, 60, says further: "The above figure is supposed to be below the actual number, the great increase of population being in the back countries, not then included in the regulation of the policy."

LOCAL 177

— *Continued*

	Men
Colleton County	732
Craven County	1,949
Welch Tract	865
Berkeley County	563
Savannah River about Horse Creek	109
New Windsor Township	67
	6,594 [6,590] b

II. CENSUS OF 1790 a

DISTRICTS AND COUNTIES	FREE WHITES			OTHER FREE	SLAVES	TOTAL
	Males		Females			
	Over 16	Under 16				
Beaufort Dist.b	1,266	1,055	2,043	153	14,236	18,753
Camden c						
Chester	1,446	1,604	2,831	47	938	6,866
Claremont	517	841	1,080	...	2,110	4,548
Clarendon	444	516	830	...	602	2,392
Fairfield	1,335	1,874	2,929	...	1,485	7,623
Lancaster	1,253	1,537	2,074	68	1,370	6,302
Richland	596	710	1,173	14	1,437	3,930
York	1,350	1,612	2,690	29	923	6,604
	6,941	8,694	13,607	158	8,865	38,265
Cheraw	1,779	1,993	3,646	59	3,229	10,706
Charleston [district]d						
Berkley e	209	152	331	60	5,170	5,922
Colleton e	209	104	272	22	4,705	5,312
Dorchester f	337	311	604	25	3,022	4,299
Christ Ch. Parish g	156	138	272	11	2,377	2,954

b In these tables for S.C., totals of columns are given as found in the source cited. When the total is incorrect, the true sum has been presented in brackets in addition to the sum given in the original.

a U.S. Bureau of Census, *Heads of Families*, S.C., 8-9.

b St. Helen's Parish, Port Isle, in Beaufort District, in *1728* had 70 families: Humphreys, S.P.G., 102. Port Royal in *1742* had 40 families: Repr. of Lt. Gov. and Coun. of S.C., in S.C. HSC, III, 289.

c Camden in *1781* had 300 men at most: Letter to Johnstone, dated Camden, April 4, 1781, in *Chalmers Coll.*, Md., II, NYPL; in *1786* had 50 dwellings: Watson, *Memoirs*, 297.

d Charleston (city) in *1680* had 100 houses: Wilson, "Acct. of Prov. of Carolina," in Carroll, *Hist. Colls.*, II, 24; in *1705*, 250 families, . . . amounting to about 3,000 souls: Oldmixon, "Carolina," in Carroll, *Hist. Colls.*, S.C., II, 450; in *1731*, 500 to 600 houses: "A Desc. of the Prov. of S.C.," in Force, *Tracts*, Vol. II, Tract XI, 6; in *1739*, 450 dwelling houses; 800 warehouses and kitchens: Anon., *State of the British and*

II. Census of 1790 — *Continued*

DISTRICTS AND COUNTIES	FREE WHITES			OTHER FREE	SLAVES	TOTAL
	Males		Females			
	Over 16	Under 16				
St. Andrew's Parish h	125	71	174	31	2,546	2,947
St. Bartholomew i	625	491	1,017	135	10,338	12,606
St. James Goose j	158	79	202	15	2,333	2,787
St. James Santee k	140	110	187	15	3,345	3,797
St. Paul's l	65	48	103	15	3,202	3,433

French Colonies in North Am., *1755*, 138; in *1742*, 700 men capable of bearing arms: Repr. of Lt. Gov. and Council of S.C., in S.C. HSC, III, 289; in *1744*, 7,000 white persons: Quoted from sermon delivered by Rev. P. Bearcroft, Sec'y of S.P.G., in London, 1744, in Dalcho, *Hist. Acct. P.E. Church in S.C.*, 156; in *1745*, 1,000 houses: "Journal of Wm. Logan," in *Pa. Mag. Hist.*, XXXVI, 164; in *1755*, 600 houses: Anon., *State of the British and French Colonies in North Am.*, *1755*. 138; in *1763*, 1,100 dwelling houses; 4,000 white inhabitants, and near the same number of Negro servants: Milligan, "Desc. of S.C.," in Carroll, *Hist. Colls.*, II, 484; in *1765*, 5,000 to 6,000 white inhabitants, and 7,000 to 8,000 Negroes: Hewitt, "Hist. Acct. of S.C.," in *ibid.*, I, 503; in *1770*, 1,292 dwelling houses; 10,863 total inhabitants: 5,030 whites; 5,833 blacks (domestics and mechanics), according to enumeration: "The State of S.C.," by Lt. Gov. Bull, Nov. 30, 1770, in *Chalmers Coll.*, Carolina, I, 15. NYPL; 1,500 houses; above 12,000 souls. (The date not given specifically, apparently about 1770. Rossiter gives 10,863 for 1770): Wm. G. de Brahm, "Philosophico-Historica-Hydrogeophy of S.C., Ga., and E. Fla.," in Weston, *Docs. Connected with the Desc. of S.C.*, 195; 1,292 dwelling houses; 11,330 total inhabitants: 5,030 whites; 6,276 slaves; 24 free Negroes, etc., in *North Am. and W. Ind. Gazetteer*, under "Carolina, South"; in *1773*, 14,000 inhabitants; 1,400 men on the muster rolls: *Ibid.*; 1,000 houses: Smyth, *Tour in the U.S.*, II, 82: in *1778*, 1,800 houses previous to the fire: Watson, *Memoirs*, 67; in *1779*, 15,000 inhabitants: Bancroft, V, 376. Wilton in Charleston Precinct in *1706* had 80 houses: Oldmixon, "Carolina," in Carroll, *Hist. Colls.*, S.C., II, 453.

e St. John's Parish (Berkeley and Colleton County are St. John's Parish) in *1705* had 70 families, and 180 slaves: Rev. S. Thomas to S.P.G., Docs. Concerning the Rev. S. Thomas," in *S.C. Hist. and Gen. Mag.*, V, 32-33. Colleton County in *1706* had 200 freeholders: Oldmixon, "Carolina," in Carroll, *Hist. Colls.*, *S.C.*, II, 453.

f Dorchester (Dorchester County is St. George's Parish) in *1706* had 350 souls: *ibid.*, II, 452; in *1719*, 15 English families amounting to about 500 persons, and 1,300 slaves: Smith, "The Town of Dorchester in S.C.," in *S.C. Hist. and Gen. Mag.*, VI, 80. St. George's Parish in *1728* had 500 English, 1,300 Negro slaves: Humphreys, S.P.G., 115.

g Christ-Church Parish in *1712* had 105 heads of families: Humphreys, "Missionaries sent to Carolina," in Carroll, *Hist. Colls.*, S.C., II, 556; in *1724* had 407 free born inhabitants; 700 slaves: Quoting the Rev. Mr. Pownall, in Humphreys, S.P.G., 111. .

h St. Andrew's Parish in *1728* had 180 families: *Ibid.*, 112.

i St. Bartholomew's Parish in *1713* had 120 families: *Ibid.*, 93; in *1736*, 120 white families; 1,200 Negroes: Mr. Thomson to S.P.G., in Dalcho, *Hist. Acct. of P.E. Church in S.C.*, 368.

j St. James Goose Creek Parish in *1706* had 100 families and 1,000 persons: Humphreys, "Missionaries sent to Carolina," in Carroll, *Hist. Colls.*, S.C., II, 540; 120 families and about 200 slaves: Rev. Samuel Thomas to S.P.G., Docs. Concerning the Rev. S. Thomas," in *S.C. Hist. and Gen. Mag.*, V, 31-32.

k Santee River in *1770* had 70 families, mostly French: Lawson, *Hist. of Carolina*, 28. St. James Santee Parish in *1728* had 100 French families or more; 60 English families, besides free Indians and Negro slaves: Humphreys, S.P.G., 117.

l St. Paul's Parish in *1742* had 4,000 Negroes: Letter from Orr to S.P.G., in N.C. CR,

II. Census of 1790 — *Continued*

DISTRICTS AND COUNTIES	FREE WHITES			OTHER FREE	SLAVES	TOTAL
	Males		Females			
	Over 16	Under 16				
St. Phillips and						
St. Michael's [m]	2,810	1,561	3,718	586	7,684	16,359
St. Stephen's [n]	81	45	100	1	2,506	2,733
St. Thomas' [o]	145	67	185	34	3,405	3,836
	5,060	3,177	7,165	950	50,633	66,985
Georgetown [p]						
All Saints Parish	104	102	223	1	1,795	2,225
Pr. Frederick	907	915	1,596	32	4,685	8,135
Pr. George's [q]	1,345	1,450	2,236	80	6,651	11,762
	2,356	2,467	4,055	113	13,131	22,122
Ninety-six [r]						
Abbeville	1,904	1,948	3,653	27	1,665	9,197
Edgefield	2,333	2,571	4,701	65	3,619	13,289
Greenville	1,400	1,627	2,861	9	606	6,503
Laurens	1,969	2,270	3,971	7	1,120	9,337
Newberry	1,992	2,232	3,962	12	1,144	9,342
Pendleton	2,007	2,535	4,189	3	834	9,568
Spartanburg	1,868	2,173	3,866	27	866	8,800
Union	1,500	1,809	3,121	48	1,215	7,693
	14,973	17,165	30,324	198	11,069	73,729
Orangeburgh						
Northern Pt.	1,780	1,693	3,258	21	4,529	11,281
Southern Pt.	1,421	1,478	2,782	149	1,402	7,232
	3,201	3,171	6,040	170	5,931	18,513
Grand Total [s]	35,576	37,722	66,880	1,801	107,094	249,073

IV, 609; in *1743*, had 65 men, women, and children in the Cusoe Indian nation: Same to Same, in *ibid.*, 622.

m The Charleston city parishes.

n St. Stephen's Parish in *1784* had 5,000 Negroes: Mills, *Statistics of S.C.*, 484.

o St. Thomas' Parish in *1713* had 120 families; and in *1728*, 565 whites; 950 Negroes; 60 Indian slaves; 20 free Negroes: Humphreys, S.P.G., 104.

p Georgetown in *1773* had 100 houses: Smyth, *Tour in the U.S.*, II, 86.

q Prince George's Parish in *1728* had 500 Christian souls, besides Negroes and Indians: Humphreys, S.P.G., 119.

r Ninety-six in *1781* had 70 men at the most: Letter to Johnstone, dated Camden, April 4, 1781, in *Chalmers Coll.*, Md., II. NYPL.

s It will be seen that localities referred to in the preceding footnotes sometimes bear the names of the districts in which they are included, e.g., Charleston, Georgetown, Ninety-six.

GEORGIA

GENERAL

1733 152 emigrants sent out: 141 British, 11 foreign Protestants; 61 men. "An Acct. Shewing the Progress of Ga.," in Force, *Tracts*, Vol. I, Tract V, 15.

500 souls in Ga. in Nov. last [1733] and of them 100 fighting men. "Journal of Earl of Egmont," Feb. 27, 1733-34, in *British Hist. MSS. Comm. Rept.*, LXIII, 36.

1734 600 persons in Ga. in Jan., 1734. "Diary of Earl of Egmont," March, 1733-34, *ibid.*, LXIII (4), 54.

400 persons in Ga., according to letter from Oglethorpe. "Journal of Earl of Egmont," *ibid.*, LXIII (4), 69.

437 souls, as follows: Savannah, 259 souls; Ogekie, 22 souls; Highgate, 3; Hamstead, 39; Abercorn, 33; Skidaw, 18; Hutchinsons I., 5; Tybee, 21; Cape Bluff, 5; Westbrook, 4; Thunderbold, 28. "Diary of Earl of Egmont," June 19, 1734, *ibid.*, LXIII (4), 112.

1736 2,300 people. "Diary of Earl of Egmont," *ibid.*, LXIII (4), 262.

500 men able to bear arms, more than 300 of them are in the town of Savannah. Mr. Causton to Lt. Gov. Broughton, in Ga. CR, XXI, 343.

1737 700 fighting men. Estimate of Oglethorpe, "Diary of Earl of Egmont," in *Brit. Hist. MSS. Comm. Rept.*, LXIII (4), 376.

1740 500 souls left in colony, exclusive of the regiment and the Saltzburgers. Estimate of Mr. Seward, "lately arrived from Ga.," "Diary of the Earl of Egmont," *ibid.*, LXIII (4), 376.

200 fighting men, according to Stephens.[1] "Diary of the Earl of Egmont," *ibid.*, LXIII (4), 183.

1,000 militia. *See* Thirteen Colonies: General, 1740.

1,200 inhabitants. Rept. of Lt. Horton, in "Journal of Earl of Egmont," *ibid.*, LXIII (5), 184.

142 houses and good habitable huts in Savannah;

100 Indians in Euchee Town and Mt. Pleasant;

600 white men — inhabitants and traders — in Augusta;

5,000 warriors among the Cherokees;

1,000 warriors among the lower Creeks;

700 warriors among the upper Creeks.

State of the Province of Ga., 1740. Taken on oath Nov. 10, 1740, and transmitted to the Trustees and by them to the BT, in CO 5: 368, G: 48.

---

[1] Stephens favored the introduction of slaves, and therefore his estimate would tend to be low. Egmont distrusts it, and says that the trustees had sent 1,521, and 500 had gone on their own accounts.

1741 14,000 inhabitants. Rept. of the Trustees, "Journal of Earl of Egmont," in Ga. CR, V, 610.

1749 6,000 inhabitants, including Negroes. Warden, *Statist., Polit., and Hist. Acct. of the U.S.*, II, 466.

6,000 inhabitants. *See* Thirteen Colonies: General, 1749.

1751 1,700 whites and 420 blacks. "State of Ga. as presented to the King by the Trustees, Aug., 1751," in *Chalmers Coll.*, Ga., 27. NYPL.

1752 [2] 2,000 to 3,000 people. Memorial and Repr. of Trustees, CO 5: 372, K:14 and K:15.

3,000 white inhabitants. Rept. of BT, NYCD, VI, 993.

1753 2,381 whites; 1,066 blacks. Gov. Wright, Ans. Quer., Nov. 29, 1766, *Kings MS.*, 205, fol. 312, pp. 640-41, in LCT.

2,261 white persons and 1,600 slaves. Establishment of Royal Gov't. in Ga., p. 1, in *Chalmers Coll.*, Ga., 35. NYPL.

1754 5,000 white, 2,000 black inhabitants. Bancroft, II, 389-91.

1755 6,500 population, black and white; 756 militia.[3] Stevens, *Hist. of Ga.*, I, 409.

3,000 whites; or 6,000 population. *See* Thirteen Colonies: General, 1755.

6,000 people may at present inhabit it. Anon., *State of British and French Colonies in North Am., 1755*, 138.

1756 800 men capable of bearing arms. Gov. Ellis to BT, reported to Privy Council, *Acts of the Privy Council*, IV, 345.

1758 10,000 population. Stevens, *Hist. of Ga.*, I, 456, citing BT Ga., VIII, 93.

1760 6,000 white people; 3,578 Negroes by returns "which I soon found greatly exceeded the real number." Stevens, *Hist. of Ga.*, II, 54. (Quoted from Gov. Wright's rept. to the Earl of Hillsborough.)

895 militia in Dec., 1760. Gov. Wright, Ans. Quer., Nov. 29, 1766, *Kings MS.*, 205, fol. 312, pp. 640-41, in LCT.

1761 6,100 white inhabitants and 3,600 blacks. Gov. Wright, Ans. Quer., Nov. 29, 1766, *ibid.*, 205, fol. 312, pp. 640-41. Also in his Ans. Quer., Sept. 20, 1773, in Ga. HSC, III, 167, and *Chalmers Coll.*, Ga., 79. NYPL.

1765 6,800 whites and 4,500 blacks; 1,100 militia. Gov. Wright, Ans. Quer., Nov. 29, 1766, *Kings MS.*, 205, fol. 312, pp. 640-41, in LCT.

40,000 inhabitants; 10,000 men, in Ga., and E. and W. Fla. *See* Thirteen Colonies: General, 1765.

1766 9,900 or 10,000 white inhabitants; 7,800 Negroes; 1,800 militia. Gov.

---

[2] Dexter quotes Jones, *Ga.*, I, 460, "2,700 whites; 1,700 blacks." Rossiter says 5,000 total population.

[3] Draws figures from Gov. Reynold's Rept. to B.T., but does not cite reference.

Wright, Ans. Quer., Nov. 29, 1766,[4] *Kings MS.*, 205, fol. 312, pp.
640-41.

1769   11,000 inhabitants. "Estimate of the Annual Loss of Revenue by
       Illicit Trade," in *Chalmers Coll.*, Ga., 81. NYPL.

1773   18,000 whites; 15,000 blacks; 2,828 militia.[5] Gov. Wright, Ans.
       Quer., Sept. 20, 1773, in Ga. HSC, III, 167-69; and *Chalmers
       Coll.*, Ga., 79. NYPL.

1774   100,000 souls, white and black, of which one-fifth are white. Smyth,
       Tour in the U.S., II, 46.

       17,000 whites; 15,000 blacks. Bancroft, IV, 181.

       30,000 total population; or by another estimate, 18,000. *See* Thirteen
       Colonies: General, 1774.

1776   3,000 men; 15,000 slaves.[6] Col. Lachlan McIntosh to Gen. Wash-
       ington, in White, *Hist. Colls. of Ga.*, 92.

1777   1,500 or 2,000 militia at the uttermost, "what with the numbers
       who have quitted the State, entered into the Army, etc." Joseph
       Clay to Henry Laurens, "Letters of J. Clay," Ga. HSC, VII, 54.

1779   400 militia. Gov. Wright to Sec. Lord G. Germain, in Ga. HSC, III,
       258-59.

1783   25,000 population. *See* Thirteen Colonies: General, 1783.

1786   56,000 total inhabitants. *See* Thirteen Colonies: General, 1786.

1787   90,000, including 20,000 negroes; or by another estimate, 27,000.[7] *See*
       Thirteen Colonies: General, 1787.

1790   82,548 total population, as follows: free white males over 16, 13,103;
       free white males under 16, 14,044; free white females, 25,739;
       other free persons, 398; slaves, 29,264. U.S. Bureau of Census,
       Heads of Families, 8.[8]

[4] Same figures given by Gov. Wright to Lord Shelburne, April 6, 1767, p. 5. See
Chalmers Coll., Ga., 45. NYPL.

[5] Cf. number of land grants, 1754-75, given on page 183.

[6] Dexter estimates 45,000 to 50,000; Rossiter says 50,000 population.

[7] This estimate given to the Constitutional Convention is manifestly too low.

[8] There is no individual volume for the Ga. census. This digest is included in every
volume under Heads of Families.

LOCAL

Parishes	Number of Grants, 1754-75 [a]	Parishes	Number of Grants, 1754-75 [a]
St. Paul's	557	St. John's	186
Augusta	33	Medway	48
Goshen	11	Sunbury	362
St. George's	753	Hardwick	47
Halifax	8	St. Andrew's	310
St. Matthew's	491	Sapello	16
Ebenezer	84	Newport	68
Ogeechee	24	Darien	6
St. Phillip's	220	St. David's	81
Great Ogeechee	40	Brunswick	136
Christ Church	313	St. Thomas'	24
Savannah	237	St. Patrick's	37
Vernonburgh	7	St. Mary's	76
Little Ogeechee	33	St. James'	16
Skedaway	11		

Total number of Head Grants, 4,235.

Augusta

1739 600 whites. Mertyn, "Impartial Inquiry into the State and Utility of Ga.," in Ga. HSC, I, 179.

1764 540 whites; 501 Negro slaves; 90 Chickesaw Indians. Rev. S. Frink to S.P.G., Hawkins, *Hist. Notices*, 101.

Augutches [Augusta?]

1733- 10 families. "Diary of Earl of Egmont," in *Brit. Hist. MSS.*
1734 *Comm. Rept.*, LXIII (4), 545.

Barrimacki

1741 24 families. Mertyn, "Impartial Inquiry," in Ga. HSC, I, 181.

Bethany

1751 1,500 inhabitants. De Brahm, *Hist. of Ga.*, 20.

Cape Bluff, or *Oglethorpe*

1733- 40 houses begun. "Journal of Earl of Egmont," *Brit. Hist. MSS.*
1734 *Comm. Rept.*, LXIII (4), 545.

Cornhouse Creek

1733-

a The "Head Grants Manuscript," from which these figures are taken, is an unpublished bound volume of land grants in the office of the Secretary of State in Atlanta, Georgia. When the system of holding land in tail was abandoned in 1754, the land was regranted in fee simple, and the names of the grantees, together with the number of lots or acres given each, were recorded in the "Head Grants Manuscript." Accordingly, it is a complete record of landowners for the period 1754-75. These figures were kindly supplied by Miss Sutherland.

1734   10 families. "Journal of Earl Egmont," *ibid.*, 545.

Darien

1736   150 Scots Highlanders sent over in 1735 . . . arrived in Jan. of
       the year following . . . settled a district called Darien and soon
       after a town to which they gave the name New Inverness. Anon.,
       Hist. of North Am., 214.

       250 persons settled there. Tailfer, Anderson, and Douglas, "A True
       and Hist. Narrative," in Force, *Tracts*, I, Tract IV, 72.

1739   40 families. Letter from Mr. Auspurger, "Journal of Earl of Eg-
       mont," Ga. CR, V, 251.

1740   80 inhabitants. Acct. of R. Lawley, "Journal of Earl of Egmont," in
       Ga. CR, V, 452.

       60 fighting men can be furnished. "Journal of Earl of Egmont," in
       Brit. Hist. MSS. Comm. Rept., LXIII (5), 90.

1741   53 inhabitants, above ⅔ of which are women and children. Tailfer,
       Anderson, and Douglas, "A True and Hist. Narrative," in Force,
       Tracts, I, Tract IV, 72.

       86 inhabitants. "Journal of the Earl of Egmont," in Ga. CR, V,
       508.

Ebenezer

1738   146 Saltzburghers settled in Ebenezer. Computation of "one of two
       ministers." "An Acct. Shewing the Progress of Ga.," in Force,
       Tracts, I, Tract V, 33.

1740   64 families, containing 127 grown people and 72 big and small
       children. [Total, 199 persons.] Letter from Mr Bolzius, minister,
       "Journal of Earl of Egmont," in *Brit. Hist. MSS. Comm. Rept.*,
       LXIII (5), 212.

1742   256 souls. Rept. of Mr. Bolzius, "Journal of Earl of Egmont," in
       Ga. CR, V, 418.

1751   156 men, women, and children sailed from England intending to
       settle in Ebenezer. "List of families and single persons intending
       to settle at Ebenezer," in CO 5: 372, I: 8.

Frederica

1738   60 families. "Journal of Earl of Egmont," in Ga. CR V, 170.

1739   60 families. Rept. of Mr. Anspenger, "Journal of Earl of Egmont,"
       ibid., V, 251.

1745   200 houses. "Wm. Logan's Journal," in *Pa. Mag. Hist.*, XXVI, 178.

Highgate

1733- 10 families. "Journal of Earl of Egmont," in *Brit. Hist. MSS.*
1734   *Comm. Rept.*, LXIII (4), 545.

New Hanover

1758   60 families. Acct. of the Establishment of Royal Govt. in Ga., p. 8, in *Chalmers Coll.*, Ga., 37. NYPL.

St. Simons

1741   120 inhabitants. Tailfer, Anderson, and Douglas, "A True and Hist. Narrative," in Force, *Tracts*, I, Tract IV, 71.

Savannah

1732   130 odd souls. Extract of letter, March 22, 1732, App. to "Acct. Shewing Progress of Georgia," in Force, *Tracts*, I, Tract V, 36.

1733- 48 houses. "Journal of Earl of Egmont," in *Brit. Hist. MSS.*
1734   *Comm. Rept.*, LXIII (4), 545.

1734   91 houses including the public buildings. Lee and Agnew, *Hist. Recds. of Savannah*, 9.

1736   600 inhabitants and 200 houses, according to Mr. Quincey, "our former minister at Savannah." "Journal of Earl of Egmont," in *Brit. Hist. MSS. Comm. Rept.*, LXIII (4), 294-95.

       700 souls estimated by Mr. Westley. *Ibid.*, 313.

1736- 386 inhabitants, besides wives and girls, according to return made
1737   to the Board by Mr. Causton: freeholders, 132; widows, 9; boys, 40; infants, 8; inmates, 72; servants, 86; absent freeholders, 32; dead freeholders, 6; runaway, 1. "Journal of Earl of Egmont," in *Brit. Hist. MSS. Comm. Rept.*, LXIII (4), 399.

1737   518 inhabitants, according to John Wesley's census. Jones, *Hist. of Ga.*, 285n.

1739   109 freeholders, according to return to Trustees. Stevens, *Hist. of Ga.*, I, 298.

1740   100 people. Acct. of R. Lawley, "Journal of Earl of Egmont," in Ga. CR, V, 451.

       142 houses. "State of the Prov. of Ga., 1740," in Force, *Tracts*, I, Tract III, 4.

       130 houses at least. "An Acct. Shewing the Progress of Ga.," *ibid.*, I, Tract V, 32.

       Not 40 English families left in Savannah. Letter from John Pye to Trustees, in Ga. CR, XXII, Pt. ii, 366.

1741   42 freeholders only left; whole number of souls — men, women, and children — are not above 100. Ric'd Lawley, late freeholder of Frederica, to Egmont, "Journal of Earl of Egmont," in *Brit. Hist. MSS. Comm. Rept.*, LXIII (5), 188.

1742   69 fighting men. "Journal of the Earl of Egmont," in Ga. CR, V, 657.

       287 inhabitants: 87 men, 92 women, 59 boys, 49 girls. Letter from Mr. Dobel, *ibid.*, 667.

1743 353 houses exclusive of public buildings. Lee and Agnew, *Hist. Recds. of Savannah*, 19.

1747 602 inhabitants. Rept. of Rev. Mr. Zouberbugler to S.P.G., Hawkins, *Hist. Notices*, 100.

1748 613 inhabitants. Letter from Mr. Zouberbugler to Rev. Mr. Bearcroft, Ga. CR, XXV, 315.

1754 150 houses. Gov. Reynolds to BT, in Lee and Agnew, *Hist. Recds. of Savannah*, 27; also in *Chalmers Coll.*, Ga., 29, 35. NYPL.

1765 400 dwelling houses. Lee and Agnew, *Hist. Recds. of Savannah*, 32.

1776 250 houses and more. *North Am. and W. Ind. Gazetteer*, under "Savannah."

1779 400 houses and about 750 inhabitants. Lee and Agnew, *Hist. Recds. of Savannah*, 65.

   600 houses. *Letters from Brunswick and Hessian Officers*, 236.

1785 200 houses. Webster, in *N.Y. Directory for 1786*, 22.

   300 inhabitants. Mandrillon, *Le Spectateur américain*, 323.

THE NORTHWEST

THE ILLINOIS COUNTRY

1723 334 inhabitants according to census made by M. Diron in June, 1723, as follows:

	Settlers	White Workmen	Women	Children
Kaskaskias	64	41	37	54
Fort Chartres	39	42	28	17
Cahokia	7	1	1	3
	110	84	66	74

"Archs. de la Marine," Ser. F 3, XXIV, fol. 163, in *Rept. on Canadian Archs.*, 1905, I, 453. Also for year 1724 in "Mémoire concernant les postes de Illinois, juillet, 1724," *Archs. Nationales: Colonies*, C 13, A 8: 226, in LCT.

1726 700 men. Memoir (by Bienville) on Louisiana, 1726.[1] *Archs. Nationales: Colonies*, C 13, A 10: 10, in LCT.

   280 "masters," 37 hired persons or servants, 129 Negro slaves, 66 Indian slaves. "Recensement général des habitants de la Louisiane, 1 janvier, 1726," *Archs. Nationales: Colonies*, G 1: 464, n.p., in LCT.

[1] For authorship of Bienville, see N, M. M. Surrey, *Calendar of MSS. in Paris for Hist. of Miss. Valley*, I, 447.

1732 672 [699] total inhabitants according to census as follows:

| | WHITES | | | | SLAVES | | | | |
| | | | | | Negroes | | | Indians | |
	Men	Women	Legitimate Children	Orphans and Bastards	Men	Women	Children	Men	Women
La Prairie du Fort Chartres	43	27	66	6	13	6	18	19	20
Cascassias	48	36	87	14	38	23	41	30	38
Cahoquias	5	..	..	..	3	1	..	7	3
Concession de Renault	12	3	17	..	14	3	5	1	1
Officers	3								
Soldiers	41								
Jesuits	4								
Priests	3								
	159	39 [66]	170	20	68	33	64	57	62

"Recensement des Illinois, 1 janvier, 1732," *Archs. Nationales: Colonies*, G 1: 464, n.p., in LCT.

1743 2,000 to 3,000 whites in the Illinois settlements of Kaskaskia, St. Philippe, Cahokia, and Prairie du Rocher. Winsor, *Mississippi Basin*, 259.

1750 140 families in the 5 French villages. Father Vivier, S.J. to a Father of the same Society, Nov. 15, 1750, in *Jesuit Relations*, LXIX, 221.

1,100 white people, 300 blacks, and about 60 red slaves in the 5 French villages. Father Vivier, to Father —, June 8, 1750, *ibid.*, LXIX, 145.

1763 670 white inhabitants and 300 Negroes in all Illinois:

Kaskaskia	400	100 Indian warriors besides
Fort Chartres	100	40 Indian warriors besides
Prairie du Rocher	50	
St. Philippe	20	
Cahokia	100	60 Indian warriors besides
	670	200 Total Indian warriors

"Aubry's Acct. of Ill., 1763," in *Ill. Hist. Colls.*, X, 4-5.

1764 1,400 inhabitants, including women and children, according to last census. Letter from Dabbadie, in *Ill. Hist. Colls.*, X, 209.

600 fighting men and 1,000 Negroes. Col. Bradstreet's "Thoughts on Indian Affairs," in NYCD, VII, 693.

1765   90 families: 50 in Kaskaskias, and 40 at Cahokia. "Those [villages] of Prairie du Roche, Fort Chartres, and St. Philippe are almost totally abandoned." Capt. Stirling to Gen. Gage, Dec. 15, 1765, in *Ill. Hist. Colls.*, XI, 125. Also in *Pls. Genl.*, S : 110, B (9); in HSPT.

2,950 inhabitants: white men able to bear arms, 700; white women, 500; white children, 850; Negroes of both sexes, 900; also Indians able to bear arms, 650. Official estimate enclosed in letter from Lieut. Fraser to Gage, in *Ill. Hist. Colls.*, X, 492.

1766   400 French families. Estimate of Sir Wm. Johnson, in "Reasons for Establishing a British Colony at Ill.," July 10, 1766, in CO 5: Vol. 67, fol. 197, p. 131, in LCT.

700 white men able to bear arms. Fraser to Gen. Haldimand, May 4, 1766, in *Ill. Hist. Colls.*, XI, 231.

168 French families plus 80 houses, as follows:

Kaskaskia	80 houses	15 cabins of Indians
Prairie du Roche	14 families	
St. Philippe		
Cahokia	43 families	20 cabins of Indians
Pointe Coupée	110 families	

"Capt. Gordon's Journal," in *Ill. Hist. Colls.*, XI, 297-99.

1767   1,100 families in Illinois. British Cabinet Minutes, 1767, in *Ill. Hist. Colls.*, XI, 467.

Census:

Kaskaskia	600 whites	142 Negro men
		81 Negro women
		80 Negro boys
Cahokia	60 families	
Prairie du Roche	25 families	
St. Philippe	3 families	
Fort Chartres	3 families	

Ill. Hist. Colls., XI, 469.

1770   2,000 white inhabitants of all ages and sexes in the Illinois country including Vincennes.

Kaskaskia, 65 families, an officer and 20 men.

Prairie de Roches, 12 dwelling houses and 1 company militia.

Fort Chartres, 3 or 4 families.

Cahokia, 45 dwelling houses.

Pittman, *Present State of European Settlements on Mississippi*, 85-87, 90, 92, 102.

1771   300 fencible men, and 230 Negroes on the eastern side of the Mississippi. Hutchins, *Topographical Desc. of Va., etc.*, 111 and n.

1772 1,500 inhabitants. Boggess, *Settlement of Ill.*, 70.
900 whites; 560 or 660 blacks:[2]

Kaskaskia	500 whites	400 to 500 blacks
Prairie du Roche	100 whites	80 blacks
St. Philippe	1 to 3 families	
Cahokia	300 whites	80 blacks

Ibid., 12.

1786 550 or 600 souls in Illinois nearest to the Mississippi; about 200 white settlers in the Mississippi towns, including Americans, who number about 50; about 250 slaves. Translation by John Pintard of Gabriel Cerres Testimony on Ill., given before Congress, 1786, in *Ill. Hist. Colls.*, V, 385.

1787 606 males, according to census, as follows:[3] Cahokia, 239 French; Kaskaskia, 191 French; Prairie du Rocher, 79 French; American male inhabitants, 97. *Ill. Hist. Colls.*, II, 624-32; V, 414-23.

1788 146 or 147 families, according to report of Congressional Committee, as follows: Kaskaskia, 80; Prairie du Rocher, 12; Fort Chartres and St. Philippe, 4 or 5; Cahokia, 50. Boggess, *Settlement of Ill.*, 70.

THE WABASH VALLEY AND THE GREAT LAKES BASIN

Fort Miamis

1765 9 or 10 French houses. "Croghan's Journal," in Ill. HSC, XI, 36.
1769 9 heads of families, according to census. *Ind. Hist. Soc. Publ.*, II, 439. Also in "Haldimand Collection," in *Rept. on Canadian Archs., 1885*, 203.

Fort Ouiatanon

1765 14 French families. "Croghan's Journal," in Ill. HSC, XI, 33.
1769 12 heads of families, according to census. *Ind. Hist. Soc. Publ.*, II, 439. Also in "Haldimand Collection," in *Rept. on Canadian Archs., 1885*, 203.
1775 12 cabins surrounded by a stockade. Hutchins, *Topographical Desc. of Va.*, etc., 30.

St. Joseph

1780 48 inhabitants, according to census. "Haldimand Papers," in *Mich. Pioneer Colls.*, X, 406-7.

[2] Practically the same estimate is given for 1778 by Alvord, in "Intro." to *Ill. Hist. Colls.*, II, xv-xvi.
[3] On the basis of these returns Alvord estimates the total population of Cahokia at 400 and that of Kaskaskia at 341. See Intro. to Vol. II, cxlvi and cxliii, respectively.

Vincennes

1733 10 men in garrison and some French settlers. *Jesuit Relations,* LXVII, 342.

1758 18 to 20 habitants, besides the 50 men who composed the garrison. Phillips, "Vincennes and French Colonial Policy," in *Ind. Mag. of Hist.*, XVII, 335.

1763 70 families. *Ibid.*

1764 60 houses of French people. "Banishment of the Jesuits from Louisiana," by François Philibert Watrin, Paris, Sept. 3, 1764, in *Jesuit Relations*, LXX, 235-37.

1765 80 or 90 families (French). "Croghan's Journal," in Thwaites, *Early Western Travels*, I, 141.

1767 232 inhabitants (white); 168 strangers; 10 Negro slaves; 17 Indian slaves; according to census. *Ill. Hist. Colls.*, XI, 469.

1769 50 men able to bear arms; 50 women; 150 children, according to census. *Ind. Hist. Soc. Publ.*, II, 439. Also in "Haldimand Collection," in *Rept. on Canadian Archs., 1885*, 203.

1775 60 settlers and their families. Hutchins, *Topographical Desc. of Va., etc.*, 100.

1778 621 inhabitants, of whom 217 are fit to bear arms, according to census. Lt. Gov. Hamilton's Rept., in *Ill. Hist. Colls.*, VIII, 182.

1787 320 French, 103 American males, by census. *Ibid.*, V, 449.
500 souls, French, and about half as many Americans. Major Denny, Sept. 15, "Military Journal," in *Pa. Hist. Soc. Mem.*, VII, 311.
400 houses; 900 French inhabitants, and 400 Americans. Letter of Gen. Harmar, Aug. 7, 1787, *ibid.*, VII, 422.

1788 300 houses or cabins and the inhabitants nearly all French. Dr. Saugrain, "Note-Books, 1788," in *Amer. Antiq. Soc.*, XXX, 227.

Detroit

1701 80 to 100 dwellings; 600 population. Walker, "The North-West during the Revolution," in *Mich. Pioneer Colls.*, III, 13 (no citation).

1704 400 inhabitants able to bear arms; 2,000 savages.[4] "Memoir of M. De la Mothe Cadillac," in *Mich. Pioneer Colls.*, XXXIII, 205.

1706 270 persons; 25 families. "Points concerning Canada," (from Cadillac's Rept.), *ibid.*, XXXIII, 316.
563 persons, according to census, as follows: Habitants, 144 Garçons, 163; Filles, 146; Esclaves, 45; Engagés, 65. *Mich.: Detroit Census (1706?)*, in LC MSS.

1707 120 French houses; 1,200 savages. "Cadillac Papers," in *Mich. Pioneer Colls.*, XXXIII, 340.

---

[4] Apparently Indian warriors were included among men able to bear arms.

1708 63 French Settlers. Letter from the Sieur d'Aigremont, in "Cadillac
      Papers," *ibid.*, XXXIII, 426.

1710 48 male inhabitants: 35 farmers; 3 resident soldiers; 8 resident
      Canadians; 2 resident Frenchmen. "Cadillac Papers," *ibid.*,
      XXXIII, 492-94.

1718 28 or 30 inhabitants. Letter of Intendant Dupuy to the Minister,
      in *Wis. Hist. Colls.*, XVI, 471, citing *Archs. du Ministère des
      Colonies, "Canada, Corr. Gen."* XLIX, C 11, fol. 274.

1736 17 soldiers; 40 families; 80 men capable of bearing arms. Extract
      from "Bouquet's Journal," in *Mich. Pioneer Colls.*, XIX, 27-28.

1759 120 French families;[5] 200 soldiers in the garrison. Extract from
      "Bouquet's Journal," *ibid.*, XIX, 27-28.

1760 70 or 80 houses within the fort. Letter from Capt. D. Campbell to
      Col. Bouquet, *ibid.*, XIX, 48.

1765 80 houses in the fort in a large stockade, and 300 to 400 French
      families. "Croghan's Journal," in Thwaites, *Early Western
      Travels*, I, 152.

      600 French, including women and children. Memorandum on De-
      troit, in *Pls. Gen.*, S : 79, in HSPT

      799 total inhabitants, according to census: Men capable of bearing
      arms, 243; women, 164; children, 294. NB. the French families
      consist of: men capable of bearing arms, 33; women, 24; chil-
      dren, 41. Slaves included in the numbers mentioned may amount
      to 60 men, women, and children. *Mich.: Detroit Census, 1765*,
      in LC MS.

1767 500 or 600 families. Extract of a letter on American Affairs sent by
      Shelburne to BT, Oct. 5, 1767, in CO 5 : 216, fol. 62/63, in LCT.

      600 French inhabitants; few English. "Memorial of Officers wish-
      ing to settle in Detroit," in CO 5 : 67, fol. 376, p. 250; in LCT.

      500 families at Detroit. "British Cabinet Minutes," in *Ill. Hist.
      Colls.*, XI, 467.

1769 2,500 inhabitants, of which 500 capable of bearing arms. Estimate
      of Major Rogers, cited by Walker, "The North-West during the
      Revolution," in *Mich. Pioneer Colls.*, III, 13.

1771 2,000 inhabitants, most of whom were French. Hutchins, *Topo-
      graphical Desc. of Va., etc.*, 119-20.

1773 1,367 inhabitants, according to census. "Haldimand Papers," in
      Mich. Pioneer Colls., IX, 649.

1778 2,144 inhabitants, according to census. *Ibid.*, IX, 469.

1779 2,653 inhabitants. *Ibid.*, X, 312-27.

1782 2,290 inhabitants, according to census, besides about 100 in the
      army. *Ibid.*, X, 601-13.

[5] Probably included families on farms outside the town.

1788   4,000 inhabitants in the town and settlement. Mr. Robertson's Ans.
        to Mr. Finlay and Mr. Baby, *ibid.*, XI, 633, 636.

Missilimackinac or Mackinaw

1686   400 population. Walker, "The North-West during the Revolution,"
        in *Mich. Pioneer Colls.*, III, 13.

1730   30 French in the garrison and a vast concourse of traders, some-
        times not less than 1,000. Pls. Gen. S: 33 in HSPT.

THE SOUTHWEST

KENTUCKY [1]

GENERAL

1775   150 immigrants, but no women. Durrett, "Ky. Centenary," 35, in
        Filson Club Publs., No. 7.

1777   5,000 souls in all the region south of the Ohio. Monette, *Valley of
        the Mississippi*, III, 108.

        102 in military population. Albach, *Annals of the West*, 256.

1780   3,000 men able to bear arms. [2] S. Deane to Robert Morris, "Deane
        Papers," in NYHSC, XXII, 126.

1781   1,050 militia: Fayette County, 156; Lincoln, 600; Jefferson, 300.
        Col. John Todd to Gov. Jefferson, in CVSP, II, 44.

1782   1,000 men. Col. Wm. Christian, Sept., 1782, in CVSP, III, 331.

        8,000 inhabitants. Brissot de Warville, *New Travels*, 475.

1783   12,000 souls. Monette, *Valley of the Miss.*, II, 143.

1784   30,000 souls at present in Ky., Filson, "Discovery, Settlement, and
        Present State of Ky. (1784)," in Imlay, *Topographical Desc. of
        Western Countries of U.S.*, 321. [3]

        20,000 souls and over. Monette, *Valley of the Miss.*, II, 143.

1785   30,000 people. *Ibid.*, II, 172.

1786   25,000 souls of every description, a great many of them Negroes
        and transient trading persons. "Diary of Major E. Beatty," in
        Mag. of Amer. Hist., I, Pt. I, 311.

1787   50,000 inhabitants. Brissot de Warville, *New Travels*, 475.

1790   73,677 total inhabitants, according to "a rough census": whites,
        61,133; slaves, 12,430; free blacks, 114. Rossiter, *Cent. Pop.
        Growth*, 9. [4]

LOCAL

Beargrass Creek

1780   600 serviceable men. Albach, *Annals of the West*, 321.

[1] This area became the state of Kentucky in 1792.
[2] Rossiter estimates 45,000 population for this year.
[3] A note adds: "It is asserted that 20,000 migrated hither in 1787."
[4] There is no "Heads of Families" for Ky.

Bryant's Station

1782   40 cabins; 44 men in the garrison. Ranck, *Hist. of Lexington, Ky.*, 77-78.

Fayette County

1782   130 militia. Col. Daniel Boone to Gov. Jefferson, Aug., 1782, in CVSP, III, 276.

1786   1,100 militia exclusive of officers. Col. Levi Todd to Gov. Henry, June 22, 1786, in CVSP, IV, 151.

Greenbrier County

1781   550 militia. "Petition to Gov. Jefferson," in CVSP, I, 468.

Jefferson County

1781   400 men able to bear arms. John Floyd to Gov. Jefferson, in CVSP, I, 437.

354 militia between the ages of 16 and 50, including officers. John Floyd to Gov. Jefferson, April, 1781, *ibid.*, II, 48.

300 militia in October. John Floyd to Gov. Jefferson, Oct., 1781, *ibid.*, II, 530.

1782   370 men and about 850 women and children. Estimate of Col. John Floyd, *ibid.*, III, 122.

Lexington

1782   60 effective men in the garrison. Ranck, *Hist. of Lexington, Ky.*, 77.

Louisville

1778   20 families brought by Gen. Geo. Rogers Clark. Durrett, "Centenary of Louisville," 29, in *Filson Club Publs.*, No. 8.

1779   100 inhabitants. *Ibid.*, 47.

1784   63 finished houses; 37 houses in the process of construction; 22 houses with walls up without being covered by roofs. *Ibid.*, 45.

1784   63 houses finished; 37 partly finished; 22 raised, but not covered, and more than 100 cabins. Albach, *Annals of the West*, 419.

TENNESSEE [5]

GENERAL

1776   7,700 population. Letter of Thos. Dillon, mentioning enumeration, in *Va. Mag. of Hist.*, XII, 260.

1786   400 to 500 families east of Cumberland and south of the Tennessee Rivers. Alex. Outlaw to Gov. Caswell, in *N.C. State Recds.*, XVIII, 758. (Exec. Letter Book.)

[5] This area, comprising the counties Washington (formed in 1777 partly from Wilkes and Burke counties, N. C.) Sullivan, Greene, Davidson, Sumner, Hawkins, and Tennessee, was under the jurisdiction of North Carolina until 1792, and became a state in 1796.

1788 25,000 inhabitants. Brissot de Warville, *New Travels*, 475.[6]
1790 35,691 inhabitants. Rossiter, *Cent. Pop. Growth*, 9.[7]

LOCAL

Cumberland County

1776 13,000 population. Letter from Thomas Dillon, in *Va. Mag. Hist.*, XII, 260.
1784 2,415 whites according to census, and 459 houses. CVSP, III, 590.
1788 8,000 inhabitants. Brissot de Warville, *New Travels*, 475.

Holston

1775 2,000 inhabitants. "A Short Desc. of State of Tenn., lately called the territory of the U.S. south of the river Ohio, March 9, 1796." Imlay, *Topographical Desc., etc.*, App. V, 513.
1788 5,000 inhabitants. Brissot de Warville, *New Travels*, 475.

Nashville

1788 800 families. Letter from St. Jean de Crevecoeur, June 6, 1788, in MHSP, LV, 44.

Watauga

1772 300 militia. Notice of First Settlements of Tenn., in MHSC, 2d Series, VII, 58.
1776 700 to 800 riflemen could have been raised here. *Ibid.*, 60. (No author mentioned.)

WESTERN INDIANS [1]
NORTHERN DEPARTMENT

1677 2,150 fighting men in the Five Nations: Maques, 300; Onyades, 200; Onondagos, 350; Gaiongos, 300; Senecques, 1,000. "Observations of Wentworth Greenhalgh in a journey from Albany, May 28 to July 14, 1677," in CSPC, 1677-80, 95-97, No. 271, citing *Col. Papers*, XL, No. 94.
1689 2,800 fighting men in the Five Nations, according to census (?). Mohocks, 270; Oneidas, 180; Onondagos, 500; Cayonges, 300; Senecas, 1,300. River Indians, 250. CSPC, 1697-98, 175, No. 381, citing BT, N.Y., No. 59, and 52, pp. 481-82.
1694 1,300 fighting men in the Five Nations. Col. Fletcher to Sir John Trenchard, Sept. 25, 1694, CSPC, 1693-96, 361, 1340.

[6] This estimate is given for "Frankland," probably intended for the so-called state of Franklin.

[7] "Heads of Families" for Tenn. is not published.

[1] This term indicates in general Indians living outside the jurisdiction of the seaboard provinces and states. The division of the Indians into Northern and Southern Departments was not, of course, made until 1756, but since the demarcation is a natural one, it was thought best to use it from the beginning. Indian names follow spelling in the sources.

1697 1,320 fighting men in the Five Nations according to census: Mohocks, 110; Oneidas, 70; Onondagos, 250; Cayonges, 200; Senecas, 600. River Indians, 90. CSPC, 1697-98, 175, No. 175.

1699 1,100 men in the Five Nations. Gov. Bellomont to BT, April 13,
1699, in CSPC, 1699, 135, No. 250, citing BT, N.Y., 8 A, No. 21,
53, and 45.

1710 2,000 in all the Five Nations at the most, and of these the Senecas
are near 1,000. Rev. T. Barclay to S.P.G., in NYDH, III, 899.

1718 Northwest Indians:

Detroit: Hurons	100 men
Poux	180 men
Outaouacs	100 men
12 Leagues from Detroit: Misisaguay	60 or 80 men
Lake Huron: Saginaws	60 men
N. Miss. R.: Puants	80 or 100 men
Saqui	100 or 120 men
Renards	500 men
Mascoutins	200 men
Illinois: La Roche	400 men
Miamis	400 men
Wabash	1,000 or 1,200 men

List incomplete. "Memoir on the Savages of Canada as far as
the Mississippi River," *Archs. of Ministère des Colonies*, Paris,
"Canada Corr. Gen.," XXXIX, C 11, fol. 354, in *Wis. Hist.
Colls.*, XVI, 370-76.

Indians of Mississippi and Great Lakes: Same as above. *Pa. Arch.*
2d Series, VI, 52-57.

1721 French Allies: Between Alleghanies and Mississippi: Miamis, 2,000
in number; Illinois, 3,000 men; Ottoways, 500, formerly 3,000;
Nokes, 100; Follesavoins, 200; Sakes, 200; Puans, 600. "On the
Mississippi and branches are 60,000 men . . . The Indian nations
lying between Carolina and the French settlements on the Missis-
sippi are about 9,200 fighting men . . . 3,800 of them are Chero-
kees . . . About 1,000 savages dispersed in several parts between
Carolina and Va., from whom we have not much to apprehend . . .
English allies to the northward of Carolina not 1,500 warriors."
Repr. BT, to King, Sept. 8, 1721, in *Kings MS.*, 205, fol. 24-25,
pp. 44-45, and fol. 35-36, pp. 66-67, in LCT. Also in *Mich.
Pioneer Colls.*, XIX, 7.

1,480 fighting men in the Five Nations, as follows: Mohawks, about
160; Oneidas, about 200; Onondagos, about 250; Cayonges, about
130; Senecas, about 700; Scatakooks, about 40. Memorandum of

Paul Dudley, in "Pincheon Papers," in MHSC, 2d Series, VIII, 244.

1738   1,500 fighting men in the Six Nations, including the River and Schaachkook Indians. Gov. Clarke, Ans. Quer., in NYDH, IV, 240.

1746   1,750 warriors of Six Nations: Maquaische, 100; Oneidas, 100; Tuscarrora, 150; Onondagos, 200; Cayjuckes, 500; Senecas, 700. Estimate of Conrad Weiser in letter to Chris. Sauer, 1746, in *Pa. Mag. Hist.*, I, 323.

9,300 warriors in allies and friends of Six Nations: those in Lakes regions, 5,800; those in Mississippi Valley, 2,800; North of Lake Huron, uncertain; Pa. and Ohio, 400; Mohicans, 300. Estimate of Conrad Weiser, *ibid.*, II, 407.

1748   1,700 warriors in the Six Nations; 700 or 800 more in their friends and allies. Gov. Ogle, Ans. Quer., in "Council Proc'dings," *Md. Archs.*, XXVIII, 469-70.

1754   16,000 warriors in the Six Nations. Wm. Shirley's Address to Council and House of Reprs., April 2, 1754, *Shirley Correspondence*, II, 41.

1759   9,100 warriors, as follows:

	Warriors	*Location*
Delawares	600	Susquehanna and Lakes
Shawanees	500	Ohio
Wyandots	300	Detroit
Twightwees	300	Miami River
Ouiatonons	200	Wabash
Piankishas	300	Wabash
Illinois	400	Lakes
Ottawas	2,000	Lakes
Shakies	200	Lakes
Kickapous	600	Lake Michigan
Musquakies	200	Lake Michigan
Cherokees	1,500	West of N. Carolina
Chacktaws	2,000	West of Georgia

List of Geo. Croghan, Deputy Agent for Ind. Affairs under Sir Wm. Johnson, in Jefferson, "Notes on Va.," in *Writings*, III, 209-11.

1763   3,960 men in the Six Nation Confederacy: Mohocks, 160; Oneidas, 250; Tuscaroras, 140; Onondagas, 150; Cayugas, 200; Senecas, 1,050; Oswegachys, 80; Nanticokes, Conoys, Tutecoes, and Saponeys, 200; Caghnawagas, 300; Canassadagas, Ammidacks, and Algonkins, 150; Abemaquis, 100; Skaghquanoghronas, 40; Hu-

rons, 40. Indians of Ohio: Shawanese, 300; Delawares, 600; Wyandots, etc., 200.

8,020 [7,810] men in the Ottawa Confederacy:

Wyandots or Hurons	250	
Powtewatamis	150	about Detroit
	200	about Ft. St. Joseph
Ottawas	300	about Detroit
	250	about Michilimackinac
	150	about St. Joseph
Chipeweighs	320	about Detroit
	400	about Michilimackinac
Meynomenys	100	
Folsavoins	110	
Puans	360	
Sakis	300	
Foxes	320	
Miamis or Twightwees	230	
Kickapoos	180	
Mascoutens	90	
Piankashaws	100	
Ottawas, Chipeweighs, etc.	4,000	
Illinois	Uncertain	
Sioux	Uncertain	
Total	8,020	
	[7,810]	

Present State of Northern Indians in Dept. of Sir Wm. Johnson,
Nov. 18, 1763, in *Pls. Gen.*, R: 52, in HSPT.

1764   23,330 among the western Indians:

Mohocks, Oneidas, Tuscaroras Cayugas, Onondagos, Senecas	1,550	
Delawares	600	Lakes
Shawnees	400	Lakes
Wyandots	300	Ohio
Miamis	350	Miami River
Ouiatonons	400	Wabash
Piankishas	250	Wabash
Illinois	600	Lakes
Piorias	800	Illinois River
Ponteotamees	350	Detroit
Ottawas and Chippewas	5,900	Upper Lakes
Shakies	400	Lake Michigan
Ouisconsings	550	Lake Michigan
Kickapous	300	Lake Michigan
Macoutins	500	Lake Michigan

Musquakies	250	Lake Michigan
Cherokees	2,500	West of N. Carolina
Chickasaws	750	West of Georgia
Catawbas	150	S. Carolina
Chocktaws	4,500	W. of Georgia
Lower Creeks	1,180	W. of Georgia
Natchez	150	W. of Georgia
Alibamons	600	W. of Georgia
	23,330	

Taken from rept. annexed to Col. Bouquet's Acct. of 1764 Expedition, in Jefferson, "Notes on Va.," *Writings*, III, 209-11.

1768   25,080 Indians west of the Alleghanies

Mohocks	160	⎫
Oneidas	300	⎪
Tuscororas	200	New York and Lakes, and
Onondagos	260	Upper Susquehanna
Cayugas	200	⎪
Senecas	1,000	⎭
Aughquagahs	150	⎫
Nanticoes	100	⎪
Mohiccons	100	⎪
Conoies	30	Susquehanna
Saponies	30	⎪
Munsies	150	⎪
Delawares	750	⎭
Shawanees	300	⎱ Lakes
Cohunnewagos	300	⎰
Wyandots	250	Ohio
Piankishas	300	⎫
Ouiatonons	300	Wabash
Shakies	200	⎭
Kaskaskias	300	Kaskaskia
Illinois	300	⎱ Lakes and Illinois River
Ponteotamies	300	⎰
Twightwees	250	Miami River
Ottawas and Chippewas	1,800	Northern Lakes
Shakies	550	⎫
Indians on Lake Mich.		Lake Michigan
and Mississippi River	4,000	⎭
Cherokees	3,000	West of N. Carolina
Chickasaws	500	⎫
Chacktaws	6,000	West of Georgia
Creeks	3,000	⎭
	25,080	

Taken from figures by Capt. Hutchins and Galphin, Jefferson, "Notes on Va.," *Writings*, III, 209-11. Also part in Hutchins, *Topographical Desc. of Va., etc.*, 135-37.

1770 2,000 fighting men in the Six Nations, of whom the Onondagas are about 200; the Cayugas, 260; the Senecas, 1,000; the Tuscaroras, 250. Sir Wm. Johnson to Rev. Mr. Inglis, in NYDH, IV, 427-28.

1773 25,420 warriors in all the Indians of the Northern Department, or about 130,000 souls, extending westward to the Mississippi: Long Island, 300 warriors; Mohawks, 406 souls; Oneidas, 1,500 souls; Whole Six Nations, 2,000 warriors, and 10,000 souls at least; Lakes Regions, 3,500 souls; Stockbridge Indians, 300 souls. "Rept. of Sir Wm. Johnson," in NYCD, VIII, 458-59.

1775 10,060 [10,600] warriors among the frontier Indians:

The Six Nations:	Mohawks	100	
	Oneidas and Tuscaroras	400	
	Cuyahogas	220	
	Onondagas	230	
	Senecas	650	1,600
	Delaware and Munsies		600
	Shawanees of Scioto		400
	Wyandots		300
	Ottawas		600
	Chippewas		5,000
	Pottewatamies		400
	Pyankeshas, Kiakapoos, Muscoutans, Vermilions, Weotanans, etc.		800
	Miamis or Picts		300
	Mingoes		600
	Total		10,060 [10,600]

From estimate made by Col. Morgan, in Hildreth, *Pioneer Hist.*, 129. Cf. Schoolcraft, *Indian Tribes*, III, 560-61.

1778 9,130 fighting men among the Indians in the Western Dept.:

I. Delawares		
Coochocking	400
Ouabache	100
II. Munsies and Mohickons	
Removed to Seneca country	30
Joined with Delawares	20
Dispersed in Western tribes	40
III. Christianized Indians	
Lictenane	100

IV. Shawnees
  Coochocking 50
  Removed to Miami 250
V. Wyandots
  Sandusky 80
  Detroit River 120
VI. Ottawas and Pottawatamies
  Miamis and Lake Erie 250
  Detroit and Lake Huron 330
VII. Chipewas
  Lakes Huron and Michigan and North of Lake Erie 5,000
VIII. Twixtees and Picts
  Miami River 800
IX. Ouabache Indians 1,500
X. Mingoes 60
                                                                     ———
          Total   9,130

Copied from census taken in 1778 by Wm. Wilson, in *Va. Mag. Hist.*, XXIII, 345-46.

1779

Mohocks	**100**	
Oneidas ⎫		
Tuscororas ⎬	400	
Onondagos	230	New York and Lakes, and
Cayugas	220	Upper Susquehanna
Senecas	650	
Munsies	150	
Delawares	500	
Shawanees	300	
Mingoes	60	Ohio and Susquehanna
Mohiccons	60	
Wyandots	180	
Miamis	300	
Ouiatonons	300	
Piankishas	400	
Ponteotamies	450	
Ottawas and Chippewas	5,750	Great Lakes
Kickapous	250	
Musquakies	250	
Sioux	500	

                          [11,050]

From figures of John Dodge, an Indian trader, and from other sources. Jefferson, "Notes on Va.," *Writings*, III, 209-11.

1780 1,600 men, of whom about 1,200 are warriors, in the Six Nation Confederacy. Col. Guy Johnson to Lord George Germain, in NYCD, VIII, 797, citing *Pls. Gen.*, CCLXVI.

4,000 men in arms in the Five Nations. The Senecas number about 350. Chastellux, *Travels*, I, 403.

1786

Ottawas	Uncertain	South and East of Lake Michigan
Chippewas	800 men	Lake Huron and Superior
Manominis	150 men	N. Mississippi River and Fox River
Winipigoes	600 men	N. Mississippi River
Osakies	1,300 men	Both sides Mississippi River
Outagamies	1,400 men	Wisconsin River
Sioux	3,000 men	West Side of Mississippi River

"Mem. Rel. to Indian Trade," in *Wis. Hist. Colls.*, XII, 79-81.

1788 Indians of the Northwest Territory:

Tribe	Location	Number
Delawares	Sandusky	400
Wyandots	Sandusky and Detroit	260
Munsees	Alleghany River	100
Miamis	Miami Town	100
Shawanoes	Miami River	150
Cherokees	Paint Creek	100
Wiahtanos	Wabash River	600
Kickapoos	Wabash River	1,100
Piankishaws	Wabash River	400
Kaskaskias	Mississippi River	150
Peorees	Illinois River	150
Meadow Indians	Illinois River	500
Iowas	Illinois River	300
Foxes	Lake Superior	1,000
Chippewas	Lake Michigan	4,000
Potowatomies	Lake Michigan	1,000
Sioux	Lake Superior	6,000

[16,310]

Indians of the North West Territory, Extract from the "Journal of Enoch Parsons, while on tour to the N.W. Territory," in *N.E. Hist. and Gen. Reg.*, I, 160.

1789 North West Indians:

Detroit Indians: Hurons, 150 men, and Ottowas, 100 men; Poudew, 150 men; Miamis, 350; Big Island Indians, 300; Michilimackinac, 300; St. Joseph, 300; La Bay, 200; Lake Michigan, 400; Lake Superior, 130; St. Anseor Bay, 150; Pt. Shagwannigon, 500; West end of Superior, 50; Caministicouya, 150; L.

Nipicon, 300; North side of Superior, 500. "Haldimand Papers," in *Mich. Pioneer Colls.*, XX, 305-7.

SOUTHERN DEPARTMENT

1708   8,480 men able to bear arms among the tribes: Yamasees, 500; Paleachuckles, 80; Savannahs, 150; Apalachys, 250; on Ochasee River, 600; on Chocta Sanchy River, 1,300; Chickysaws, 600; Cherokees, 5,000, in 60 towns. "The State of S.C., Sept. 17, 1708," Gov. and Council of S.C. to Lord Proprietor, in *Chalmers Coll.*, Carolina, I, 13. NYPL. Also in CSPC, 1708-9, 468, No. 739.

1712   2,000 fighting men among the Tuscaroras. Lt. Gov. Spotswood to BT, CSPC, XXVII, 15.

1715   16,000 or 17,000 men among the Yamansees and Charakees, "who are on the back of our plantations as far as New Eng." Mr. Byrd of Va. before Parl., July 15, 1715, in *B.T. Journal*, 1714-15 to 1718, 54.

28,041 [26,984] total number of souls among the following tribes:

Tribes	Villages	Men	Souls
Yamasees	10	413	1,215
Apalatchicolas	2	64	214
Apalatchees	4	275	638
Savanos	3	67	233
Euchees	2	130	400
Abikaws	15	502	1,773
Tallibooses	13	636	2,343
Ochesees or Creeks	10	731	2,406
Albamas	4	214	770
Cherokees			
Upper Settlement	19	900 ⎫	
Middle Settlement	30	2,500 ⎬	11,530
Lower Settlement	11	600 ⎭	
Chickasaws	6	700	1,900
Catapaws	7	570	1,470
Saraws	1	140	510
Waccomassus	4	210	610
Cape Fears	5	76	206
Santees	2	43 ⎱	
Congerees	1	22 ⎰	125
Weneaws	1	36	106
Seawees	1	57	Men, women and Children
Itwans	1	80	240
Corsaboys	5	95	295

28,041
[26,984]

"An exact Account of the Number and Strength of all the Indian Nations that were subject to the govt. of S.C. . . . in 1715, taken out of the Journalls of Capt. Nairn, John Wright, Esq., Price Hughs, Esq., and compared with and corrected by the Journalls & Observations of John Barnwell." Gov. Johnson, Ans. Quer., Jan. 12, 1719-20, *Proprieties Q.:* 201, Vol. X (2), in HSPT.

1716 11,210 souls among the Cherokees, of whom 4,000 were warriors. *Journal of House of Burgesses of Va.*, 1761-65, [x].

1720 2,800 souls, and 1,000 men among Indians to North-ward; 11,500 souls, and 3,800 men among the Cherokees; 10,000 souls, and 3,000 men among the Indians in the French interest. Ans. Quer., by Com. of Ass'bly of S.C., Jan. 29, 1719-20, in *Proprieties Q:* 204 and 205, Vol. X (2), in HSPT.

10,000 souls among the Cherokees; 2,500 souls among the Northern Indians; 6,000 or 7,000 souls among the Chickasaws, Albamons,[2] and a great part of the Tallaboosees Abikaws. Gov. Johnson, Ans. Quer., Jan. 12, 1719-20, in *Proprieties Q:* 201, Vol. X (2), in HSPT. *See also* 1721, page 195.

9,200 men between our settlement (S.C.) and the Mississippi; 3,400 men among those we formerly traded with, but now entirely cut off by the French; 2,000 men lying between us and the French; 3,800 men among the Cherokees; 1,000 men in the Northern Indians between us and Va. Gov. Boone and Col. Barnwell, Ans. Quer., Aug. 23, 1720, in CO 5: 358, A: 7.

1729 4,000 fighting men in 62 towns of the Cherokees. 400 fighting men among the Catawbas. Byrd, *Hist. of the Dividing Line*, I, 141.

1730 3,010 men bearing arms in the 45 villages of the Choctaw nation, according to census made by Lusser at the order of Perier, Commandant General of Louisiana. "Lusser to Maurepas, March, 1730," *Miss. Prov. Archs.*, 1729-40, 116-17.

1732 2,726 warriors in the 54 villages of the Choctaws. "Journal of Regis du Roullet," in *Miss. Prov. Archs.*, 1729-40, 150-54.

5,000 Choctaws bearing arms, and 42 villages . . . "but according to my calculation . . . there are not more than 1,466 Choctaws fit to make a campaign." Father Beaudoin to Salmon, Nov. 23, 1732, *ibid.*, 156.

1734 5,000 fighting men among the Choctaws, near the Mississippi. 1,300 fighting men among the Creeks — about 150 miles from the Choctaws. "Acct. Shewing Progress of Georgia," Repr. of S.C. Council to King, April 9, 1734, Force, *Tracts*, I, Tract V, 45.

50 fighting men among the Yamancraw Indians. "They are a branch

[2] Gov. Johnson thinks they have been much reduced by "Warr, Pestilence, and Civill Warr."

of the Crick Indians who make above 600." "Diary of the Earl of Egmont," in *Brit. Hist. MSS. Comm. Rept.*, LXIII (4), 114.

1736 400 fighting men in the Chickasaw nation. Westley [*sic*], one of the three Georgia ministers, and secretary to Oglethorpe, in "Diary of Earl of Egmont," *Brit. Hist. MSS. Comm. Rept.*, LXIII (4), 312.

1738 16,000 men among the Choctaws. Abst. of letter from Wm. Bull, Pres. of Council of S.C., to BT, in "Journal of Earl of Egmont," Ga. CR, V, 56.

1,500 warriors of the Creeks; 5,000 warriors of the Choctaws; 500 warriors of the Chickasaws. Abst. of letter from Col. Oglethorpe, "Journal of Earl of Egmont," *ibid.*, 191.

1740 4,000 Cherokee warriors; 1,700 Creek warriors. "State of the Prov. of Ga.," in Ga. CR, IV, 666-67. Also in Force, *Tracts*, I, Tract III, 4-6.

1742 3,000 men in the Cherokees; 1,500 men in the Creeks; 400 men in the Chickesaws; 300 men in the Catabaws. Gov. Bull. to BT, June 15, 1742, in CO 5: 368, G: 80.

1743 400 warriors among the Catawbas. Hewitt, "Hist. Acct. of S.C.," in Carroll, *Hist. Colls.*, S.C., II, 188n.

1745 5,000 men among the Creeks, Chickasaws, and Cherokees; 5,000 men among the Choctaws. "Humble Representation of John Fenwicke, late of the province of S.C.," in CO 5: 371, H: 73.

1747 16,000 fighting men among the Choctaws. Gov. Glen to BT, April 28, 1747, in CO 5: 371, H: 100.

1748 300 fighting men among the Catawbas; 3,000 fighting men among the Cherokees; 2,500 gunmen among the Creeks; 200 to 300 men among the Chickesaws. "The Choctaws have more than all the others combined." Gov. Glen to BT, Feb., 1748, in CO 5: 372, I: 13. Cf. Gov. Glen, Ans. Quer., 1749, in *Kings MS.*, 205, fol. 298, p. 611, in LCT, and Carroll, *Hist. Colls.*, S.C., II, 243-44.

1753 3,000 gunmen in the Cherokees; 2,500 gunmen in the Creeks; 400 in the Catawbas, and the Chickesaws rather more. Gov. Glen to the Earl of Holdernesse, June 25, 1753, in *Journal of House of Burgesses*, 1752-55 to 1756-58, 522.

1756 400 warriors among the Catawbas in N. and S. Carolina; 2,300 warriors among the Cherokees. *Va. Mag. Hist.*, XIII, 227n.

700 or 800 Indians in the Shawanese, Delaware, and Susquehanna Tribes. Gov. Sharpe, Ans. Quer., *Md. Archs.*, VI, 353-54; XXXI, 145-46.

1758 4,000 warriors and 52 villages of the Chactaws, and the Alabamons have about 3,000 warriors. M. de Kerlerec to the Minister, Nov.

9, 1758, in "Archs. de la Marine," F 25, fol. 33, in *Rept. on Canadian Archs.*, 1905, I, 466. *See also* 1759, page 196.

1761 770 hunters among the Lower Creeks, and 1,390 among the Upper Creeks. Ga. CR, VII, 522-24.

1763 500 fighting men among the Shawness, and 4,000 fighting men among the Cherokees, including upper, middle, and lower towns. Gov. Fauquier, Ans. Quer., Jan. 30, 1763, in CO 5: 1330, fol. 550, in LCT.

237 warriors among the small tribes along the Mississippi: Pascagoulas, 25; Mobilliens, 4; Chactow, 7; Allabamons, 33; Tensa, 12; Chittamasha, 27; Houmas, 25; Appalusas, 40; Tonicas, 12; Oufoe, 7; Biloxi, 45. Gov. Chester to BT, Sept. 20, 1771, in CO 5: 578, p. 319.

1764 14,000 people in the Chactaw nation, whereof 6,000 are fighting men. Major Farmar to Sec'y of War, Jan. 24, 1764, in *Miss. Prov. Archs.*, 1763-66, 14.

3,655 men among the tribes as follows: Alybamons, 440; Talapouches, 805; Abikas, 1,220; Chaouanons, 100; Tchikachas, 40; Natchez, 20; Kaouitas, 1,030. "Census of the Villages inhabited by the Creek Indians of the Porte des Alybamons," Encl. No. 29 in Maj. Farmar's letter of Jan. 24, in *Miss. Prov. Archs.*, 1763-66, 96-97. Also in CO 5: 582, pp. 162-63. *See also* 1764, page 198.

1765 3,600 fighting men among the Creeks, and 6,000 fighting men among the Choctaws. Gov. Johnston to Mr. Stuart, June 12, 1765, in CO 5: 582, p. 353.

1766 3,500 warriors among the Creeks. Gov. Johnstone to BT, June 23, 1766, *ibid.*, 583, p. 611.

3,500 gunmen among the Creeks; 60 gunmen among the Catawbas; 150 to 200 gunmen among the Natchez; 570 gunmen among the Natchez, Arkansas, and Alibamons. John Stuart to Conway, Aug. 8, 1766, *ibid.*, 67, fol. 210, p. 162, in LCT. Cf. John Stuart to BT, Dec. 2, 1766, *ibid.*, 67, fol. 400, 403, in LCT.

2,150 gunmen among the Creeks; 350 gunmen among the Chickesaws; 4,000 gunmen among the Choctaws. Gov. Wright, Ans. Quer., Nov. 29, 1766, in *Kings MS.*, 205, fol. 314, p. 645, in LCT.

1768 2,500 Cherokees in W. part of N. Carolina; 750 Chickesaws south of Cherokees; 150 Catawbas in South Carolina; 3,500 in northern and northwestern tribes; 300 Shawnees on Sciota and Muskingum Rivers in Ohio. Estimate of Capt. Hutchins, in Waddell, *Annals of Augusta Co., Va.*, 55-56. *See also* 1768, page 198.

1770 4,000 gunmen in the Creek nation. John Stuart to Lord Botetourt, Jan. 13, 1770, in *Journal of House of Burgesses*, 1770-72, xii.

1776 15,000 gunmen in tribes to the west, viz., the Creeks, Cherokees, Choctaws, and a number of small tribes. Rept. of Committees to Pres. and Council of Safety, in *Ga. Rev. Recds.*, I, 301.

1784 25 warriors in the villages of the Humas; 30 warriors in the villages of the Alibamas; 27 warriors in the Fourche de Chetimachas; 20 warriors in the village of the Tonicas; 20 warriors in the village of the Pascagoula; 30 warriors in the village of the Biloxi Indians; 140 warriors in the village of the Choctaws; 500 warriors in the villages of the Chickasaws. Hutchins, *Hist. Narr. and Topog. Desc. of La. and W. Fla.*, 415, 419-20, 427.

INDEX

INDEX

Towns now in Maine are here associated with Massachusetts because they were under the jurisdiction of Massachusetts until 1819.

Granville County, N. C., 160, 161, 162, 163, 164, 165, 167, 168, 169, 170
Gravesend, N. Y., 93 n.
Gray, Mass., 38, 44
Great Barrington, Mass., 28, 38, 44
Great Choptank Parish, Md., 130, 132
Great Falls, Mass., 36
Great Lakes Region, 196
Greenbriar County, Ky., 193
Greenbriar County, Va., 150, 152, 154
Greenfield, Mass., 27, 33, 42
Green Harbor, Mass., 12
Greenland, N. H., 76, 83
Greensville County Va. 150, 152, 154
Greenville County, S. C., 179
Greenwich, Conn., 51, 52, 53, 54, 55, 56, 57, 59
Greenwich, Mass., 27, 34, 42
Greenwich, R. I., 65, 66
Greenwich, East, R. I., 67, 69
Greenwich, West, R. I., 67, 69
Groton, Conn., 56, 57, 59
Groton, Mass., 20, 33, 41
Groton, N. H., 76. *See also* Cockermouth
Guilford, Conn., 51, 52, 53, 54, 55, 56, 57, 59
Guilford, Vt., 86, 87
Guilford County, N. C., 171
Gunthwaite (Concord), N.H., 75, 81

Haddam, Conn., 51, 52, 53, 54, 55, 56, 58
Haddam, East, Conn., 57, 58
Haddam, West, Conn., 57
Hadley, Mass., 21, 26, 33, 41
Hagerstown, Md., 133
Halifax, Ga., 183
Halifax, Mass., 28, 35, 42
Halifax (town), N. C., 169
Halifax, Vt., 86, 87
Halifax County, N. C., 165, 167, 168, 169, 170
Halifax County, Vt., 150, 152, 154
Halifax District, N. C., 170
Hallowell, Mass., 39, 45

Hampshire County, Mass., 21, 26, 30, 33, 41, 42, 46
Hampshire County, Va., 150, 152, 154
Hampstead, N. H., 76, 83
Hampton, N. H., 76, 83
Hampton-Falls, N.H., 76, 83
Hamstead, Ga., 180
Hamstead, Vt., 87
Hancock, Mass., 38, 44
Hancock County, Mass., 46
Hancock, N. H., 82
Hanover, Mass., 28, 35, 42
Hanover, N. H., 76, 81
Hanover County, Va., 150, 152, 154
Hardwick, Ga., 183
Hardwick, Mass., 26, 37, 44
Hardy County, Va., 154
Harford County, Md., 132, 133
Harpswell, Mass., 30, 38, 44
Harrington (No. 5), Mass., 45
Harrisburg, Pa., 119 n.
Harrison County, Va., 154
Hartford, Conn., 51, 52, 53, 54, 55, 56, 57, 58
Hartford (Hertford; formerly Ware), Vt., 86, 87
Hartland, Conn., 60
Harvard, Mass., 26, 37, 44
Harwich, Mass., 29, 35, 42
Harwinter, Conn., 60
Hatfield, Mass., 21, 27, 33, 42
Haverhill, Mass., 20, 24, 32, 41
Haverhill, N. H., 76, 81
Hawke (Danville), N. H., 76, 83
Heath, Mass., 42
Hebron, Conn., 58
Hempsted, N. Y., 93 n., 101 n.
Henniker, N. H., 76, 82
Henrico County, Va., 144, 145, 147, 148, 149, 151, 152, 154
Henry County, Va., 152, 159
Hertford County, N. C., 166, 167, 168, 170
Highgate, Ga., 180, 184
Hill (New Chester), N. H., 77, 81
Hillsborough, N. H., 76, 82

Kawita (Kouitas), 205; Kickapoos, 196, 197, 199, 200, 201; Mahicans (River Indians), 195; Mascoutens (Massoutins, Meadow Indians, Muscoutans), 195, 197, 201; Menominees (Menominis, Follesavoins), 195, 197, 201; Miamis (Twightwees, Twixtwees), 195, 196, 197, 198, 199, 200, 201; Mingoes (Iroquois), 199, 200; Missisaugas (Misisaguays), 195; Mobilians (Creeks, Mobillions), 205; M o h a w k s (Maques, Naquaische), 194, 195, 196, 198, 199, 200; Mohicans, 196, 198, 199, 200; Munsees (Munsies), 195, 196, 198, 199, 200, 201; Musquakies, 196, 198, 200; Nanticokes, 196, 198; Natchez, 198, 205; Nipissings (Skaghquanoghronos), 196; Noquets (Nokes), 195; Ochesees (Ocheese, Creeks), 202, 203, 204, 205, 206; Oneidas (Onyades), 194, 195, 196, 198, 199, 200; Onondaga, 194, 195, 196, 198, 199, 200; Opelusas (Appalusas), 205; Oquaga (Aughquagahs, Susqquehannahs); 198, 204; Osakies (Sauks), 201; Osewegatchies, 196; Ottawas (Ottoways, Outaoucs), 195, 196, 197, 198, 199, 200, 201; Oufoes, 205; Ouiatanons (Weas, Weatanans, Wiahtanos), 201; Outagamies (Foxes, Renards), 195, 197, 201; Paleachuckles (Apalachicola), 202; Pascagoulas, 205, 206; Peorias (Peorees, Piorias), 197, 201; Piankashaws, 197, 198, 199, 200, 201; Pickawillamees (Picts), 200; Potewatomies (Pottewotomies, Poux, Powtewatamies), 195, 197, 198, 199, 200, 201; Poudew, 201; Puans or Puants (Winipegoes, Winnebagoes), 195, 197, 201; Renards (Foxes, Musquakies, Outagmies), 195, 196, 197, 199, 200, 201; River Indians (Mahicans), 195, 196, 198, 199, 200; Saginaws, 195; Santees,

202; Saponis, 196, 198; Sauks (Sakis, Saquis, Shakies), 195, 196, 197, 198; Savannahs, 202; Scaticooks, 195; Sewees, 202; Senecas (Senecques), 194, 195, 196, 198, 199, 200, 201; Shawnees (Chaouanons), 196, 197, 199, 201; Skaghquanoghronos (Nipissings), 196; Susquehannas, 204; Talapoosas (Talapouches), 202, 203, 205; Taensa, 205; Tunicas (Tonicas), 205, 206; Tuscaroras, 196, 197, 199, 200; Tuteloes (Tutecoes), 196; Twightwees or Twixtwees (Miamis), 196, 197, 198, 200; Wabash, 195, 200; Waccomaws (Waccomassus), 202; Weas (Ouiatanons, Weatanans, Wiahtanos), 201; Winnebagoes (Puans or Puants, Winipegoes), 195, 197, 201; Winyaws (Wineaws), 202; Wisconsins (Ouisconsings), 197; Wyandots (Hurons), 196, 197, 198, 199, 200, 201; Yuchi or Yuma (Euchees), 202

Inisquamego, Mass., 22 n.
Ipswich, Mass., 14, 20 n., 23, 31, 41
Iredell County, N. C., 171
Irish Protestants, N. C., 161
Isleboro (Penobscot), Mass., 45
Isle of Wight County, Va., 145, 147, 148, 149, 151, 152, 154
Islip, N. Y., 103

Jaffrey, N. H., 76, 80
Jamaica, N. Y., 93, 101 n.
James City, Va., 143, 144
James City County, Va., 145, 147, 148, 149, 151, 152, 155
James Island, Va., 143
Jamestown, R. I., 65, 67, 68, 69
Jamestown, Va., 145
James Town and New Harbor, Mass., 20
Jefferson County, Ky., 192, 193
Jews in New York, 96 n.
Johnston, R. I., 68, 70
Johnston County, N. C., 160, 161, 162,

Unity, N. H., 79, 80
Upton, Mass., 26, 37, 44
Uxbridge, Mass., 25, 37, 44

Vasallboro, Mass., 39, 45
Vernonburgh, Ga., 183
Vienna, Md., 134
Vinalhaven, Mass., 45. *See also* Fox
Island
Vincennes, Ind., 190
Voluntown, Conn., 60

Wake County, N. C., 171
Wakefield, N. H., 79, 85
Waldoboro, Mass., 39, 44
Wales, Mass., 45
Wallingford, Conn., 51, 52, 53, 54,
55, 56, 57, 59
Walpole, Mass., 23, 31, 40, 44
Walpole, N. H., 79, 80
Waltham, Mass., 25, 32, 41
Wandoe River Parish, S. C., 173
Ward, Mass., 37, 44
Ware, Mass., 27, 34, 42
Ware (Hartford), Vt., 86, 87
Wareham, Mass., 20, 28, 35, 42
Wariscoyack, Va., 144
Warren, Mass., 39, 45
Warren, N. H., 79, 83
Warren, R. I., 67, 68, 69
Warren County, N. C., 169, 170
Warrowerguyoake County, Va., 145
Warwick (Roxbury Canady), Mass.,
27, 34, 42
Warwick, R. I., 61, 64, 65, 66, 67, 68,
69
Warwick County, Va., 145, 146, 147,
148, 149, 150, 151, 153, 155
Warwick Squeak, Va., 143
Washington, Mass., 38, 43, 44
Washington, N. H., 79, 80
Washington, N. Y., 104, 105
Washington County, Md., 132, 133
Washington County, Pa., 110, 117,
119
Washington County (Kings), R. I.,
66, 70
Washington County, Va., 153, 155

Watauga, Tenn., 194
Waterboro, Mass., 43
Waterbury, Conn., 51, 54, 55, 56, 57,
59
Watertown, Mass., 19, 24, 32, 41
Wayne County, N. C., 171
Weare, N. H., 79, 83
Welch Township, S. C., 177
Wellfleet, Mass., 29, 35, 42
Wells, Mass., 22 n., 29, 36, 43
Welsh, the, in Pennsylvania, 114
Wendell, Mass., 42
Wendell, N. H., 79, 80
Wentworth, N. H., 79, 81
West and Sherlow Hundred, Va., 143,
144
Westborough, Mass., 25, 37, 43
Westbrook, Ga., 180
Westchester County, N. Y., 92, 94, 95,
96, 97, 98, 99, 100, 101, 102, 103,
104, 105
West Dover, Del., 122
Westerley, R I., 65, 66, 68, 69
Western, Mass., 26, 37, 43
Western Shore, Md., 133
Westfield, Mass., 21, 27, 33, 42
Westford, Mass., 25, 32, 41
Westhampton, Mass., 33, 42
Westminster, Mass., 26, 37, 44
Westminster, Vt., 86, 87
Westmoreland, Conn., 61
Westmoreland, N. H., 79, 80
Westmoreland County, Pa., 117, 119,
120
Westmoreland County, Va., 146, 147,
148, 149, 150, 151, 153, 155
Weston, Mass., 24, 32, 41
West Springfield, Mass., 34, 41
West Stockbridge, Mass., 38, 44
Wethersfield, Conn., 51, 52, 53, 54,
55, 56, 57, 58
Wethersfield, Vt., 86, 87
Weybridge, Vt., 87
Weymouth, Mass., 14, 19, 22, 31, 40
Whately, Mass., 33, 42
White Plains, N. Y., 96 n.
Whiting, Vt., 86, 87